Designing the invisible

Miki!
It's great to have
you as a colleague
designer doing great
things in the world!
Love Lara ♡

BLOOMSBURY VISUAL ARTS
Bloomsbury Publishing Plc
50 Bedford Square, London, WC1B 3DP, UK

BLOOMSBURY and the Diana logo are trademarks
of Bloomsbury Publishing Plc

First published in India 2018

Cover design: Eduardo Foresti, Foresti Design

A catalogue record for this book is available from the British Library.

Library of Congress Cataloging-in-Publication Data
Names: Penin, Lara, author.
Title: An introduction to service design / by Lara Penin.
Description: London ; New York, NY : Bloomsbury Publishing, 2017. | Includes bibliographical references and index.
Identifiers: LCCN 2017022582 (print) | LCCN 2017040985 (ebook) | ISBN 9781350031913 (Epub) | ISBN 9781472572592 (Epdf) | ISBN 9781472572585 (pbk. : alk. paper)
Subjects: LCSH: Customer services. | Service industries.
Classification: LCC HF5415.5 (ebook) | LCC HF5415.5 .P454 2017 (print) | DDC 658.8/12–dc23
LC record available at https://lccn.loc.gov/2017022582

ISBN: PB: 978-1-4725-7258-5
ePDF: 978-1-4725-7259-2
ePub: 978-1-3500-3191-3

Typeset by Struktur Design
Printed and bound in India

To find out more about our authors and books visit www.bloomsbury.com and sign up for our newsletters.

AN INTRODUCTION TO SERVICE DESIGN

Lara Penin

Designing the invisible

BLOOMSBURY VISUAL ARTS
LONDON • NEW YORK • OXFORD • NEW DELHI • SYDNEY

Part I Understanding Services

Main concepts, critical aspects and implications of designing services, discussed by experts

01 Defining services

02 The service economy

Part II
The Service Design Process

The service design process, methods and tools explained through outstanding projects and discussed by the designers behind them

07
Starting the service design process

08
Research and analysis

09
Generating service design concepts

Acknowledgments

I have many people to thank for helping me in my journey preparing this book.

I'll start by thanking the interviewees who have generously shared their projects, ideas, and perspectives, a real all-stars team of service design champions: Birgit Mager; Ezio Manzini; Jodi Forlizzi; Eduardo Staszowski; Cameron Tonkinwise; Daniela Sangiorgi; Alessandro Confalonieri; Sarah Schulman; The Reboot team Nonso Jideofor, Panthea Lee, and Adam Talsma; Juha Konqvist; Alex Nisbett; and Lucy Kimbell.

Thanks to people who have shared materials about their projects and organizations: Marc Stickdorn, Rachel Lehrer, Chelsea Mauldin, Aldo Cibic, Susan Spraragen, the Mayo Clinic Center for Innovation, Bigbelly, IDEO, Studio Thick, Designit, Service Design Jam Berlin, Service Design Network, Design Council UK, MindLab, La 27éme Region, PAN Studio, City of Boston, SmartCitizen, Citi Community Development, New York City Office of Financial Empowerment, New York City Department of Consumer Affairs, Parsons DESIS Lab, Intersezioni, Hellon, InWithForward, The Reboot, and Strategyzer.

Thanks to all people who helped materialize this book. Thanks to Amy Findeiss for the whimsical illustrations and Eduardo Foresti for the marvelous cover and graphic design guidelines. Thanks to Christian Smirnow, Mashal Khan, and Cameron Hanson for their pictures. Thanks to Siri Betts-Sonstegard and Dongin Shin for sharing materials from their theses. Thanks to Clive Dilnot for the inspiring discussion on invisibility. A big thank you to Mauricio Manhães, for the careful and generous revisions, helping me cover gaps in many aspects, including guiding me through a deeper understanding of the service-dominant logic. Many thanks to Bloomsbury editors—Lee Ripley who has been such a patient and steady guide in the book development process, as well as Leafy Cummins and Miriam Davey. I have been fortunate enough to work with several brilliant research assistants who have worked with me in different stages of this book; in chronological order, Chen-Yu Lo, Lillian Shi Tong, Christopher Taylor Edwards, Mollie West, Katie Edmonds, Alix Gerber, Christian Smirnow, and Scott Brown.

A further thank you to fellow service design educators with whom I have collaborated and interacted over the years: Beatrice Villari, Stefano Maffei, Carlo Vezzoli, Anna Meroni, Katarina Wetter-Edman, Stephan Homlid, David Young, Shana Agid, Luo Qi, Yumiko Mizutani, Eduardo Staszowski, Carla Cipolla, Ezio Manzini, Cameron Tonkinwise, François Jégou, Birgit Mager, Ben Winter, Elliott Montgomery, Patty Beirne, Clive Dilnot, Terry Irwin, and Laura Forlano. Special thanks to Marshall Sitten, who has been a service design animator in New York City. Thanks to the vibrant service design community in New York City, especially Talia Radywyl, Jamie Nicholson, Jackie Cooksey, and Dave Seliger. Thanks to Citi Community Development that has been a pillar supporting service design in New York. Thanks to colleagues in the Service Design Network, the DESIS Network, and the Winterhouse Institute.

Thanks to my university The New School and Parsons School of Design, in particular the School of Design Strategies that has embraced service design in its curriculum and ethos. Thanks to my colleagues at Parsons DESIS Lab. Thanks to all my students and colleagues at Parsons School of Design, in particular my students in the Transdisciplinary Design program and the Integrated Design program. Many of their projects help illustrate this book.

Thanks to my husband and research and teaching partner, Eduardo Staszowski, a constant sounding board for this book. Thanks to my parents Sonia and Silverio Penin.

Foreword
Clive Dilnot

The play between the tangible and the intangible, the visible and the invisible, has always been integral to design. It was, after all, its *raison d'etre*. Designers have only ever been employed because the refinements they add to the simple fact of a thing contribute to its experience and hence to its desirability. But while experiences are propelled by the material qualities of the thing, it takes place In mind. It might be better to say then that the tangible *induces* the intangible.

Service design is, in a way, no more, and no less, than this—but in reverse. In designing a service, the aim is often all but intangible: the felt quality of the experience offered. Yet the paradox of this intangibility is that this experience is very largely delivered through material means (even if the "material" here might be the actions of, or encounters with, other human beings). This has always been the case. Think of religious rituals. Services of worship are, by definition, "services." Their choreography is as carefully plotted as the configuration of a building. Indeed, in this case, the latter is often servant to the former. So a service is no less an artifact than a physical thing. The difference is that here the artifact is the choreographed ensemble of places, things, communications, scripted encounters and so on—in a word the assemblage—that "delivers" the service and which the subject encounters as a set of experiences (since services unfold always over time). But there is no evasion of design. Even in those religions stressing the least ritualistic emphasis to the communion and connection with God, the quality of the spaces in which these meetings take place—think of the washed plain light of a Quaker or Shaker meeting house—is as significant and no less material, no less designed, than the Baroque interior of St. Peters. Despite what architects sometimes like to pretend, no architecture is merely physical. Site is always really situation. Situation means the encounter of a person and a context: a context that usually contains other persons and has its basis in a material human need. Situations are fundamental, they are in a sense, even prior to artifacts. Not for nothing did even that most technological of design theorists (Herbert Simon) nonetheless famously insist, back as early as 1968, that to design "is to devise of actions to change existing situations into preferred ones."[1] There are as many situations as there are human interactions. If today they proliferate as moments for design—both because of the (pseudo-)encounters that technology allows us but also because of the often egregious contemporary economic demand to monetize all human relations—the core remains the *situation* of the human encounter. It is this that gives the situation (and hence service design) its ethic, a point caught by the philosopher Alain Badiou when, in his little book on *Ethics*, he argues at one point: "There is no need for an 'ethics' but only for a clear vision of *the* situation . . . to be faithful to the situation means: to deal with the situation according to the rule of maximum possibility; to treat it right to the limit of the possible. Or, if you prefer, to draw from the situation, to the greatest possible extent, the affirmative humanity that it contains."[2]

It is important to stress the ethics of the situation—and therefore the ethics of "service design." which is

[1] Herbert Simon, *The Sciences of the Artificial* (Cambridge: MIT Press, 1969), p. 130.
[2] Alain Badiou, *Ethics* (London: Verso, 2001), p. 15 (adapted quote).

nothing more than (and nothing less than!) the design of situations—because the same monetarizing impulse which makes the seizing of intimate human moments one branch of how the contemporary economy keeps itself afloat also seizes service design, both in the private and in the public sector. The operationalizing of service design, often under a jargon that is as inflated and barbaric as the claims of the economy itself, distorts what is really at stake here, which is the experience of being human. Too easily commoditized, Badiou's double rule is too easily forgotten, too easily disposed of when profit is put in question.

Yet, outside of the profit motive, the reason why anyone takes up the mantle of service design is surely in fact to help make manifest, in concrete human situations, Badiou's ethic. Service design in this sense is an ethical act. It is using the capacities of design to establish resonance between things and persons for human ends. Technocratic and econometric formulations of "service design" tend to obscure this more fundamental truth. In fact, branding and marketing have almost nothing to do with service design—and, as we know, are often counterproductive, contributing to the wider devaluing of experience in the contemporary economy. Real service design has its ethos, by contrast, in how, out of sometimes the most constrained and difficult situations—the conditions and character of the delivery of cancer treatments, for example—we can create moments that can relieve, even in small ways, the tensions of the experience, and can do so *through* design. Through design means here undertaking that extraordinary act that all design achieves when it translates a perception about a human condition or encounter into an artifact that helps relieve or enhance it. That is why service design is necessarily ethical. It deals with how subjects are enabled to act in the world.

Now all this might seem a long way from what is essentially a working handbook for learning about, and then for doing, service design. But it is not, for this is the essential (human) underpinning to service design. I will note in particular Chapter 12, "Service Design Core Capabilities," and the five vital human capacities or capabilities that the author lays out—for "facilitation and stewardship," for "envisioning and visualizing," for "prototyping and testing," for acting as agents of "organizational change-making," and not least and indeed first in her list, for "active and empathic listening," or what she describes as "understanding people in their human complexity and being able to see the world from the perspective of an 'other'" (page 312). The "literacy" of designing in this field of encounters and situations has to come into play; the developments of professional capacities to translate perceptions into forms, experiences, ensembles, and arrangements; choreographic and choreographed structures are not less; indeed, they are often *more*, in these contexts. But capacities arise from understanding what tasks require. And this is where, as the delightful subtitle of this book has it, *Designing the Invisible*, comes into play. As a literal *Introduction to Service Design*, this book describes concisely but exhaustively the context and tasks of service design. It leaves the readers in no doubt as to what is needed and expected of them, but it also supplies the essential clues for anyone who wishes to take up service design, either as an aspect of their existing career in designing, creating, or organizing things, or as a career path in its own right.

Preface

When I started teaching service design more than ten years ago, service design literature mainly consisted of academic papers, a few doctoral theses, a few service marketing and interaction design publications, and the websites of pioneer service design consultancies. In those days, I would prepare readers and compilations, write introductory papers, and even build websites aggregating all available resources for my students. Things have changed considerably since then. Soon enough, practitioners and researchers started producing publications that made service design knowledge more accessible. A handful of pioneer books—and the list keeps growing—are still the core of any essential library of service designers everywhere. Yet, there was still the need for a book dedicated to the pedagogy of service design.

This book is meant as a resource for students and educators braving the new specialization of service design, whether they are majoring in service design at either the undergraduate or graduate level, or coming from other design or nondesign disciplines and practices and looking to gain service design literacy. It is also for service design educators who need a handy resource for their courses.

Learning (and teaching) service design can be challenging because it is in great part about designing the invisible. The core of services are social interactions that happen over time, and designing for services therefore implies designing material and immaterial conditions for interactions and experiences, flows, and systems. But most of all, we are designing the enabling conditions for people to solve a problem and improve their lived experience. While service design is connected with traditional design domains, such as visual communication and the built environment, it is equally connected to organizational policies, protocols, business models, scripts, and choreographies. So, as service design aggregates different practices and mindsets and enters new domains and possibilities, it may actually help redefine design altogether and reshape our understanding of what design really does and what capabilities it entails. This book makes a case for service design as an original and legitimate design practice in its own right, an ambitious and transdisciplinary design practice occupying a strategic space between creating visions of sustainable social and environmental futures, and negotiating these visions within organizational and political realities. Service designers therefore have the challenge of dealing with businesses, government, and the civil society at large, as our efforts can affect labor relations, economic performance, and public policy. The project examples showcased in this book were selected precisely because they embody a responsible and sensible approach of designing for services. The outcomes of these projects improve people's lives and create social value while building capacity within the communities and organizations through these service relations.

Where do we even start? The rationale for this book is that learning service design is a journey. And, while it never really ends, it needs to start from somewhere. This book hopes to offer a starting point for a lifelong learning journey in service design.

The book is structured in two parts:

Part I attempts to chart the key guiding aspects of the transdisciplinary nature of services, since services are interconnected with so many critical aspects of the world and its artificial infrastructure. Chapters 1 to 6 evoke economics, politics, labor, technology, social issues, behavior, culture, and emotions. Experts in the field discuss how all this affects and defines the practice of service design.

Part II brings the conversation to a hands-on mindset, diving into the service design process, methods, and tools through outstanding projects. Chapters 7 to 11 break down the service design process into manageable packages, through case studies of exemplary projects and interviews with the designers behind them, as well as a guide of essential methods and tools. Chapter 12 offers a final reflection on the core capabilities of service design.

Each chapter ends with a "Learning features" section that includes glossaries of terms, key points, and recap questions as well as suggestions of class activities and templates.

Here's an overview of each chapter.

Chapter 1, "Defining services," introduces the fundamental concepts and theories necessary to understand services, and establishes the basis to help us think through the service lenses, such as how interactions and relationships are the core of services that depend on people to actively participate and coproduce them. The chapter introduces the service-dominant logic, a key concept that helps us see services as the real base of our economy and the concept of product service systems (PSS) that help break the barrier between goods and services. The chapter concludes with an interview with Birgit Mager, the founder of Service Design Network, who offers some essential definitions about service design, its development as a field and a profession, and the development of a community around service design bringing together practitioners, researchers, and different industries.

Chapter 2, "The service economy," locates services in terms of an economic activity, introduces the main service industries and emergent service-based economic models such as the sharing economy and demarcates the highly service-based social economy. The chapter also discusses the current market for service design, highlighting the health-care and financial sectors. In the interview, Ezio Manzini, founder of DESIS (Design for Social Innovation and Sustainability) Network, talks about the emerging ecosystems of different economies and the opportunities for the design community can offer in the emerging economic models.

Chapter 3, "Digital services," charts the landscape of digital services, platforms, and ecologies, including the Internet of Things (IoT) and its main areas of application. It also discusses impacts and new possible roles for service design in relation to technology—for example, the possibilities for service design to help humanize technology development. The chapter concludes with an interview with Jodi Forlizzi, Associate Professor of Human-Computer Interaction at Carnegie Mellon University, who discusses emerging trends in technology and the overlaps of service design with other design specializations and practices such as interaction design or experience design.

Chapter 4, "Services for public interest," frames the main sources of services for public interest starting with a close look into service innovation in the public sector, including the spread of innovation labs within government. It also presents the phenomenon of social innovation, a dynamic and creative source of innovation in services emerging directly from active citizens. The chapter concludes with an interview with Eduardo Staszowski, director of Parsons DESIS Lab. He charts the history of the growing presence at the nexus of service innovation, public interest design, and design for social innovation, exploring future opportunities arising for designers interested in working with public and collaborative services.

Chapter 5, "The politics of service design," introduces crucial political aspects of services such as labor relationships, environmental aspects, and the challenges of dealing with organizations' cultures. In particular, it investigates the concept of *emotional labor* performed by front office staff by examining political and ethical aspects embedded in it. It also looks into environmental issues and the link between climate change and services. The chapter concludes with an interview with Cameron Tonkinwise, Professor of Design at University of New South, Australia, who offers a critical perspective on the role of service design as designing the future of work, the relationship between services, and issues of sustainability, among other insights.

Chapter 6, "Designing for services," positions service design within the design universe, affirming it as a legitimate design practice; introduces its principles; analyzes the service design practice; and maps out the community service design. In making a case for service design as a new kind of design practice, it reviews core principles of the service design work, including its people-centeredness, the centrality of participation and codesign, and the holistic/systemic nature of service design. The interview with service design researcher and author Daniela Sangiorgi offers reflections about service design core principles and considers the arc of evolution of service design, among other key insights.

Chapter 7, "Starting the service design process," charts how service design projects are typically structured and presents the specifics of creating a project brief. It showcases as a case study project the service redesign of a bus company in Parma, Italy, and features an interview with Alessandro Confalonieri, partner at design firm Intersezioni. Confalonieri navigates us through the transformational process of defining a design brief with the client organization. The project is further analyzed in a takeaway section that dissects the main processes and methods employed by the designers in the project. The "Methods and tools" section expands and details typical methods and tools used in service design projects, as well as how to develop a service design brief.

Chapter 8, "Research and analysis," presents research methods for discovery in the service design process and tools for synthesis and insights. It showcases a case study project focusing on a mental health-care service in Toronto, Canada, and features an interview with Sarah Schulman, leader of InWithForward. Schulman explains the team's research process, centered around immersive ethnography and a deep analytical process. The project is further analyzed in a takeaway section that dissects the main processes and methods employed by the InWithForward team in the project. The "Methods and tools" section gives an overview of typical methods and tools used in the research and analysis phases.

Chapter 9, "Generating service design concepts," focuses on generative processes, such as creative workshops aimed at developing new service ideas. The case study in this chapter is a project focusing on health-care management in rural Nigeria, led by the firm The Reboot. In the interview, Panthea Lee and a team of Reboot researchers and designers offer details about their ideation process and the constraints and choices made by the team, leading to the development of an innovative concept. The project is analyzed in a takeaway section that highlights the main ideation approaches employed by the team in the project. The "Methods and tools" section expands and details typical ideation approaches and techniques such as workshops and creative sessions, brainstorming, and storytelling approaches.

Chapter 10, "Prototyping, testing, iterating," explores how to prototype service concepts for both physical and digital channels. The case study describes an award-winning project of a new pharmacy service model to be implemented across Finland by Finnish company Hellon. In the interview, Juha Kronqvist, lead designer at Hellon, explains the unique prototyping techniques used by Hellon through the pharmacy project, which are further discussed in the takeaway section. The "Methods and tools" section expands on other prototyping techniques, both physical and digital, as well as hybrid prototyping methods.

Chapter 11, "Implementation and evaluation," presents methods related to implementation, business models, impact evaluation, and user feedback. The case study project features the London Olympic Games (2012), followed by an interview with Alex Nisbett (Live|Work), who led the service design team of the games. Nisbett explains the unique approach the team implemented centered around the spectator experience. The takeaway analyzes the evaluation and feedback methods employed in the games, and the "Methods and tools" section expands into evaluation and feedback methods plus business aspects and other vital considerations for the implementation of services.

Chapter 12 "Service design core capabilities," looks into the service design practice as a whole, considering its unique challenges and opportunities, framing the core service design capabilities. The interview with service design lead thinker Lucy Kimbell, from the University of the Arts London, considers the learning paths toward service design practice, core capabilities of service design, and a critical view on the future of service design careers.

Part I
Understanding Services

01 Defining services

1.1 Introduction

This chapter introduces the fundamental concepts necessary to understand services, charting the principal theories that help us think through the service lenses.

The idea of services as a glue around which our lives are structured, the concept of interactions as the heart of services as social entities, and the notion of coproduction in services help us understand that services need users to actively participate in their production.

Next, the chapter introduces the groundbreaking concept of the service-dominant logic that helps us see services as the real base of our economy, where goods and services are not two different things but rather the same integrated thing, revealing there is no divide between goods and services. The next concept is the environmentally motivated concept of product service systems, on which tangible goods and services are incorporated into an integrated benefit.

The chapter also maps out the products of service, explaining the strategic and material outputs of service design.

The final highlight of this initial chapter is an interview with Birgit Mager, the founder of Service Design Network, a foundational entity for service design practitioners around the world.

What is a service, a working definition

In economic terms, service occurs when there's a value exchange between parts. One part, the service provider, performs a certain activity that results in some benefit that includes a specific output and involves certain experiences. The other part, the service user, sees value in the output, the experience, or both combined and is willing to pay for it or exchange for something else of equivalent value. Expanding into other aspects of life, the notion of services might overlap with the idea of care, e.g., health care, personal care, or firefighters protecting people; religious services; military protecting a country; community services and public services; and care for citizens, among many others. In many of these cases, no payment is made between parts (provider and user), but the compensation for the service happens through indirect ways, such as public services. In some cases, there's no monetary exchange whatsoever, such as volunteer-based services.

1.2
Services are the soft infrastructure of society

Services permeate our busy daily journeys sometimes in invisible ways—when we take a bus, go to school, use a credit card, talk or send a message over the phone, use social media, go to a restaurant, go to the dentist, or read the news. The events of our lives are interconnected through a myriad of different services. Through them, we get things done and get to interact with different people and organizations. Services are everywhere, as life's essential scaffold, as a soft infrastructure of our lives.

Services can be organized into categories that may be very different from each other. Typical service categories include transportation (subway, buses, and taxis), restaurants, banks, phone and internet services, entertainment (such as movies, theater, concerts, live sports events), nail salons, barber shops, laundromats, and every kind of health-care and school system. Some of these services are vital utilities like water and plumbing services, gas, and electricity. Digital services are also key services in everyday life, such as social media platforms like Facebook and Twitter, along with communication and data sharing platforms such as Skype and Google Drive, or services to facilitate exchanges like eBay or Airbnb. All these services continue to evolve and shape our lives.

With technology and the increased specialization of service provisions in today's world, the presence of services in our daily lives has grown exponentially, or at least our awareness of services has grown more acute.

As we are now far into the *network society*, our lives depend heavily on service provisions such as telecommunications and the internet for all kinds of communication forms and information exchange. It is hard to imagine life without all the communication and information services we increasingly depend on.

1.1

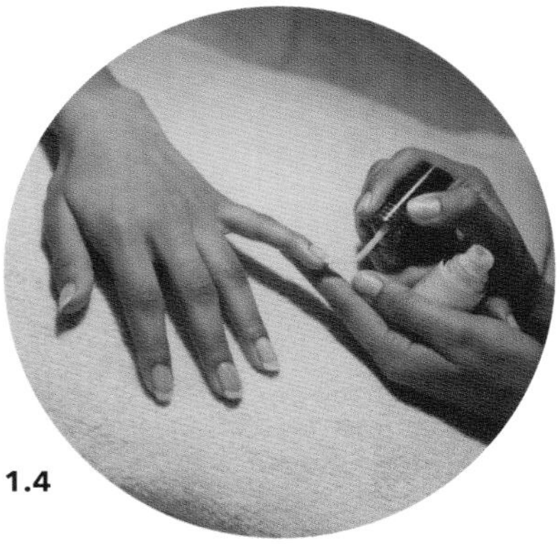

1.4

1.2

1.6

1.3

1.5

Figs 1.1 to 1.12: Typical services of everyday life: transportation, cafes, social media, school, restaurants and bars, health care, entertainment, personal care, care for others, car services.

OF US
WILL

1.7

BAR & CAFE

1.10

1.8

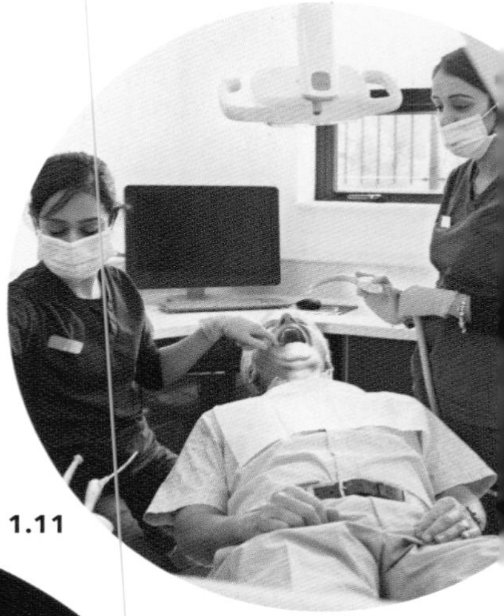

1.11

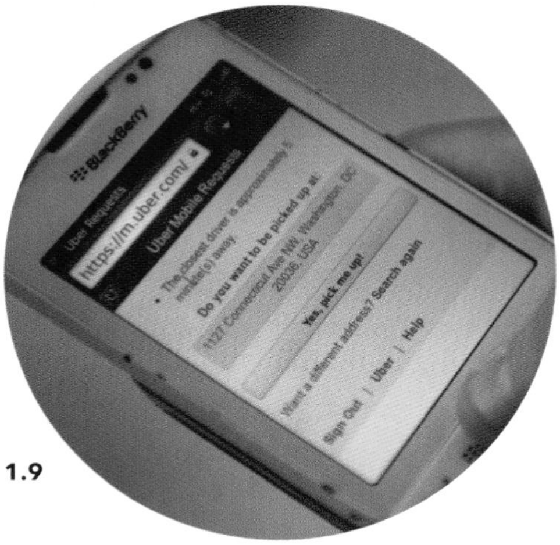
BlackBerry
https://m.uber.com/
Uber Mobile Requests
Do you want to be picked up at:
1127 Connecticut Ave NW, Washington, DC 20036, USA
Yes, pick me up!
Want a different address? Search again
Sign Out | Uber | Help

1.9

1.12

1.3 Interactions are the core of services

As designers, we look at services primarily as human experiences, not necessarily as economic activities. Some social science scholars argue that services are not always monetized and do not always involve a company or an organization. Instead, services are a foundation of the human condition in a deeper sense.

Services are people-centric entities that are essentially relational and social. They are also temporal, because relationships happen over time. Because human actions and relationships are at the basis of services, it is essential that we acknowledge the uncertainty and unpredictability as contingent to services. Service interactions are therefore unpredictable; we have no guarantees that things will happen in a certain way.

Service management literature acknowledges interactions as "the moment of truth" of services, the moment when value in services is constituted. "Service encounters" occur when a person (user) interacts with a service via a touchpoint. *Touchpoints* are the material face of services and comprise the artifacts that support the service's interactions. They not only physically enable the interactions but also are key to make them better, more efficient, more meaningful, and more desirable. Services are therefore also material because they are anchored or supported by some kind of artifact.

The interaction that happens in the *moment of truth* is crucial in determining the perceived value of the service for people, who at that point are able to assess results against cost and effort of the service provider.

Apart from the role that touchpoints play in the perception of quality in service encounters, services are bound to a myriad of other factors, many beyond the control of service designers and of the service-providing organizations themselves, and they might vary over time. The reason is that services can be delivered through unique face-to-face encounters, through automated digital interfaces, and through a number of different channels or a combination of them. Each one of these channels and the processes behind them need to be accounted for when orchestrating services. The consistent delivery of positive moments of truth over time is a critical challenge for service organizations of all kinds.

For designers, the idea of designing for interactions poses a vital question: can interactions be designed at all? The question reveals the limits of design. Several authors address this conundrum. Some of them consider that interactions involve the details and particularities of daily life, unscripted and unpredictable as they are, considering all kinds of interactions—whether between people and objects, services, or systems. Others point out that service interactions are, to a large extent, undesignable and talk about designing *for* services rather than designing services and that we can design the *conditions* for interactions to happen but never the interaction itself.

On one hand, for some designers, previously accustomed to the assurance of tangible artifacts, entering the unpredictability of services and interactions will seem painfully complicated, or at least challenging. Product designers know that they will design a three-dimensional object, graphic designers knows they will be designing a two-dimensional visual piece, and architects know they will be designing a physical space. Service designers might not know what they will be designing until further into their research process.

On the other hand, designing for interactions presents designers with a new world of possibilities that takes them beyond *form and function* into a more intellectual and strategic practice in which they are able to create a deeper social impact.

Let's discuss a few key dimensions to help the designers' adventure in the sphere of interactions.

The first dimension is related to the nature of social interactions as tacit behaviors. Tacit behavior means the opposite of formal or codified behavior. Social interactions are dynamic interactions happening between people, individuals, or groups and are connected to social norms, bound to contextual, cultural, emotional, and aesthetic aspects that are dynamic and ever evolving in any society. Understanding tacit behavior is therefore vital for design. And it is the reason that service design needs to be essentially user-centric: it depends on directly observing and documenting people in their own contexts as well as iterative consultations with people through participatory methods and codesign processes throughout the development of a service proposition. It makes designers' work messier, nonlinear, contradictory, but also exciting.

The second dimension is related to the medium through which interactions happen, when they are mediated through technology-based devices and interfaces. In these interactions, we are affected both by the hardware design of the equipment as well as the software that is written based on protocols and coding (e.g., "if x, then y"). The design of interfaces and interaction systems relies on defining predetermined protocols (programming) that direct users to take certain routes and reach certain results. The field of philosophy offers useful principles to guide designing for interactivity. One such principle is the notion that, as human beings, we are not naturally cognitive, reflective thinking individuals, but rather, we are individuals in the world, situated beings relying on

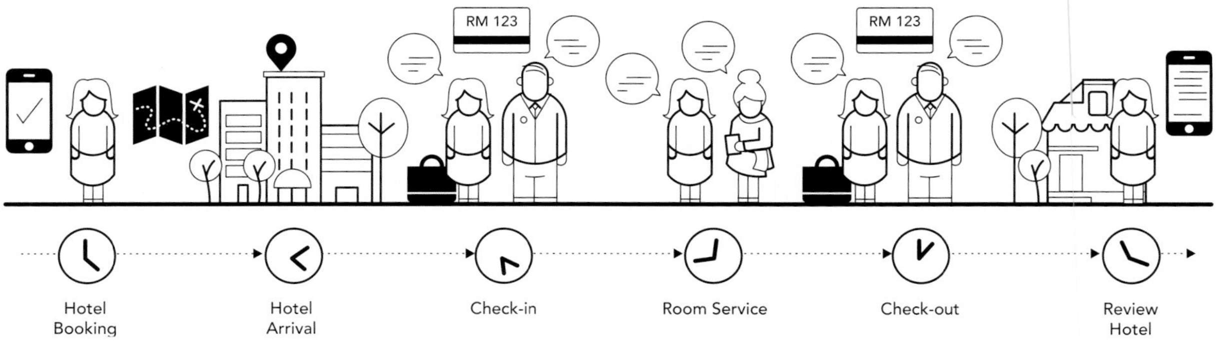
RM 123
RM 123
Hotel Booking
Hotel Arrival
Check-in
Room Service
Check-out
Review Hotel

Fig 1.13: Service interactions through multiple channels over time: some interactions are face to face, whereas others are mediated through technology.

intuitive behavior. In other words, we don't think first and act later; in fact, it's quite the opposite. In this sense, people's reactions toward designed protocols are never predictable. Designers of interactions not only need to spend a lot of time trying to anticipate people's reactions to automated protocols but also—and foremost—they need to get their interaction ideas out there and test them with users in context throughout the development process.

The third dimension of interactions to be factored in is the plural nature of interactions. Services are typically based on interactions that happen over time, following more or less predetermined frequencies. We interact with certain services daily, with others weekly, monthly, yearly, and with some, occasionally, and with some, just once in a lifetime. They may never repeat exactly in the same way, even if we're using automated protocols. It's through the continuous negotiation of interactions across time that our perceptions of value in services are shaped: good service is consistent; bad service is inconsistent and contradictory. When we interact with a service through different media and channels, the challenge of consistency is even higher.

As anticipated previously, time is the fourth dimension to be considered in service design. Balancing perceptions of the experiences being delivered over time across different aesthetic and functional channels—both through human-to-human and human-machine/computer—requires some specific tools. The main time-based tools developed and used by designers are time-based narratives, notably *service blueprints* and *user journeys* on which actions and interactions are described as a sequence of frames or a timeline. *Enactment*, either live or captured through video, is also a popular tool to help envision service design narratives. It helps service designers create narratives and stories that capture how services are going to unfold and look at them from different viewpoints.

How do you define service design?

Service design is the activity of choreographing people, infrastructure, communication, and material components of a service in order to create value for the multiple stakeholders involved. In the very early times, we were focused on designing interfaces, touchpoints, and artifacts that were usable, useful, and desirable for users. Today we see that value should be distributed equally among all stakeholders. Considering the entire system is one way to bridge the gap between concept and implementation, which would make service design more attractive to different industries.

Services and related fields like service management and service sciences have been around for a long time. Designers have only entered the scene in the last ten years or so. What is design contributing that is unique?

Initially, design brought the ability to gain deep insight into people's needs, preferences, and desires, combining both qualitative and quantitative research to really bring the user's perspective into focus. Designers also introduced the use of participatory approaches in interdisciplinary teams. Over the past ten years, these skills became a commodity for marketing people or other service business managers. We are losing some of our uniqueness, but design can still provide a very valuable contribution in our ability to envision scenarios that do not yet exist and to prototype those scenarios for service improvement and innovation.

Is service design a field or a profession?

Both. It's a field, but it's also a profession. Anyone can bring service design into their company's culture, but the service design professionals are those who bring new expertise into an organization's processes. For example, when I teach service design in a company for just ten days distributed over one year, many people come out with a lot of service design knowledge, even if they don't frame it that way. Still, for certain projects the company would probably hire external design partners that bring expertise, a concrete time commitment, and an external perspective.

Can you talk about the development of a community around service design, specifically the history of the Service Design Network? How do industry and academic research come together in this community?

Even though service design is young, a strong community has developed around it. The Service Design Network was created to support exchange between businesspeople, consultants, and researchers. Today, there is quite an equal distribution of participants from these three sectors at the events, as well as representation from many different fields—especially public, health, and finance. Academic research on service design still needs to be strengthened and communicated more effectively to practitioners who don't take time to read academic papers. We are also creating special interest groups to build deeper knowledge and networks within specific service fields.

Are there other areas in which our society can benefit from services that are still underdeveloped?

I definitely see these opportunities in social innovation, in new types of sharing communities, new types of financial solutions, among others.

In your view, can we talk about different "genealogies" of service design, or different schools of thought and approaches from different parts of the world? For example, service design took off in Europe, responding to demands from specific service sectors such as health care, whereas in the United States service design has emerged very much related to technology, using interaction design as a primary disciplinary scaffolding.

There are two main genealogies: one led by design and the other by service science. The science stream is more academic, building on theories of new service development and service innovation to create consistent methods for improving or innovating services. Meanwhile, the designers are trying to connect service design with UX design and interaction design. I don't think that these streams will ever come together, but we should definitely be careful not to create too many confusing areas.

Are we ready to move toward a service-dominant logic mindset, with services as the basic unit of exchange in our economy? In the United States, when we hear a politician campaigning for job creation, they only seem to mention manufacturing jobs, but never service jobs. What is missing for a mindset transition?

I've seen a major change happening. Twenty years ago, it seemed farfetched for an automobile company to focus on broad solutions rather than just producing cars. Today we see Mercedes, BMW, and Volkswagen putting service-based offerings on the market. The relevance of service industries for growth and creation of new jobs is quite clear in Europe. A developing desire for ecologically feasible lifestyles has shown manufacturing industries that real value comes from the combination of manufacturing and service together. In fact, we are discussing how much service the economy can digest, and how much manufacturing we need to retain a good balance.

How is designing for services different than designing for products or communication?

Both service and product design require the designer to work between disciplines to turn a concept into reality. While product designers work with a few people in marketing, engineering, and production, service designers must coordinate between a diverse array of stakeholders who will make a service real across multiple channels. This demands a clear strategy around company politics and cultural frameworks. Since services are being produced and consumed simultaneously, designers must create flexible systems that adapt to changing environments and requirements. Ultimately, services are cocreated by many different actors, so motivation and behavior are often a crucial part of the design process.

What are the limits to service design?

Often service design intervenes into political systems of power within organizations and within established structures and processes. So it demands a good understanding of change processes in order to go beyond colorful sticky notes to implementation of innovative concepts.

Why is it important to learn about service design?

Service design provides an opportunity to create value on many different scales—economic value just as much as social or environmental value. And it can be a lot of fun designing with and for people!

1.10 Learning features

Key Points

- Services, not goods, are the basic unit of human exchange and the invisible glue of our everyday lives.
- Interactions are at the core of services because services are essentially people-centric. Interactions can be human-to-human or mediated through technology-based devices and interfaces.
- Services are experienced through interactions that unfold over time, and are delivered through different channels.
- Users are active participants in generating value by bringing their own knowledge to the service process. Users' actions and interactions with service providers affect the final outcome of the service.
- Service-dominant logic theory argues that services are the real base of our economy and that all economies are service economies. The real exchange is services even if mediated through goods.
- In product service systems (PSS), instead of acquiring a product, you acquire the function of said product by paying per use or shared ownership. A successful example of PSS is the *car-sharing model*.
- Designers can never fully design services. Instead, they can design the conditions of the interaction, its details, conditions, and touchpoints, but never the interaction itself.

Recap questions

- What characterizes the "service-dominant logic"?
- What are the practical implications of coproduction for service designers?
- What is the IHIP framework?
- What are other successful cases of product service systems?
- What are the main aspects of service interactions?
- What are the main "products of services," the material outputs of services as well as strategic ones?

Activities

- Map out the services you interact with daily, weekly, yearly, and those you interact with once in a lifetime. Pick a weekly one. Describe its main service offering (what is the benefit of this service?); analyze all the interactions that are part of it and the channels through which they are delivered. Draw the main physical and digital touchpoints and all the servicescapes where key service interactions happen. Draw or enact the main service scenes.
- Pick an item out of your household (for example, a power drill, an inflatable air mattress, or a

garbage bin) and imagine that instead of an individually owned good, it was a product service system (PSS). Design the service behind the service system behind the product. How would it be shared with other users? How would this change the experience of the product for you? How would this change the business model of the organization behind the product?

Glossary

- *Service-dominant logic*: The concept that argues that services are the primary mode of economic activity.
- *Product service systems (PSS)*: Systems that satisfy the users' needs through a system of services and products, rather than through individually owned products.
- *Touchpoint*: The material evidence or material systems that support the service experience.
- *Service channel*: The medium through which the user accesses the service touchpoints.
- *IHIP framework*: A framework that identifies services by four key qualities: intangibility, inseparability, heterogeneity, perishability.
- *Intangibility*: Part of the IHIP framework: Services are largely intangible, whereas goods can be sensed, touched, felt, or tasted.
- *Heterogeneity*: Part of the IHIP framework: Service provisions are performed and experienced in an irregular, heterogeneous fashion.
- *Inseparability*: Part of the IHIP framework: The production and consumption of services occur simultaneously, in contrast with products or goods (mass-produced products).
- *Perishability*: Part of the IHIP framework: Services, in general, cannot be stored, rendering them perishable and requiring the synchronization of demand and supply.

Recommended reading

Polaine, A., Løvlie, L., and Reason, B. (2013). *Service Design. From Insight to Implementation*. Rosenfeld Media.

Lusch, R. F., and Vargo, S. L. (2014). *Service Dominant Logic: Premises, Perspectives, Possibilities*. Cambridge University Press.

02 The service economy

2.1 Introduction

This chapter locates services in terms of an economic activity and also introduces the main service industries and emergent service-based economic models such as the sharing economy.

In spite of the notion that all economies are service economies in service-dominant logic, the world economy is still organized around the three classic areas of manufacturing, agriculture, and services. The service sector has an increasing importance in national and international economies worldwide and is the most common workplace worldwide.

The chapter looks into the current market of service design that has expanded over the years, thanks to some key industries commissioning service design work such as health care, the public sector, and the financial sector with great demand for service innovation.

The following section investigates the challenge of balancing standardization and customization of services. On one hand, it looks at how customer experience, or CX, is a professional role embedded in large organizations focusing on bridging this gap. On the other hand, it looks at service design's own contribution in this aspect, through the use of one of service design's most typical tools—the service blueprint.

Next, the chapter looks into the broad concept of social economy comprising parts of the economy that are not necessarily geared toward private profitability, including government and nonprofits, health care, and other social areas that are regarded as a major source of innovation, economic growth, and job creation. We look also at how service design is contributing to the highly service-based social economy.

The following section introduces the sharing economy in its two main and competing versions. One is the peer economy that is based on peer-to-peer collaboration and exchange such as *Timebanks*, *Freecycle*, the solidarity economy, and many other bottom-up initiatives. The other version of the sharing economy is associated with digital platforms such as *Uber* and *Airbnb* that became multibillion-dollar commercial entities operating as intermediary logistics companies between users and providers.

The chapter concludes with an interview with Ezio Manzini, founder of DESIS (Design for Social Innovation and Sustainability) Network, professor, and expert in design and social innovation.

2.2
The economics of services

Service-dominant logic (see Chapter 1) introduces the idea that there is no real divide between goods and services because services encompass goods as one integrated thing. Therefore, all economies are service economies and "everything is service," because the value created by goods is, in fact, generated by services as design, engineering, manufacturing, marketing, logistics, sales, and so on, that are embedded in it.

However, the world economy still persists in organizing industries (and their regulations and policies) around the three classic areas of manufacturing, agriculture, and services. In this approach the so-called service sector is known to be the main source of economic activity in the United States and Europe, in contrast to the manufacturing and agriculture sectors. Throughout the second half of the twentieth century, what is considered the service sector was the largest-growing building block of the U.S. economy, which is now considered a service-based economy. Many competing theories have been proposed to explain this structural shift toward a service-based economy. Forces behind this shift are complex and can be attributed to many factors, such as the offshoring of manufacturing with companies focusing on core service-related functions such as bundling of services with products. They also include the development of high-growth service industries such as in high technology and knowledge-intensive areas or in less-skilled and labor-intensive areas.

According to a 2014 report from the U.S. Bureau of Economic Analysis, the U.S. has a current trade surplus in services with a corresponding decline in the trade of goods. According to a report from the Australian government, China is the global manufacturing powerhouse but has recently opened its service sector to foreign investment by joining the World Trade Organization (WTO), which might result in growth in the Chinese service sectors. Some services are essential to sustain the manufacturing sector. Services and manufacturing clearly overlap to mutual benefit, including some promising design strategies such as product service systems (PSS), in which products are replaced by services as a way to reduce material consumption and lower environmental impact (see Chapter 1).

The service sector has an increasing importance in national and international economies worldwide and is composed of a constellation of different industries and subsectors. Each country, region, and city has its own unique combination of priorities and investments in the various service areas, responding to private sector inputs as well as governments' strategic visions and regional development plans.

What exactly are the service industries composed of? It is difficult to circumscribe the service sector, since it includes a wide variety of industries. Let's look at some specific data to have a better sense of the service economic landscape.

In the United States alone, the service sector corresponds to nearly 80 percent of the *gross domestic product* (GDP) from which the main contributing industries are as follows, according to the Bureau of Economic Analysis: real estate (13 percent), government services (14 percent), finance and insurance (8 percent), health and

2.2 The economics of services

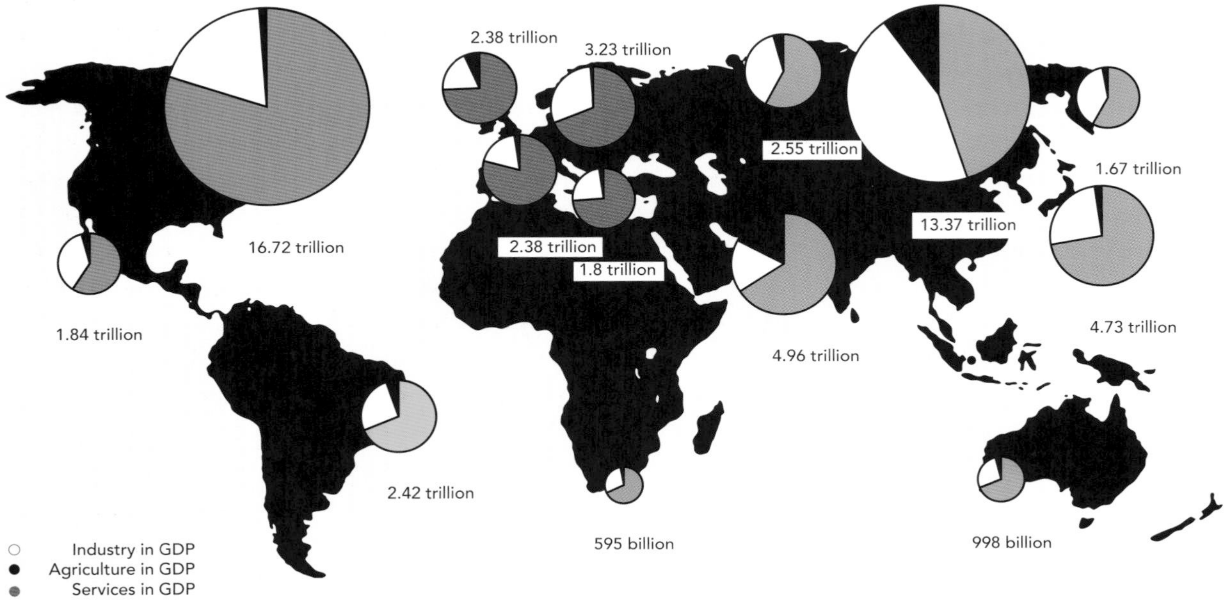
16.72 trillion
1.84 trillion
2.42 trillion
2.38 trillion
3.23 trillion
2.38 trillion
1.8 trillion
595 billion
2.55 trillion
13.37 trillion
4.96 trillion
1.67 trillion
4.73 trillion
998 billion
Industry in GDP
Agriculture in GDP
Services in GDP

Fig 2.1 Gross domestic product (GDP) composition of selected countries, showing manufacturing, agriculture, and service inputs. Data given in U.S. dollars.

social care (8 percent), information (4 percent), and arts and entertainment (4 percent). At the local level, however, different areas might differ in the percentages of each sector that are represented.

The North American Industry Classification (NAIC) system classifies "services" in thirteen distinct industries, excluding government services.

Other classification systems are similar to NAIC's, for the most part, but can include variations. Although classifications enable us to make sense of complex economic arrangements, we should recognize that goods or services classification systems are also arbitrary. For instance, a hamburger sold at a fast-food restaurant is part of a service, while its ingredients sold at a supermarket are considered goods.

Another important consideration when analyzing the economics of services is related to employment. Services industries are the most common workplace worldwide: from a global labor workforce of about 3.3 billion people (2013), 41.8 percent are employed in services, 35.4 percent in agriculture, and 22.8 percent in manufacturing, according to the American Coalition of Services Industries (2008). In other words, one in five human beings alive today is employed in providing services. In the United States, the service sector employs 80 percent of the workforce, and while the *service economy* continues to grow, there is a great wage disparity across service industries. Some provide part-time jobs, whereas others provide full-time jobs. Some industries pay low wages, such as fast-food service jobs, whereas others pay high wages, such as investment bankers. There are many contradictions within service jobs, and some trends should be viewed with concern. For example, an increase in temporary, low-wage, and low-skill jobs may contribute to widening income inequality and a decline in the standard of living for large segments of the population. But how does the design world connect to the service economy and relate to the topics discussed so far? In the next section, we look into how service design firms and consultancies have been engaging with different service industries and clients.

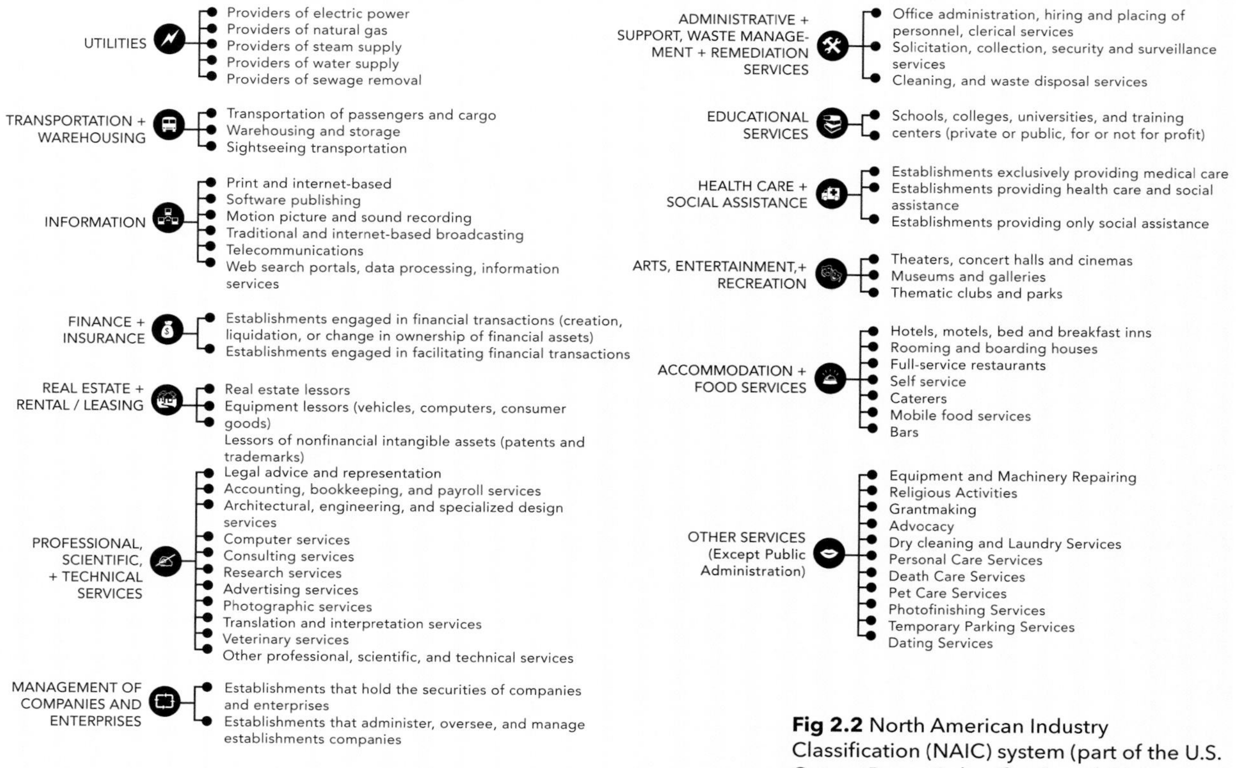
UTILITIES
Providers of electric power
Providers of natural gas
Providers of steam supply
Providers of water supply
Providers of sewage removal
TRANSPORTATION + WAREHOUSING
Transportation of passengers and cargo
Warehousing and storage
Sightseeing transportation
INFORMATION
Print and internet-based
Software publishing
Motion picture and sound recording
Traditional and internet-based broadcasting
Telecommunications
Web search portals, data processing, information services
FINANCE + INSURANCE
Establishments engaged in financial transactions (creation, liquidation, or change in ownership of financial assets)
Establishments engaged in facilitating financial transactions
REAL ESTATE + RENTAL / LEASING
Real estate lessors
Equipment lessors (vehicles, computers, consumer goods)
Lessors of nonfinancial intangible assets (patents and trademarks)
PROFESSIONAL, SCIENTIFIC, + TECHNICAL SERVICES
Legal advice and representation
Accounting, bookkeeping, and payroll services
Architectural, engineering, and specialized design services
Computer services
Consulting services
Research services
Advertising services
Photographic services
Translation and interpretation services
Veterinary services
Other professional, scientific, and technical services
MANAGEMENT OF COMPANIES AND ENTERPRISES
Establishments that hold the securities of companies and enterprises
Establishments that administer, oversee, and manage establishments companies
ADMINISTRATIVE + SUPPORT, WASTE MANAGEMENT + REMEDIATION SERVICES
Office administration, hiring and placing of personnel, clerical services
Solicitation, collection, security and surveillance services
Cleaning, and waste disposal services
EDUCATIONAL SERVICES
Schools, colleges, universities, and training centers (private or public, for or not for profit)
HEALTH CARE + SOCIAL ASSISTANCE
Establishments exclusively providing medical care
Establishments providing health care and social assistance
Establishments providing only social assistance
ARTS, ENTERTAINMENT, + RECREATION
Theaters, concert halls and cinemas
Museums and galleries
Thematic clubs and parks
ACCOMMODATION + FOOD SERVICES
Hotels, motels, bed and breakfast inns
Rooming and boarding houses
Full-service restaurants
Self service
Caterers
Mobile food services
Bars
OTHER SERVICES (Except Public Administration)
Equipment and Machinery Repairing
Religious Activities
Grantmaking
Advocacy
Dry cleaning and Laundry Services
Personal Care Services
Death Care Services
Pet Care Services
Photofinishing Services
Temporary Parking Services
Dating Services

Fig 2.2 North American Industry Classification (NAIC) system (part of the U.S. Census Bureau) classification of thirteen distinct industries of "services."

2.3
The market for service design

The emergence of service design as a field and a market has many affiliations. One lineage traces back to government-led initiatives pioneered in the United Kingdom in the early 2000s. Another lineage is associated with the introduction of digital technologies that created the demand for new service-based business models, where cell phones and handheld computers were bundled to a new ecosystem of digital services. This technological transformation continued to enable other service models to flourish, many of which transformed more traditional industries such as music, retailing, media, and banking.

But what are the main industries currently generating demands for service design?

A report by Forrester Research, a global research and advisory firm, that surveyed more than 100 design agencies around the world revealed a few important trends: some are global, and others are specific to cities, regions, or countries.

The health-care industry has been a key client for service designers in North America and in Europe. The public sector is another leading procurer of service design work, especially in Europe, but with a

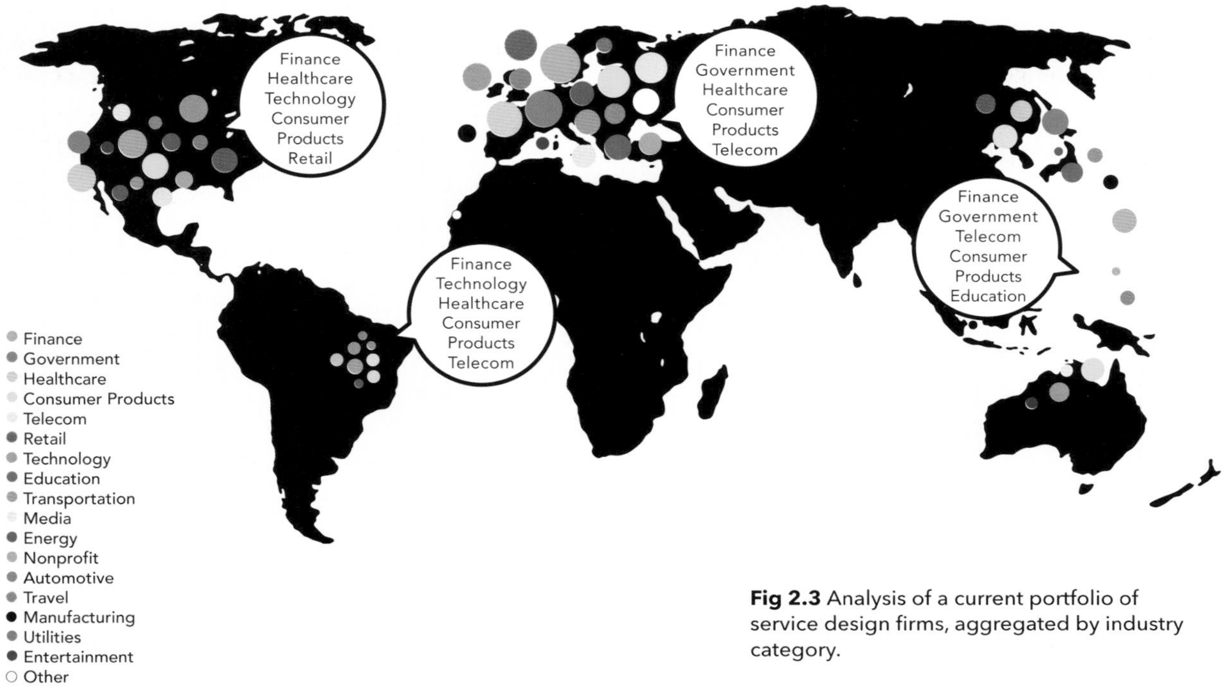

Finance
Healthcare
Technology
Consumer
Products
Retail
Finance
Government
Healthcare
Consumer
Products
Telecom
Finance
Government
Telecom
Consumer
Products
Education
Finance
Technology
Healthcare
Consumer
Products
Telecom
Finance
Government
Healthcare
Consumer Products
Telecom
Retail
Technology
Education
Transportation
Media
Energy
Nonprofit
Automotive
Travel
Manufacturing
Utilities
Entertainment
Other

Fig 2.3 Analysis of a current portfolio of service design firms, aggregated by industry category.

growing market in North America, Asia-Pacific, and in South America. (Read more about service design and the public sector in Chapter 3.)

IT-related high-tech industries appear as an emerging market for service designers both in North America and South America (especially in Brazil), followed by Europe and Asia-Pacific. Interestingly enough, neither consumer products nor manufacturing industries appear to show major demands for service design in the Asia-Pacific area, considering the extent of these industries in the region.

Financial services appear as the top industry hiring service design work. With high demand for service designers in every continent, the financial sector has been increasingly creating demand for service design. A quick analysis of top service design firms' online portfolios might show banks and insurance companies as prominent clients with a sustained demand for projects.

Not only is the financial sector the leading industry commissioning service design agencies worldwide, but also some financial institutions are creating in-house teams or acquiring design firms so that they work for them exclusively.

Banks are, after all, the quintessential service on which basic aspects of services can be demonstrated (including interactions, channels, touchpoints, but also intangibles such as expectations, relationships, and trust). Banks represent a service whose own name references the definition of service. The word *bank* comes from *banca* in Italian, meaning "counter." During the Renaissance, Florentine bankers conducted their transactions on high counters where clients would deposit their metal coins—their savings from labor, inheritances, possessions, and fortunes—onto the table top. The tall surface demarcated space for this special transaction, symbolizing mutual trust, with the service roles determined by the physical separation: service providers (bankers) on one side, and service users (clients) on the opposite.

Fig 2.4 Counting house scene from British Library collection.

The financial services sector is undergoing some important transformations. On one hand, the 2008 financial crisis changed the public's perception of traditional financial providers. On the other hand, new technology and new service models have emerged, changing the scene of the financial sector. Peer-based lending systems, microfinance, frictionless payments (such as money transfer via text messages), and crypto-currency (such as *bitcoins*, a peer-to-peer payment system enabled by the *blockchain* technology, also described as digital currency) are among some of the most recent trends transforming the traditional service models in the financial sector. In particular, the developing world emerges as a major market that can benefit from such service innovations, offering different types of project opportunities and solutions, as we see in the following case studies.

Case Study: Replacing cash with digital repayments by One Acre Fund and Citi

One Acre Fund is a nonprofit organization offering microloans to small farmers in East Africa. Farmers make an initial deposit of US$5, for an average nine-month loan of US$90. The loans give farmers access to seeds and fertilizer, financing for farm inputs, plus training in agriculture techniques and ways to better market their products and maximize their profit. To participate, farmers must join their village group, which employs a local field officer who coordinates and facilitates all transactions, distribution of supplies, and training. In partnership with Citi, through its Citi Kenya and Citi Inclusive Finance units, One Acre Fund has recently introduced the use of the digitally mobile money service M-Pesa for loan repayments, replacing the previous cash-based system.

In the previous cash-based system, farmers would meet weekly to make the repayments. The farmers would give cash to the local One Acre Fund field officer, who entered their repayments in a receipt book and gave each farmer a paper receipt. The field officer would transport the collected cash and deposit into the district bank. It would take up to two weeks to update the loan balances and reconcile the bank statements, in a process prone to uncertainty, inefficiency, and insecurity. The change has benefited the farmers on many levels.

Farmers using the digitally mobile money service to make their loan repayments reported a unanimous preference for the digital payments instead of cash in great part related to convenience, transparency, and safety. Farmers, especially women, were afraid of holding cash. In addition, farmers were also freed from the burden of a long process and higher processing costs, and the system is much less prone to fraud. The success of the new system is also related to an already-thriving digital payment ecosystem because farmers were already familiar with M-Pesa, the Kenyan digital payment system.

Fig 2.5 Farmers in Kenya, using the loan payment system of One Acre Fund and Citi.

Case Study: Advancing Financial Inclusion project by Continuum for The World Bank

In this financial service design project, the design team at Continuum worked for World Bank's branch Consultative Group to Assist the Poor in partnership with Habib Bank Limited (HBL), the largest bank in Pakistan. The project focused on the recipients of the Benazir Income Support Programme (BISP), a financial assistance program set by the Pakistani government to distribute cash payments to low-income families.

The main challenges involved irregular payment schedules and communication barriers with the end users, in great part illiterate women. The project was aimed at improving the women's ability to access BISP benefits through ATMs or directly with an employee at their local branches. The design team started the project with situated interviews and observations to learn about the clients' lifestyles, their financial and savings habits, and overall experiences with BISP. This highly immersive fieldwork resulted in a series of recommendations on how to better communicate with the women, including the design of guidelines for ATM screens using photographs instead of words.

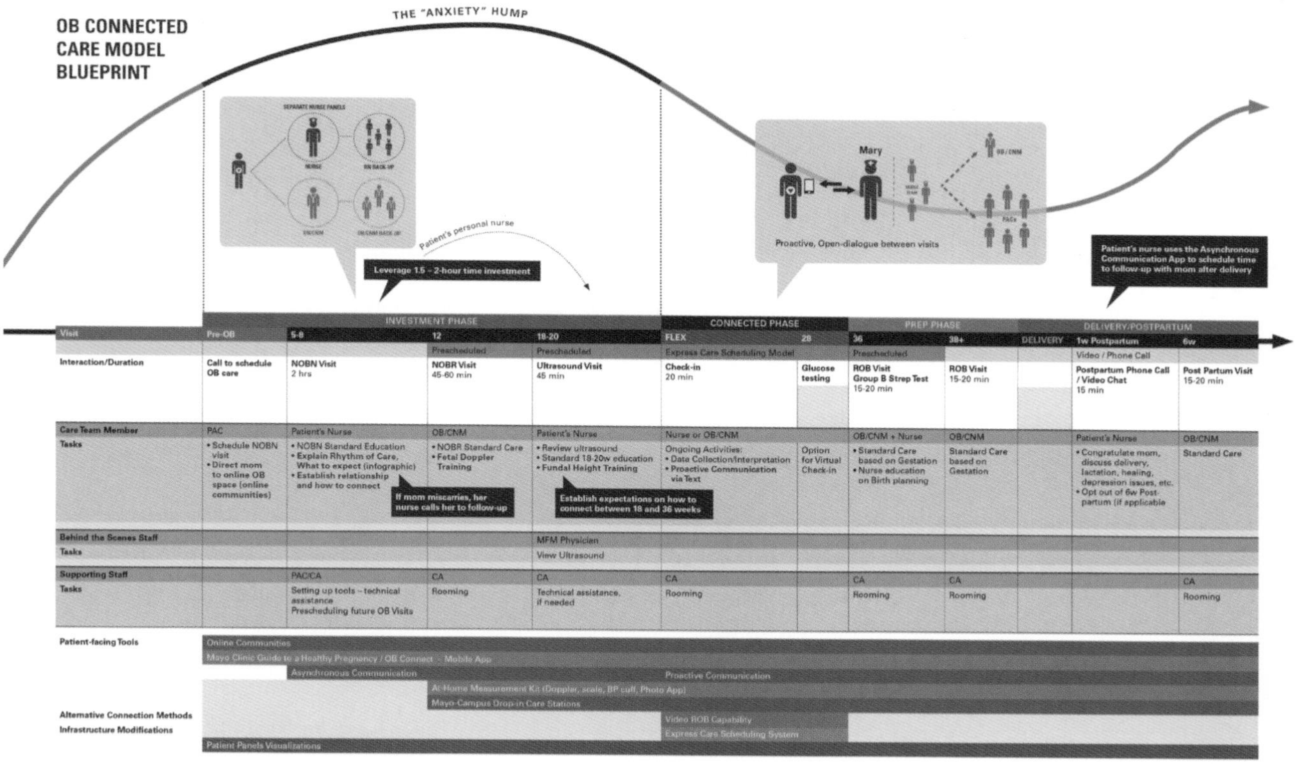

OB CONNECTED CARE MODEL BLUEPRINT
THE "ANXIETY" HUMP
Patient's personal nurse
Leverage 1.5 – 2-hour time investment
Mary
Proactive, Open-dialogue between visits
Patient's nurse uses the Asynchronous Communication App to schedule time to follow-up with mom after delivery
INVESTMENT PHASE
CONNECTED PHASE
PREP PHASE
DELIVERY/POSTPARTUM
Visit
Pre-OB
5-8
12
18-20
FLEX
28
36
38+
DELIVERY
1w Postpartum
6w
Prescheduled
Express Care Scheduling Model
Video / Phone Call
Interaction/Duration
Call to schedule OB care
NOBN Visit 2 hrs
NOBR Visit 45-60 min
Ultrasound Visit 45 min
Check-in 20 min
Glucose testing
ROB Visit Group B Strep Test 15-20 min
ROB Visit 15-20 min
Postpartum Phone Call / Video Chat 15 min
Post Partum Visit 15-20 min
Care Team Member
Tasks
PAC
• Schedule NOBN visit • Direct mom to online OB space (online communities)
Patient's Nurse
• NOBN Standard Education • Explain Rhythm of Care, What to expect (infographic) • Establish relationship and how to connect
OB/CNM
• NOBR Standard Care • Fetal Doppler Training
Patient's Nurse
• Review ultrasound • Standard 18-20w education • Fundal Height Training
Nurse or OB/CNM
Ongoing Activities: • Data Collection/Interpretation • Proactive Communication via Text
Option for Virtual Check-in
OB/CNM + Nurse
• Standard Care based on Gestation • Nurse education on Birth planning
OB/CNM
Standard Care based on Gestation
Patient's Nurse
• Congratulate mom, discuss delivery, lactation, healing, depression issues, etc. • Opt out of 6w Post-partum (if applicable
OB/CNM
Standard Care
If mom miscarries, her nurse calls her to follow-up
Establish expectations on how to connect between 18 and 36 weeks
Behind the Scenes Staff
Tasks
MFM Physician
View Ultrasound
Supporting Staff
Tasks
PAC/CA
Setting up tools – technical assistance Prescheduling future OB Visits
CA
Rooming
CA
Technical assistance, if needed
CA
Rooming
CA
Rooming
CA
Rooming
CA
Rooming
Patient-facing Tools
Online Communities
Mayo Clinic Guide to a Healthy Pregnancy / OB Connect – Mobile App
Asynchronous Communication
Proactive Communication
At-Home Measurement Kit (Doppler, scale, BP cuff, Photo App)
Mayo-Campus Drop-in Care Stations
Alternative Connection Methods
Infrastructure Modifications
Video ROB Capability
Express Care Scheduling System
Patient Panels Visualizations

Fig 2.11 Blueprint example of Mayo Clinic's OB Connected Care. The blueprint maps out the interactions of patients with the OB. The top row, or "swim lane," shows the sequence of interactions between patient and staff, and the swim lanes below show actions and tasks by staff in three levels—front office, behind the scenes, and supporting. Note the different phases of the service interaction along the pregnancy: investment phase, connected phase, prep phase, and delivery/postpartum. Note also the arc of emotions at the top showing the "anxiety hump" of patients in the first phase of pregnancy and how that changes as the patient gets more connected and proactive.

2.5
The rise of the social economy

A part of the economy that is not necessarily geared toward private profitability is on the rise. Driven by government, philanthropies, nonprofits, social enterprises, and cooperatives to create solutions for social, economic, or environmental issues, the so-called *social economy* is said to become a major source of innovation, economic growth, and job creation.

How might service designers be part of the social economy?

A growing number of designers are working for government and nonprofits in health care and other social areas. Today there is evidence of a demand for service design coming from these industries and a growing awareness of the impact of design as an effective approach to develop better solutions to social problems. A great part of the social economy is service-based. Looking at top service design firms worldwide, we note that a good part of their portfolios are related to social economy projects and clients.

Health care is among the most notable areas of the social economy that has been attracting service design talent, in great part by establishing in-house design teams.

The Mayo Clinic's Center for Innovation is a leader in service innovation applied to the health-care sector. A top-ranked not-for-profit medical practice, research, and educational group based in Minnesota, it has a nearly 150-year history connected to medical innovation with pioneering treatments and new methods of delivery and service.

In the early 2000s, Mayo Clinic's leadership reached out to IDEO and other design firms with the aim of using design methods to improve the health-care experience, focusing on doctor-patient interactions and transforming "the way healthcare is experienced and delivered." The initial pilot soon expanded into a Center for Innovation (CFI), with a series of dedicated physical spaces at different hospital and care facilities, such as collaborative work areas located on patient floors and *living labs* placed within a senior care center. The Multidisciplinary Design Clinic is a living lab where patients collaborate with providers in the design of new methods, processes, and prototypes of health-care solutions. Currently, design research capabilities at CFI include design strategy, product design, and service design, among others.

CFI's projects include the design of new online consulting systems (eConsults), models for integrating informal caregivers into the wellness system (Caregivers), the mapping and improvement of prenatal care journeys (OB Nest), the development of a decision aid tool for patients with diabetes and other diseases (Decision Aids), among others.

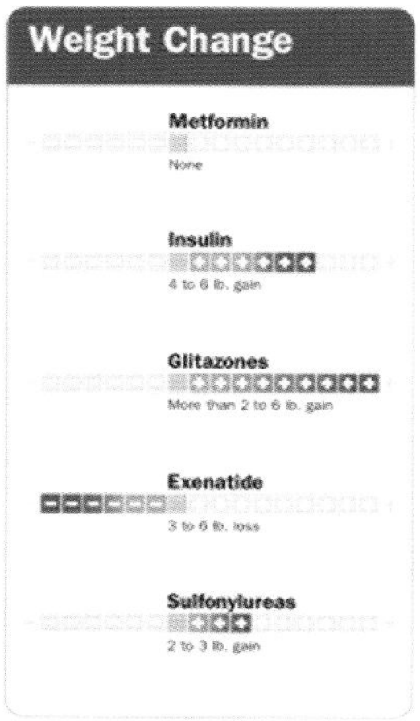
Weight Change
Metformin
None
Insulin
4 to 6 lb. gain
Glitazones
More than 2 to 6 lb. gain
Exenatide
3 to 6 lb. loss
Sulfonylureas
2 to 3 lb. gain

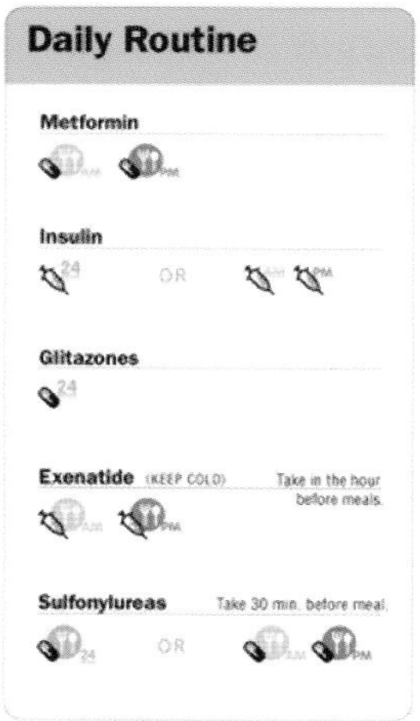
Daily Routine
Metformin
Insulin
OR
Glitazones
Exenatide (KEEP COLD)
Take in the hour before meals.
Sulfonylureas
Take 30 min. before meal.
OR

Daily Sugar Testing
(Monitoring)
Metformin
S M T W T F S
Monitor 2 - 5 times weekly, less often once stable.
Insulin
S M T W T F S
Monitor once or twice daily, less often once stable.
Glitazones
S M T W T F S
Monitor 3 - 5 times weekly, less often once stable.
Exenatide
S M T W T F S
Monitor twice daily after meals when used with Sulfonylureas, as needed when used with Metformin.
Sulfonylureas
S M T W T F S
Monitor 2 - 5 times weekly, less often once stable.

Figs 2.12 to 2.16 Mayo Clinic's Center for Innovation (CFI) space and images from Mayo Clinic Center for Innovation projects: Decision Aids cards to help patients with diabetes managing their condition; eConsults, an online consulting system; and the "Jack and Jill" consult rooms that improve the patient experience by giving physicians a place to talk with patients together with family members in conjunction with an exam room with a new layout that enables more seamless physical exams.

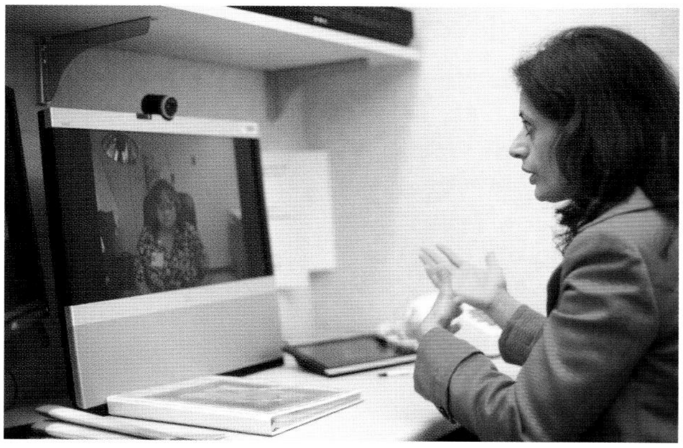

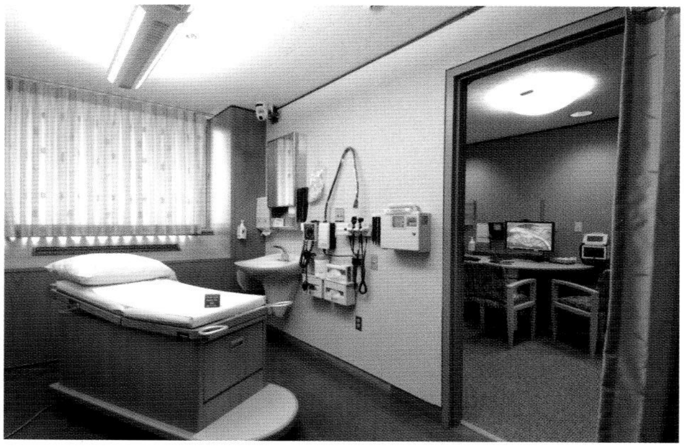

2.6 The sharing economy

The term *sharing economy* became somewhat of a buzzword in recent years, often expressing very different ideas. In fact, there are two main competing approaches.

The first one overlaps the concepts of *sharing economy* and *peer economy*, which is an alternative socioeconomic system developed around the idea of borrowing, bartering, lending, swapping, and exchanging resources, assets, or goods by different people. Examples of sharing modalities include everything from tools, home appliances, houses, and cars; to bartering time; supporting each other via *crowdfunding*; or many others ideas based on collaborations and *peer-to-peer* exchange. Think of Timebanks (in which one person helps another for an agreed number of hours in exchange for the equivalent amount of time the other person will help the first person), Wikipedia (the free online encyclopedia, created and edited by volunteers), Couchsurfing (the practice of staying temporarily in other people's homes), or Freecycle (groups of people giving away unwanted items to others instead of disposing of them). These examples challenge the traditional notions of intellectual property, private ownership, and the traditional ways of consuming goods and services.

At the origins of this version of the sharing economy is the search for a less material-intense and more ecologically sustainable society, a socioeconomic shift based on mutual trust to promote shared access to things without having to own them. The sharing economy is therefore part of a broader *social movement* built on bottom-up, grassroots initiatives aiming to solve today's biggest challenges. Solidarity economy, open source software, transition towns, collaborative services, open innovation, and others are models proposing not only practical, do-it-yourself responses to economic and environmental crisis, but also a new cultural mindset and political worldview (for more on service design for social innovation, see Chapter 4).

The other version of the sharing economy is associated with digital platforms. The original ideas behind the sharing economy soon ended up attracting entrepreneurs and investors intrigued by the potential of monetizing people's unused time and assets, and together with the swift evolution of smartphones, social media, and Internet accessibility, a complete new category of services was born. A new business model enabled by digital platforms or on-demand apps emerged to manage and *commodify* daily life.

Platform-service companies such as Uber (the on-demand car service company that connects drivers who use their own personal cars with clients through a smartphone app) or Airbnb (the online apartment-rental platform that enables people to list or rent their residential properties short term) quickly turned into multibillion-dollar commercial entities. Ultimately, they became "middleman" logistics companies in which users and providers pay them a percentage in service fees in conjunction with every transaction—without owning any physical infrastructure of their own.

These services tapped into market gaps and quickly became very successful. Despite their growing popularity among consumers, the implications on the economy are now being calculated, and not without controversy. These companies are still in great part underregulated, and some are being accused of unfair competition with previous occupants of these markets (such as hotels and taxi services) or contributing to the deterioration of labor standards.

While the disruptions caused by the different versions of the sharing economy are still being negotiated, designers cannot avoid debating its implications for their practice. Designing in this space represents not only the ability of shaping new digital interfaces and touchpoints, but the possibility of affecting society in terms of social relations, ecological sustainability, and economic opportunity.

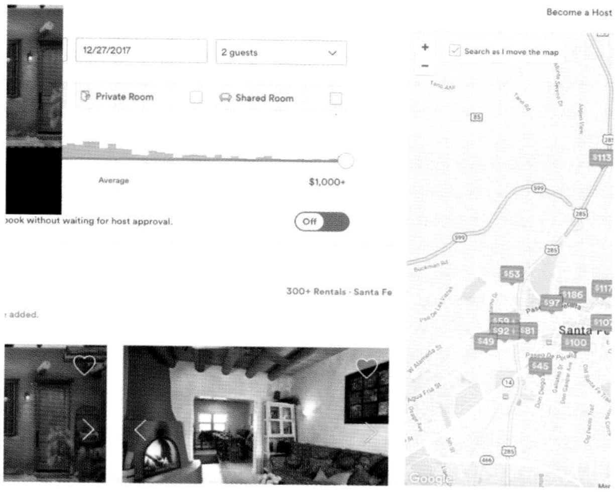

Become a Host
12/27/2017
2 guests
Private Room
Shared Room
Average
$1,000+
Off
300+ Rentals · Santa Fe
Search as I move the map

2.17

View Photos
$86
Per Night
Overview
Reviews
The Host
Location
Check In
Check Out
Casita Encantador
Guests
2 guests
Paddy
Entire home/apt
2 Guests
0 Bedrooms
1 Bed
$95 x 16 nights
$1520

2.18

モトタバコヤ

2.19

2.20

Figs 2.17 to 2.20 The Airbnb interface showing the mechanics of the service: renters can select houses by location and price range and get in touch with hosts and see reviews from previous guests, while guests are also reviewed by hosts. Images showing both interior and neighborhood are key to the Airbnb platform. (The bottom images show a listed apartment in the Konohana-ku neighborhood in Osaka, Japan.)

2.7 Interview with Ezio Manzini

Ezio Manzini is an Italian design strategist, one of the world's leading experts on sustainable design, author of numerous design books, professor of Industrial Design at Milan Polytechnic, and founder of the DESIS (Design for Social Innovation and Sustainability) Network of university-based design labs.

What is your definition of service design?

A service is an interaction between people, things, and places targeted to produce value. Service design is whatever can be designed to make this interaction more probable, interesting, and effective for all stakeholders.

To be able to understand services, we need to position services in relation to the economy. What's your vision for the current and future economy?

The economy is moving toward unprecedented forms. There are ecosystems of different economies. They may include the traditional market and state economies, but there are also economies of sharing, exchange, self-help, and of the gift. The organizational and economic models of these ecosystems are complex combinations of different motivations, goals, and points of view.

It is not by chance that these new economic models have developed side by side with growing waves of social innovation and the maturation of the digital revolution. In fact, social innovation and the digital are often blurred, creating new forms of organizations adapted to live in hybrid environments and based on equally innovative economic models.

As far as designers are concerned, we need to learn how to navigate the complexity of these new ecosystems. This includes developing clear opinions on emerging conflicts, such as the ones between emergent service models and old ones (think Uber versus taxis or Airbnb versus traditional hotels). But also between the new ones as well. For example, there are different directions the same emerging service models may take (think again Uber and Airbnb versus more platform-based cooperatives). This is, in part, the conflict between a new form of neoliberalism and the first examples of authentic collaborative economies.

What do you think service designers must pay attention to in order to embrace the complexity inherent to the services, particularly relating to new economic ecosystems?

Compared to other professional communities, the design community is already thinking more about complexities than other industries are. Designers are not in a bad position considering the traditional flexible and open nature of design.

But what is currently missing for the design ethos and community is a better understanding of their role and their tools. In a connected world, everything is designed and everybody designs, so design experts must understand how to use their specific culture and knowledge. It's even more important now for designers to understand what their specific contribution is to complex, open-ended, and contradictory codesign processes.

As you mention, designing services involve open-ended and contradictory codesign processes. Do service designers put greater emphasis on the design process rather than the design outcome? What are the outputs of service design work, the products of service design?

I think that we should redefine what is the product of our design activity. In dealing with the complexity, unpredictability, and networked nature of services, we rely greatly on codesign processes. An important aspect of codesign processes is the production of intermediate artifacts that can materialize as tools or design activities. These are the products of this kind of design.

More specifically, these tools and design activities include ethnographic research, scenario building, storytelling exercises, concept cogeneration workshops, prototyping, conceptualization of digital platforms, or other specific communication tools. These activities may take place as part of larger and open-ended codesign processes, but should be considered as unique and relatively autonomous results. These are the intermediate design products and artifacts I am referring to here. Designers must clearly communicate the value of their tools and design activities, what they can uniquely bring to these processes, and what they will produce for the overall codesign process.

Social innovation has drawn attention in relation to projects that are focused on community and social welfare. However, most design firms still work for clients who are part of the "old economy," such as financial service firms, insurance companies, and retailers. How do you see the balance of clients changing in the future?

The balance will depend on how the ecosystem of economies evolves and the various components that make up that evolution.

Of course, many design firms will go on working for what will remain of the old economy. However, there could be many more design firms working for the emerging economy if only they were capable of presenting themselves in the right way. That is, to be recognized as actors capable of making meaningful contributions. In my view, the demand of designers capable to work in the framework of emerging economies is larger than the offer.

Today, what should be done well (i.e., in an expert way) by service designers is often done by others. That is, by other practitioners who extended their original field of activity toward service design (even though they are not calling themselves service designers and haven't been trained as such). This is the case with architects and urban planners who are working with local authorities designing new kinds of urban services; software developers, developing applications that are technology-based services; social workers, developing new social services; NGO activists, inventing empowering services with under-served communities.

Facing all that, it is clear that service designers should better communicate what their capabilities are and what (potentially, at least) they would be capable to bring to these emerging design processes.

Products, communication elements, and systems offer certain affordances. Yet, how they are adopted or used often depends on how humans respond to them. This challenge of use is central to the job of service designers. How do you understand the relation between the potential of an affordance and human participation or adoption of a service?

Traditionally, if you design a product, you will not see how, once in use, this product will really interact with people. That is, you will not see how users, in their practical interaction with your object, will reinvent the way to use it. In contrast, when you design a service, which by definition is *per se* an interaction, the way it will be "used" directly affects the service providers, and therefore, in some ways, the related service designers. In short, because—luckily—interactions cannot be designed, what can be designed is a system that makes certain kinds of interactions more probable. This can be said for both products and services. But, since we started to design services, this reality appears in a much clearer way.

You've argued that the human component of services needs to be nurtured and cultivated. Are designers prepared for that? Are there new kinds of the capabilities and skills that service designers need to have?

Over the past two decades, service design has developed into a discipline with its own range of useful tools. Nevertheless, I think there is something highly important still missing. It is that very special "tool" that is culture. I think that we still are far from having a sufficient service design culture. For example, service design has yet to develop a culture comparable with the one that has been developed for product design. When dealing with products, designers have the appropriate language, knowledge, and special sensitivity to deal with tridimensional forms in space. Something similar should be produced for services and service design. A good service design expert should have a language, a knowledge, and a special sensitivity to deal with interactions. That is, with something taking place in the four dimensions (the fourth dimension being time), in which service encounters happen.

Why learn service design?

We now live in a highly connected world. Designers have the opportunity and responsibility to influence these encounters in unprecedented ways. They have the capability to develop support systems that influence and empower the interactions of our connected world.

2.8 Learning features

Key points

- Services are chiefly important in the global economy and are the main source of wealth generation in industrialized countries.
- The main industries creating a market for service design include the financial sector, public services, and health care.
- Balancing between standardization and customization is a critical challenge for service organizations.

  The social economy, composed of the public sector, health care, education, and many others, is growing its economic weight and represents important markets for service design work.
- The sharing economy has two main competing versions—one related to the bottom-up peer economy, and the other related to digital platform services such as Uber and Airbnb.

Recap questions

- What is the importance of the service sector in terms of job creation?
- What are the main industries within the service economy?
- Why are standardization and customization contradictory in services?
- What is CX and what is its role in organizations?
- What is the service design blueprint?

Activities

- Analyze your financial (or health-care) service. Map out the organizations involved and identify the different service streams coming from different parts of the system. In the case of financial services, consider your bank and all its channels that you interact with, and also related services such as credit card, PayPal, and credit scores. Prepare a service blueprint describing the main services over time. Identify critical moments where standardization and customization appear.
- Working in teams, identify the services of the sharing economy that you have already used. Identify which version of the sharing economy they represent. Find out about regulations pertaining to these services in your city or region. Debate the implications of these different services for users, the economy, and for people working for them. Debate pros and cons of each service.

Glossary

- *Service economy*: A service-based economy, in which the main source of economic activity comes from the service sector (as opposed to manufacturing and agriculture sectors), as in the United States and Europe.
- *Customer experience (CX)*: A newly defined area of expertise within organizations dedicated to integrating the customers' needs, using tools that are familiar to user-centered designers and advocating for user/customer needs within organizations.
- *Service blueprint*: A time-based matrix that reveals the sequential actions and touchpoints of a service from the perspective of both the user and the provider.
- *Social economy*: All those areas of the economy that are not geared to commercial profitability.
- *Sharing economy*: Two competing versions—one based on peer-to-peer exchanges, and the other based on digital platforms intermediating between users and providers.
- *Financial inclusion*: Accessible and affordable financial services catering to low-income populations as an alternative to mainstream financial systems, considered as a key strategy to reduce poverty. It may include microcredit, peer-based lending, and accessible technology such as payment through text message.

Recommended reading

Botsman, Rachel, and Rogers, Roo (2010). *What's Mine Is Yours: The Rise of Collaborative Consumption*. Harper Business.

Gravity Tank (2015). *Change Agents. Four Trends Disrupting the Way We Spend, Save and Invest*. Service Design Network Special Interest Group Trend Report, Fall.

Manzini, Ezio (2015). *Design, When Everybody Designs: An Introduction to Design for Social Innovation*. The MIT Press.

Julier, Guy (2017). *Economies of Design*. Sage.

03 Digital services

Nest proposes intuitive interfaces in the artifact itself and in the applications. The information loop from object to person helps individuals more consciously monitor their own energy consumption and, hopefully, make smarter decisions. The continuous connections between device, usage, data, and smart technology have disrupted the thermostat business and transformed the market. They drove Google to purchase Nest outright to run their internal devices division. In early 2014, Nest launched the Nest Developer Program, which essentially opens its platform to software developers who can create new applications and devices able to interface with Nest. This means that other artifacts and applications will be able to "talk" to each other using Nest as a translator or hub for their smart communication. For instance, Nest will be able to communicate with smart Mercedes Benz cars, smart Whirlpool washing machines and dryers, and the Jawbone UP wearable (see the first case study, earlier in this chapter).

In this case, the benefit of a smart system to control thermostats seems really clear and meaningful: improved energy efficiency. However, similarly to the wearable activity trackers, technology seems to be ahead of the service aspect. There is room for integration of the thermostat control system not only with appliances and cars, as suggested previously, but also with utilities companies. If the service model were based on a broad integrated system, such devices could play a role in helping change the current energy consumption model and influence how households choose energy sources, directing the market toward clean energy, for example.

While fitness wearables and smart home systems are the first taste of the IoT in the consumer market, it includes many systems beyond those, including smart cities and industrial applications of the IoT, also called *Industrial Internet of Things*, or IIoT. In terms of approach, there seem to be different philosophical streams cutting across these different application spaces for the IoT.

One is efficiency-driven; it is all about monitoring, control, and optimization of systems, either related to our bodies, homes, workplaces, or cities. Nest and other home devices as well as wearables seem to build on this trend. The IIoT is also strongly based on this approach for industrial infrastructures with applications including Internet-managed assembly lines, connected factories, and warehouses. Similarly, urban management also takes an efficiency-driven approach with applications such as intelligent traffic management systems or optimized waste management systems that allow trucks to be directed to collect only the waste disposal containers that are already full.

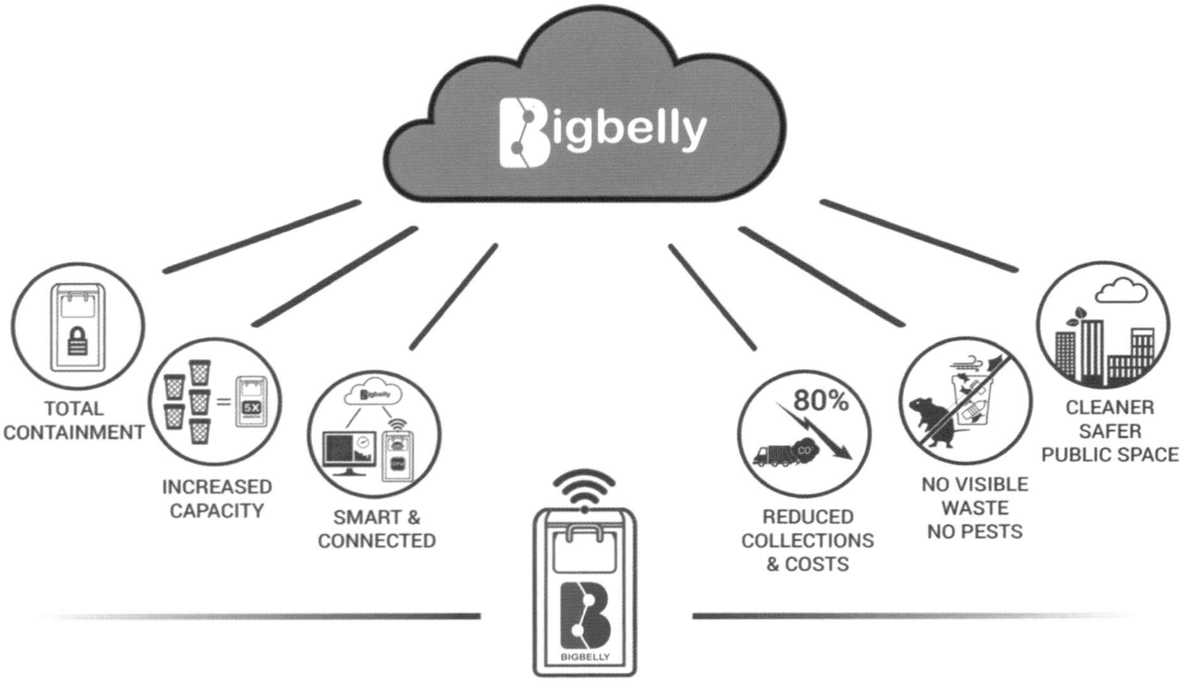
Bigbelly
TOTAL CONTAINMENT
INCREASED CAPACITY
SMART & CONNECTED
REDUCED COLLECTIONS & COSTS
NO VISIBLE WASTE NO PESTS
CLEANER SAFER PUBLIC SPACE
80%
5X
BIGBELLY

BROADWAY
TOSHIBA
TDK
PUSH
PAPER
TRASH
@TSqArts

Figs 3.7 and 3.8 Bigbelly is a Smart Waste & Recycling System whose solutions include smart bins that are equipped with a sensor that measures level of waste inside, and alerts the collection system only when completely full through real-time data, reducing the need for collection by 80 percent and consequently reducing CO_2 emissions associated with trucks.

3.5 The role of service design in digital services

What is the designer's mandate in the development of digital services in a broader sense? What are the possible contributions of service design into this growing cross-sector economy? What is the dialogue with other design specializations and traditions such as interaction design or experience design?

Increasing use of technology-enabled services requires design more than ever. As introduced earlier, a great deal of the controversy about the IoT revolves around the human impact of creating the new connectivity of new product service system ecologies. It seems that as technology becomes more accessible, the social scenarios and protocols around them haven't matured at the same rate. This is the point at which design can help, with its tradition of being interpreter of social values and capturing "signifiers."

Because designers tend to look at the bigger picture and work in a people-centric way, they can help putting people back at the center of digital and technology developments, counterbalancing the tech-centric mindset of engineers and developers. Service design is a well-positioned field with its integrative and multidisciplinary nature, building on human-centered design approaches, participatory methods, management and organizational sciences, marketing and product development, as well as links with social sciences.

The design community constantly questions the differences between the various design specializations dealing with interactions affecting services, systems, organizations, and government, unleashed by technology. How is service design different from interaction design or user experience (UX) design? Interaction design professor Jodi Forlizzi notes (see interview below) that whereas service design draws from management research, experience and interaction design draw from consumer and cognitive psychology. And because of the coproduced nature of service design, it has embraced participatory methods and cocreation methods. In contrast, UX designers have focused on understanding the essence of the experience and embraced experience prototyping as a methodology to aid in anticipating social and intangible outcomes.

From the business and management side, customer experience (CX) also converges with service design, as noted in Chapter 2. CX experts normally work inside organizations, looking into the customer experience while also designing the behind-the-scenes activities, under a business-driven mindset. Service designers often interact with CX, working from within organizations.

As services continue to evolve, design needs to be able to aggregate these complementary capacities and infuse the technological and business discussions with meaning and purpose. In practical terms, not every service designer will dive deeply into the technical aspects related to UX or CX practices because service design work tends to focus more on aspects such as social interactions, aesthetics, and meaning. It is critical, however, that service design integrate some UX and CX capabilities. Service designers need to consider economic and business implications of services and be fluent enough in technology aspects so that they can foster the consideration of the social implications of technology and help humanize IoT.

3.6 Interview with Jodi Forlizzi

Jodi Forlizzi is a professor in the Human-Computer Interaction Institute within the School of Computer Science, Carnegie Mellon University.

With the ubiquity of digital interfaces mediating our lives, there has been an explosion in thinking about "user experience," or UX. What role can service design play in enhancing the user experience of a digital service?

When technology moved off of the computer and desktop, I think UX happened. Designers realized that they needed to think about more than just a product. They needed to think about the whole context of use. At the same time, service design began to grow from operations research and marketing, two disciplines rarely mentioned in UX design.

Both service and UX focus on the experience of the customer or stakeholder. The way that they've come to it, however, is different. UX is still focused on one product or one thing and maybe one user, but service looks holistically across touchpoints and across many stakeholders.

You talked a little bit about the distinction between service design and UX as an individual outlook versus a more holistic approach. Are there any methods or approaches or aspects of the field's origin that you could share?

I think both UX and service design, and even user-centered design, use a lot of the same methods. We use research methods like interviews and observations. We use prototyping methods. We develop personas and scenarios. One thing that makes service different is its multistakeholder or systemic view.

If I gave a set of user-centered design students the task of designing a ride-sharing service like Uber, they would think about the driver and the passenger. But if you gave that same problem to someone who's really thinking in terms of service or systems, they would start thinking about taxis, and public transportation, and other traffic on the road. They would be more aware of multiple stakeholders as they affect ride sharing.

I think another difference is that service implicitly suggests that we need to think of value, and that's often economic value. A lot of times in user-centered design contexts, people aren't thinking about the business case.

Finally, I think, at the extreme, I would say, that all UX designers need to have some service knowledge and methods in their toolbox now because we're not really designing products anymore. We're designing platforms for people to interact with product service systems.

3.6 Interview with Jodi Forlizzi

How do you understand the role of service design for digital services?

I think that you can look at typography, color, and composition as the building blocks of interaction design, or even communication design. I think you can look at service design as a building block for designing these complex things. It helps us think about what people will experience when they use a digital service. Service design helps us think about all of the stakeholders, not only the main user and service provider, but other people who might be impacted. And service design helps us to think of the value flow, whether the value is economic or not. Take Flipboard as an example. Flipboard could not exist without other content providers. It would not be as rich without the likes, tags, and comments of the people that read the content. So while there is no economic exchange, there's a lot of value exchange. I think people need to consider that, especially if they're designing apps that are free or 99 cents. How is a service at this price point going to pay for itself?

Digital services can be seen as facilitating various kinds of social action. However, the models in which they do so vary considerably; for example, some are free to users, others are based on modes of sharing, while others require formal payment. What is the relationship between different modes of exchange and the development of digital services?

I don't know that there's necessarily a relationship, but I would note that there are multiple ways that people derive value from things. Everything seems to be a value in exchange. The software industry is a great example. For Microsoft and Adobe, we used to buy DVDs and load them on our computer. Then Adobe moved to a cloud model where you pay a subscription price per month and things are driven to you. But an even more radical model would be Google. Instantly you have a lightweight program that you can use that you never own. You can easily collaborate. Your software is always up-to-date. But in return for that, Google is monitoring your actions. They're watching what you do with their software. So, that's an interesting kind of value exchange, where nothing is purchased, but there is a trade-off for what the customer gets for free.

Digital services have become increasingly mobile largely through the use of smartphones. What are the new trends in this space, and how do you think they will affect process of design?

For a while, we saw this burgeoning rise of apps. Now things are starting to bundle. For example, Google on Tap and Siri app on the iPhone attempted to collapse things together around what they think a user's actions might be. The trend is to condense things and try to look at people's probable, or likely, behavior.

So for designers that suggest in addition to understanding how to design an app, we have to be able to think about what would users' typical actions through a task flow be. How are we going to design for them?

We're starting to see machine learning come, not only in the back end as they make sense of the data about you, but in the front end as it tries to predict and anticipate what your actions will be and, thus, project interfaces and response. For designers that means that we have to understand and design things in new ways. I think that it's a really interesting and different context for design.

How might digitally enabled services build on more traditional brick-and-mortar models of service provision?

In the days of physical service delivery, when the service provider did something special for someone, they felt rewarded. It felt like a luxury service and people would pay more. For example, Nordstrom department stores, some of the service actions are lovely. There's personal shoppers roaming when you're in the physical store, and when you're finished with the purchase, they step around the counter and hand you your bag. And for this you pay more. We don't have that kind of thing in digital services. I think there's an opportunity to try and create it.

Another interesting thing about digital services is that a lot of information is created about a customer but not leveraged. We've got these cards that track our purchases. We also have all the data that traditionally comes with customer relationship management. I think that if we were to blend, or extend, what digital services are doing with what is rich and good about services in the physical world, it is possible to leverage some of this data and create new personalized and even luxury services.

This could lead to interesting kinds of service actions that would not only make customers feel rewarded, but make service providers feel like they're doing a better job. And when you move those into contexts like education, or health care, I think the impact could be profound.

3.6 Interview with Jodi Forlizzi

With the rise of the Internet of Things and ubiquitous computing, the range of everyday life that falls under the umbrella of digitally enabled services is increasing. Our lives are more and more connected with products and services which are, in turn, connected with other products, services, communities, and businesses. In your mind, what is the future of our connected life? What are some of the emerging trends in this field?

IoT is huge. I work in a computer science department, and I see a lot of people working on it; however, there are still are very few people working on the human actions of Internet of Things. The basic theme is, we have all this data coming from all these different things. How are we going to use it to help people's experience? I think that's the big, unanswered question. And then underneath that, I think there are some other interesting questions. So, for example, I'll cite some examples from industry. There was a recent incident with VW cheating on its emissions. So now a company is able to go in and fake the data that its products are creating, and actually cheat the customer. What does that mean for us? I think that in other arenas, whole new kinds of services and products are going to emerge. Services that bend laws and public policies. For example, some countries are developing their own Bitcoin economies by selling their poorly valued currency, and turning it into Bitcoins, yet the notion of an economy is that there's a fixed amount of money. New laws and policies will be needed to guide these kinds of actions.

So, I think the designer's role is, number one, to advocate for the human experience of all this data, and number two, to make sure what we're designing is ethical and purposeful.

I went to the Service Experience Conference a couple of years back, and service designers were all over. They were designing fresh drinking water systems, policy, etc. You know, I don't think designers can do that alone. But I think what we can do is to do the work of design within teams of people who are writing policies and who are governing laws, and to bring to light these human examples. So that, instead of thinking about IoT and other systems as big pots of technology, we think about them as big pots of technology that are going to affect human existence.

When society operates in ways increasingly mediated through digital services, those who lack access may find themselves left behind. Additionally, issues of net neutrality, surveillance, and open data raise important concerns about the need for transparency and accountability in the digital domain. How do you understand these issues and the implications they have for service design?

I think that there is a concern that all this data collected about us is infringing on our privacy. And certainly it is, and there are interesting cases. But I think, in general, people need to understand more about privacy, and what is happening with their data. People's attitudes will change as time goes on, and people will make trade-offs in revealing data about themselves in return for the kinds of services they can have. For example, when location-aware services first became available, nobody wanted to make their location known because they felt it was an infringement on their privacy, but now we have whole apps that are just about checking in. In this area, society has really evolved beyond its original anxiety of making your location known.

With so much emphasis being placed on the power of digital technology, questions of unintended consequences are often overshadowed by enthusiasm for innovation and change. Digital services have implications for a wide range of everyday life—for example, the future of work or the nature and form of contemporary politics. What is the role of service design in considering the ethical, social, and political implications of digital services?

Designers can't decide these things alone, but designers can take equal roles on teams where people who are experts in these areas are trying to make judgments and to afford people making judgments a rich sense of the people who are using these services. I think that's what design can bring. I'm not going to be the person to say that a designer could directly impact law, ethics, or social consequences, but I certainly think we could contribute to a team who's doing that.

As an educator, what is a key lesson for students entering into the field of designing for digital services?

I think the core design lessons for service designers would be a multistakeholder view. That is understanding the impact of what you're proposing to design, both positive and negative, and understanding the value of what is designed, whether that's economic value or just human value. Those, I think, would be the big things.

3.7 Learning features

Key points

- Technology increasingly penetrates all aspects of people's everyday lives, enabled by increasingly widespread broadband Internet connectivity, mobile technology, and cloud computing.
- Trends in the digitally enabled services landscape include peer-to-peer exchanges (such as eBay, Yelp), freelance marketplaces (such as TaskRabbit), and on-demand services (such as Uber, Zipcar, and Airbnb).
- The Internet of Things is a new technological frontier that combines three main elements: sensor devices, connectivity, and people and processes. Examples of IoT systems include activity-tracking systems, smart home systems, but also smart city applications and Industrial Internet of Things.
- Service design has an important role in making sure that technology is not the sole force driving decisions but considering social implications of technology and help in humanizing IoT.

Recap questions

- What are some of the key trends in digital technologies affecting our everyday life?
- How does access to digital technologies and infrastructures affect people?
- What are the main elements and applications of IoT systems?
- What are some of the implications and threats related to digitally enabled services and the Internet of Things?
- How does service design differ from UX design?

Activities

- Map your current personal ecosystem of digital services. Think about how simple actions such as waking up in the morning, eating a meal, navigating the city, or spending time with friends are affected by digital services. Describe the same activities done by someone your age fifty years ago. From there, extrapolate a future scenario fifty years from now. Describe the same actions in the future and compare to the present and the past. Explore different scenarios, utopias, and dystopias. Describe what happens to laws, governance, politics, democracy, and power in these different alternative futures.

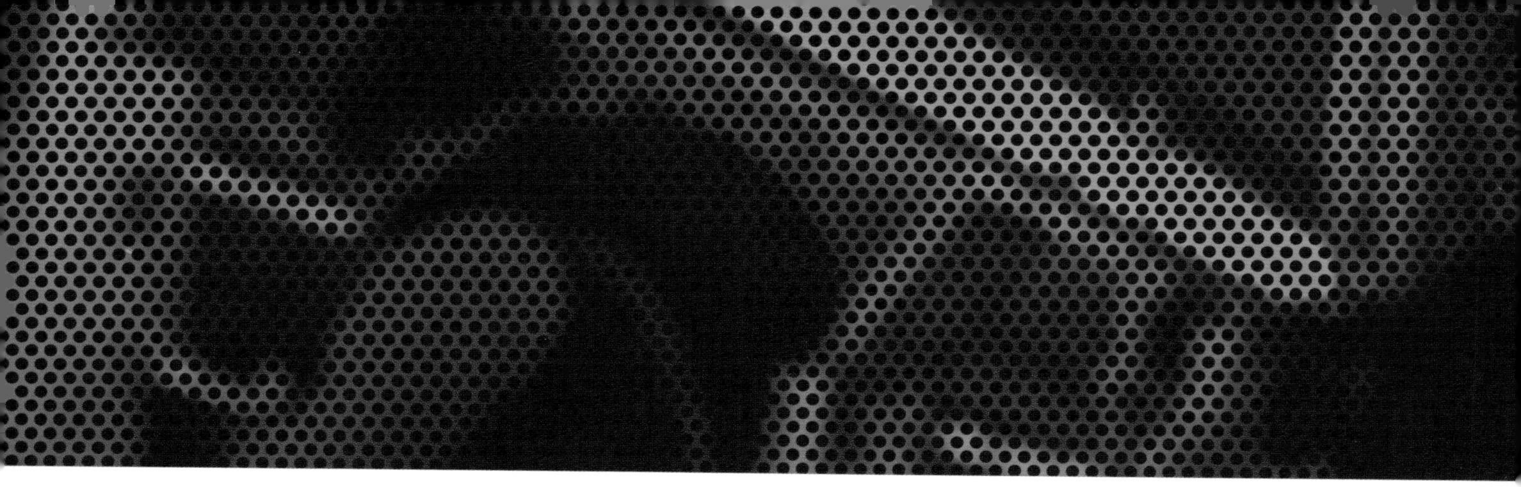

Glossary

- *Social media*: Peer-to-peer communication platforms through which people share information with each other, where users decide who they want to connect with, configuring networks and communities.
- *E-commerce*: Platforms enabling direct or indirect commercial transactions.
- *Crowdfunding*: Platforms that allow people to raise money for specific projects, usually aggregating small amounts from personal donors.
- *Wearable devices*: Devices equipped with sensors that collect data related to the physical activity of people, such as number of miles run, steps taken during the day, hours of sleep, and heart rate. The device is part of a system including an application that stores data normally with an easy-to-use interface.
- *Smart cities*: Concept on which cities' infrastructures (physical such as roads and utilities, but also institutional such as libraries and schools) are equipped with smart technology and systems, with the purpose of improving efficiency and integration of urban services.
- *Smart homes*: Automated homes equipped with smart technology to control and integrate lightning, heating and cooling, security, and appliances.

Recommended reading

Hinman, Rachel (2012). *The Mobile Frontier. A Guide for Designing Mobile Experiences*. Rosenfeld Media.

Kolko, Jon (2011). *Thoughts on Interaction Design*. Elsevier.

Greengard, Samuel (2015). *The Internet of Things*. The MIT Press Essential Knowledge Series, The MIT Press.

Scholz, Trebor (2016). *Platform Cooperativism. Challenging the Corporate Sharing Economy*. Rosa Luxemburg Stiftung.

04
Services for public interest

4.1 Introduction

This chapter describes services for public interest and how designers are approaching them.

The concept of services for public interest means creating the best solutions for achieving societal welfare through services by improving the well-being of individuals and communities. It takes the idea of services explored in previous chapters—and their intrinsic value—beyond the realm of private organizations and their mission to serve primarily the economic interests of shareholders to organizations that provide services for public interest. This notion connects and expands on the concept of social economy, as described in Chapter 2.

In this chapter, we investigate two main sources of services for public interest. One is the public sector, and the other is related to bottom-up social innovations.

The chapter first introduces service innovation and the public sector by framing what the public sector and public services are, what the main challenges for service design in this realm are, and what kind of service design projects are currently being done in the public sector.

The following section examines the service design capability for the public interest by looking into the possible configurations for incorporating design in the public sector. More specifically, this section explores the spread of *innovation labs*, design-based units dedicated to develop special projects, and other design challenges either as an entity inside governments or as an outside organization.

Next, we look into social innovation, a phenomenon based on initiatives that emerge directly from active citizens and are considered a dynamic and creative source of innovation in services for the public interest. Building into the concept of the sharing economy discussed in Chapter 2, we look into the model of collaborative services and discuss different configurations such as private cooperatives as well as public collaborative services.

The chapter concludes with an interview with Eduardo Staszowski, director of the Parsons Design for Social Innovation and Sustainability Lab (DESIS Lab).

1 http://data.worldbank.org/indicator/SE.XPD.TOTL.GB.ZS
2 http://data.worldbank.org/indicator/SH.XPD.TOTL.ZS?name_desc=true

Occasionally, service design projects such as those presented here can have an impact on existing policies or influence the formulation of new policies. Typically, designers are still assigned to design services as an implementation of existing policies. The ultimate ambition for service design applied in the public sector is that of being able to participate in the policy creation so as to affect the system as a whole, beginning with the identification of a policy need and then with design of the services that respond to the policy goals.

NYC Housing Connect
Find and Apply for Affordable Housing
Ask Us About Affordable Housing
NYC
Department of Housing Preservation & Development
www.nyc.gov/hpd

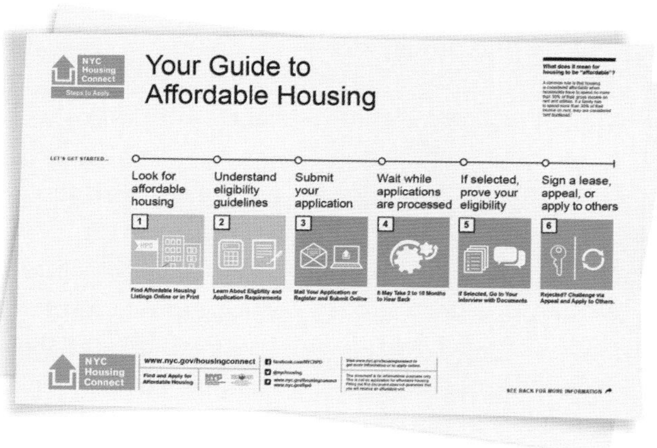
NYC Housing Connect
Steps to Apply
Your Guide to Affordable Housing
Look for affordable housing
Understand eligibility guidelines
Submit your application
Wait while applications are processed
If selected, prove your eligibility
Sign a lease, appeal, or apply to others
1
2
3
4
5
6
www.nyc.gov/housingconnect

Figs 4.4 to 4.6 Redesigned guide map of the housing lottery process, pilot of a market presence of HPD staff to explain about the lottery system, hyper-local marketing strategy with informational materials placed in laundromats.

4.3
Service design capability for the public sector

Can we imagine a more widespread presence of service design for the public interest? What possible configurations would allow incorporating design for and within the public sector to create the best possible impact? And what are the limitations of design in this space?

There have been enough precedents to date, so we can map out a range of successful practices. The Design Council in the United Kingdom identifies three major categories of applications of design in the public sector.

The first category, defined as "Design for discrete problems," includes cases in which public government agencies commission ad hoc projects to design agencies and professionals, much like the private sector does when hiring design work. Pioneer design studios such as *thinkpublic* or the now-closed *Participle*, also in the United Kingdom, specialized in applying design for the public interest, working on projects ranging from health care, senior support, youth empowerment, and employment services.

Well-known multidisciplinary design firms such as *IDEO* and service design-only firms such as *Livework* have a share of public sector clients in their portfolios. The public sector portfolios of these and other design firms are occupied with projects trying to improve rather opaque processes of public services such as immigration and social security. The service design capability therefore seems to be valuable for government clients to help untangle complex systems and streamline processes that might be trapped into siloed structures. The case of New York City's Department of Housing Preservation and Development is an example of this kind of project.

The second category of design in the public sector, "Design as capability," involves nurturing design as an internal capability of governmental agencies. One way this can happen is by training public servants in service design approaches and techniques through design workshops. The impact of such a strategy relates to its potential penetration in the daily work of public servants. Another strategy is that of hiring in-house designers in public agencies and departments, a relatively novel practice. In-house designers can work either on smaller projects within their agencies but also help liaise with external design consultancies.

The third category is "Design for policy" and involves the creation of spaces or labs, much like *research and development departments*, dedicated to develop special projects inside government, and able to affect policy in the long run. A whole constellation of design and innovation labs working from within or outside government has proliferated in the last decade or so.

One of the most notable examples of an in-house lab is MindLab in Denmark, which is configured as a "cross-governmental innovation unit" sitting between three ministries (federal level) and one municipality. MindLab is a physical space resembling a typical design agency employing a mix of designers, ethnographers, and public policy specialists who work in projects defined by the governmental entities they serve. Projects can be as broad and ambitious as redesigning the national Danish school system. Many of MindLab's projects focus in streamlining interactions between citizens and governmental systems—for example, cutting red tape for young taxpayers, facilitating small business setup for young entrepreneurs, dealing with labor regulation, and providing financial and fiscal empowerment initiatives.

The main innovation of MindLab has been to involve citizens and businesses to participate in the development of new public services and programs, opening the existing bureaucracies, which are naturally change-averse, to codesign and coproduction so that users or citizens are repositioned back in the center of services. MindLab's space itself has both a physical and symbolic meaning, functioning as an "authorizing environment" with the right mandate to explore and test new ideas. The philosophy of MindLab is centered on creating "ecosystems for public sector innovation" involving public managers and leadership, so that ultimately new models of governance can be defined beyond simply discreet interventions.

Figs 4.7 and 4.8 MindLab's goal is to nurture cultural change in the public sector. Figure in top shows an illustration that was part of a project on which MindLab reached out to hundreds of educators from Denmark's daycare centers to discuss a new educational curricula. The figure below shows an image of consultation with citizens, related to a project focused on how to streamline bureaucracy for citizens.

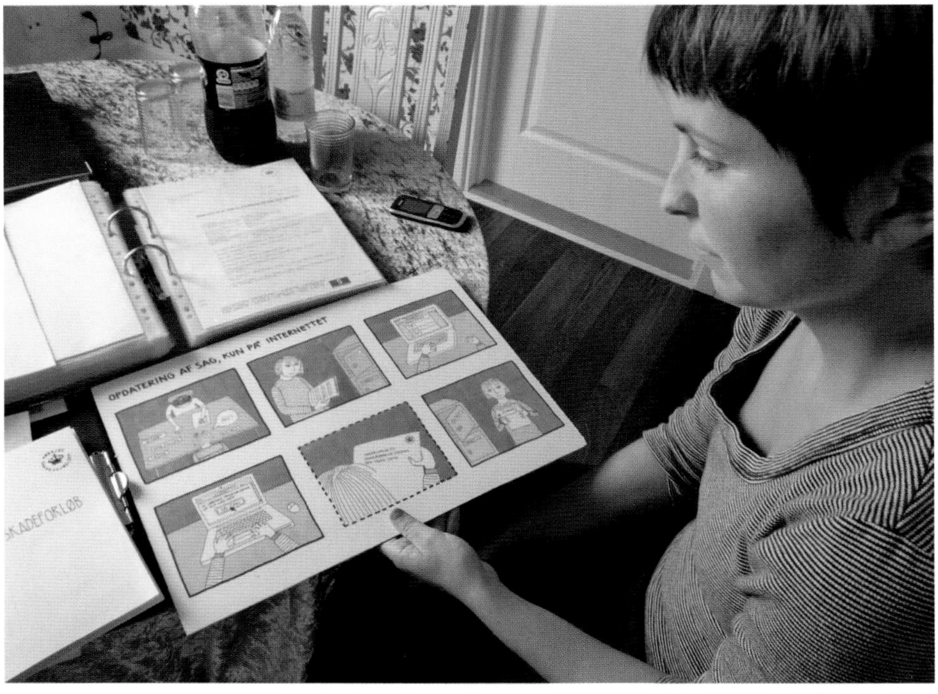
OPDATERING AF SAG, KUN PÅ INTERNETTET
SKADEFORLØB

In France, La 27ᵉ Région, or the 27ᵗʰ Region, is a public transformation laboratory working with the Associations of Regions of France. Its main principle is that social innovation transforms public policy using action research and service design. La 27ᵉ Région defines local challenges in specific regions across the country and creates residency programs and regional labs involving designers, technologists, architects, researchers, and others. These temporary labs investigate needs and opportunities for regions and their towns and rural areas and finally work on design briefs emerging from their research. Projects relate to the redesign of public spaces, schools, nursing homes, and museums. Superpublic is a venue created by La 27ᵉ Région, envisioned as a more permanent physical space meant to enable the creation of a community of practitioners around public sector innovation. This space enables the cooperation between designers, researchers, and public servants from different levels of government.

If we take a closer look at this wider trend of design-led government innovation labs dedicated to improve public service outcomes, we can see different ways in which these organizations situate themselves in relation to government structures. In some cases, government is the owner of the lab; in others, government is a funder or cofunder; and in others, government is a partner, a client, or just an endorser of the lab's activities. These modalities reflect different contexts and opportunities, and there is no claim as for which model works best. While MindLab in Denmark sits within government, La 27ᵉ Région and its affiliate Superpublic are deliberately positioned outside as a third-party partner.

c'est un lieu
pour l'ingéniosité
et l'astuce

€
VALENTINE
VERNE

Figs 4.9 and 4.10 Headquarters of La 27ᵉ Région's affiliate Superpublic that hosts events and workshops; "forum des villages du future," a pluridisciplinary seminar during the program La Transfo in the Bourgogne Region by La 27ᵉ Région (2013).

DESIGN FOR EUROPE
Design and the public sector
Local authority
Lab para la Ciudad
Mexico
Creation date
2013
Address
Tlaxcoaque 8, 2o Piso, Cuauhtémoc, Centro, 06090 Ciudad de México, D.F., Mexico
Website
http://www.labcd.mx
Lab Para La Ciudad is an experimental programme aimed at developing civic innovation and urban creativity in Mexico City.
See more
Lab para la Ciudad
North Atlantic Ocean
South Atlantic Ocean
South Pacific Ocean
Indian Ocean
EUROPE
WORLD

Whether they are working within one of these dedicated labs or directly with governments as clients, there is growing evidence that designers can be valuable partners in improving public services. Designers are indeed well positioned to not only improve service touchpoints but also contribute in policy formulations as part of multidisciplinary teams working to tackle complex social, political, cultural, and economic challenges.

Fig 4.11 Map of design-based government innovation labs, including in-house labs and independent labs having government as a partner or client.

4.3 Service design capability for the public sector

One of the main design contributions for governments in tackling complex challenges is its user-centered (or citizen-centered) approach that considers a more nuanced understanding of the aspirations of users and communities through their direct participation in the codesign of solutions to their needs. This approach can be critical in helping civil servants and policymakers redefine and open the problem space, starting from the point of view of the main beneficiaries (rather than government institutions) while also unlocking creative responses among all stakeholders.

Another design contribution is centered on the designer's ability to help imagine and visualize alternative futures and make ideas and concepts tangible and easily testable through prototyping before they get fully implemented. In addition, the service designer's ability to look at users' requirements in a holistic way can be very useful in terms of imagining ways for unifying experiences and service provisions across different departments and organizations and therefore reducing waste of resources and duplication of efforts.

We should, however, acknowledge the criticisms and alleged weaknesses of design in this emerging space. Observers have pointed to the high cost of design services, making it difficult in many instances of government and social impact organizations to afford such services, especially in economically depressed areas. Another criticism is related to the typical short engagements of designers with projects and clients, which is aggravated in the public sector when considering the need for longer approvals and the need for generating measurable impacts. Finally, while praised for stretching the imagination and generating creative inputs in the early stages of a project, designers are criticized for not having equally strong skills to guide organizations in the implementation stages of a project.

Among the recommendations of experts to realize the full potential of design within the public sector, we will find what many of the design-led innovation labs are already trying to do. In particular, many experts recommend placing designers within multidisciplinary teams that can act complementarily, and most critically, having designers recognize the organizational limitations and acknowledge the complex political environment in which the design work is situated.

4.4
Social innovation and collaborative services

In the search for better ways of organizing resources and processes that can generate better public outcomes, it is important to shed a light on social innovation practices emerging directly from communities and citizens themselves. Social innovation initiatives emerging directly from active citizens are now considered among the most dynamic and creative sources of innovation, and governments around the world are beginning to pay particular attention to them.

Simply defined as "new ideas that work in meeting social goals," *social innovation* includes a whole range of transformative actions (services or otherwise) that are not technology-based nor market-driven innovations, but rather they come "from the people," either individuals or groups, often beginning as small initiatives that at some point are adopted by large audiences. Although social innovations may also emerge from the public sector or private initiatives, it's the bottom-up social innovations, promoted by community groups, individuals, or nonprofit organizations that most capture the people-centric nature of social innovation. People are considered experts and partners.

Far from being a new phenomenon, lately there has been a growing interest in grassroots social innovations as an alternative to tackle critical social problems that remain unresolved solely by governments. Social innovations often are manifested through resourceful and efficient solutions emerging directly from the people trying to solve their own problems, implying a sense of ingenuity and agency among citizens. In many cases, social innovations result in what are called *collaborative services*, a service model that defines new patterns of citizen engagement and participation.

These new ways of purposing and repurposing resources, typical of social innovations, are especially welcome in moments of crisis, economic challenges, and limited budgets. Examples of social innovations, from urban farming to skill sharing to carpooling or home-based child care, are in fact to be found around the world, both in developing and industrialized contexts. Researchers from different fields are documenting these practices and trying to evaluate how they can inform new models of services and even new policies and legislation.

A crucial component of these initiatives is their collaborative nature. Collaborative services are services based on collaborations mostly between the users themselves. While the main interactions of services typically occur between service users and service providers, in collaborative services this line is often blurred: service providers are service users and vice versa. There is an overlap between collaborative services and initiatives defined as part of the sharing economy (see Chapter 2). The connection between socially innovative collaborative services and the

public sector is quite a promising and fertile terrain for service designers working in the public sector.
One successful model of collaborative services is the food cooperative. Food co-ops are membership-based grocery shops, where only members are allowed to shop. Becoming a member may involve working a certain monthly shift or helping with the whole operation of the shop, whether working in the stock room or as the cashier or performing many other tasks. Food co-op members are simultaneously service users and service providers.

In Chapter 1, we delineated how service users are always coproducers, since it is through the interactions between users and providers that value is generated. Coproduction is an intrinsic foundation of services. In collaborative services, coproduction is taken to the next level. And if properly incorporated back into public services, these models can increase accessibility, efficiency, trust, and the overall quality of services.

BEST
Park Slope
FOOD COOP
BROOKLYN, NY
TOMATOES

Some examples of collaborative services involve the government, which brings together citizens, helping define what public services might mean in the twenty-first century.

One such example is the community gardens in New York City. Community gardens are small urban gardens found in between buildings in different neighborhoods in New York City. Most of them were empty lots, resulting from demolished buildings where the land belongs to the city. The gardens have been in great part initiated by local residents and rely on their work for maintenance. With time, local authorities have incorporated the residents as coproducers, leaving to them the governance and maintenance of the parks, helping with some infrastructure. Members have keys to the gardens but open them to the public every day. Members might have privileges such as having their own plot to cultivate vegetables. As in the food co-op model, members are therefore both service providers and users of the gardens.

Another example of collaborative services on which a new public service is designed with people as assets is the Circles of Care in the UK. Circles was an experimental service designed by Participle, a design-led social enterprise based in London focused on reforming public services.

Fig 4.12 Park Slope Food Co-op in Brooklyn New York, an independent, nonprofit, membership-based grocery shop, founded in 1973.

Case study: Circles of Care

Launched in 2007, Circle of Care moved away from current services for elderly care that proved inadequate and out of step from end users. Circle was created as a community-based elderly care service that supports members with practical everyday life tasks, improves members' social connections, and helps them learn and develop new capabilities. Circle's model works on a membership basis through small monthly fees, giving access to organized events, shared transportation to and from events with fellow members, practical help with everyday tasks when needed, discounts for events and local businesses, and access to members with similar interests.

The local community sets up its local Circle and gets to codesign the specific services its Circle will have. It does need government investment up front, but this funding is expected to be phased out with time, as it becomes a self-sustaining social enterprise. Circles in the United Kingdom are still finding a way to survive, with some of them being interrupted after they run out of funds to scale up and develop a clear plan of how to integrate them in the broader ecosystem of government services and benefits. Nevertheless, Circle and other similar services are promising examples of new approaches to delivering public services.

As discussed earlier in this chapter, service designers are being asked to develop proposals to improve channels, interfaces, and touchpoints between government and the public. Designers are also joining innovation labs working in multidisciplinary teams to resolve complex social, political, cultural, and economic challenges. In this context, we also learned about social innovation practices and citizen participation and engagement in the design and production of public services. Overall, designing for the public interest represents an exceptional professional opportunity for service designers interested in playing a transformative role in the public realm and affecting positively the lives of individuals and communities, particularly those who are more vulnerable, such as the poor and marginalized.

Nottingham Circle
Call us on 0115 9787846
Log in
Home
How it works
Join
Calendar
Our story
News
Contact us
Monthly view
Weekly view
Past events
Get away
January 2015
Mon
Tue
Wed
Thu
Fri
Sat
Sun

Pub Games, Sept
Hucknall Heritage Tour, Sept
Bestwood Lodge Afternoon Tea, Sept
Segway, Aug
Ice-cream, Sept
Trentham Gardens, August

Figs 4.13 and 4.14 Gallery of images of Nottingham Circle showing members involved in activities (left) and an example of a monthly calendar of activities (far left).

4.5 Interview with Eduardo Staszowski

Eduardo Staszowski is the director of The Parsons Design for Social Innovation and Sustainability Lab at The New School in NYC and editor of *Public and Collaborative: Exploring the Intersection of Design, Social Innovation and Public Policy*.

There has been a veritable explosion of design activity across the globe at the nexus of service innovation, public interest design, and design for social innovation. Can you talk about the history of these developments?

Within the design profession we have seen a continuous expansion of roles that followed the evolution of how we live and work, urgent environmental and social concerns, and the need for improved design practices to meet them. Design associations and academic conferences have been constantly revising and updating their own definition of design. At first we saw industrial design moving beyond product-oriented activities to incorporate notions of immateriality such as services and systems with an increased sense of responsibility towards sustainability. In other words, a design that wants to be part of the solution and not part of the problem. More recently there is new evidence on how design is increasingly being adopted as an approach for public agencies, policymakers, and not-for-profits to develop solutions to social problems, public services, and policies.

How distinct is service innovation in the public sector from service innovation in the private sector?

In the private sector, service innovation is aimed at acquiring and satisfying clients who can choose from a pool of different companies and ultimately creating economic value for their shareholders. Governments, on the other hand, are sometimes the sole responsible for the provision of essential services that a major part of the population depends on. Service innovation in the public sector therefore cannot leave anyone behind and it is held to a very different standard of [public] accountability.

In the public sector, professional design roles are new and are being created as we speak. Who they are beholden to, the spaces in which they work, the kinds of problems they will be tasked with addressing, as well as the kinds of constraints they face.

4.5 Interview with Eduardo Staszowski

In the private sector, service innovation finds itself in a more mature stage of development where designers can influence a company's strategy and the design of complete product-service systems. While this is changing very quickly, in the public sector, service design still happens in isolated and fragmented ways and deployed to resolve problems in a more discrete and incremental way within a larger and complex cycle of policy making and implementation.

In addition to the traditional design consultancy, new venues are emerging for service design in the public sector such as innovation labs. Whereas most service designers are brought in from the outside of an organization to do projects, innovation labs are more and more situated within the organizations they serve, for example, in government. What has been the influence of these new kinds of spaces on the practice of service design in the public sector?

We are starting to see new venues where designers are being called to support experimentation and engaging people inside and outside government to see the problems they face through a different set of lenses facilitated by design. This is leading to a more careful consideration of various perspectives in the formulation and resolution of problems, for example, from the point-of-view of frontline civil servants or their constituents. In other words, design is helping to bring people's concern before the bureaucratic processes and their institutions.

Innovation labs were originally created to rethink how public sector entities operate in times of crisis and deep complexity, where problems can no longer be solved by one expert or agency alone. The result of experimenting with these new institutional forms has been the creation of opportunities for designers to enter into multidisciplinary spaces as new arenas for design practice. The result of this process has been the beginning of new design careers in various areas of government.

How do you think public services can be improved by incorporating greater citizen collaboration in service design and implementation?

In my own practice, I have worked with the concept of collaborative services, a term used within our lab to describe services that are based on the collaboration between and among the users of services, where the users become providers, and the providers become users.

In our projects with the public sector, we try to establish conversations with the policymakers to see if there is a way for the public sector to support notions of increased collaboration amongst citizens and service providers facilitated through a design-driven approach and how collaborative services can contribute to services for the public good/ public interest.

What we managed to do so far is creating participatory design events to our public agency partners to test these approaches. In part, it is about showing how the services that these agencies provide are already participatory and could be made to be more open by engaging with more people, and understanding the capacities that already exist in local communities and organizations.

Designing public and collaborative services often requires the negotiation of a complex array of diverse stakeholders; government agencies, not-for-profit organizations, community groups, private citizens, businesses, etc. The range of interests and perspectives that are brought to the table reflect the complexity of the issues at hand. What are some strategies you've learned in navigating these kinds of projects?

One strategy is to understand that working in the public sector often means working in a different professional culture than the one that characterizes traditional spaces of design practice. Designers tend to be experimental and iterative. There is a premium placed on these values. In the public sector, there is greater risk aversion; there is a higher degree of accountability and therefore conservatism. This is in part a result of the kinds of responsibilities public sector organizations have. All of these factors result in new kinds of constraints for design activity.

It is important for designers not to start with an attitude of trying to change everything all at once. You have to find the spaces where everybody feels comfortable. Designers need to cultivate a humble approach. It takes a different kind of creativity to make innovation happen under those constraints. To do this takes a level of understanding where these constraints come from. You need to understand the culture and how to operate effectively within it. This requires being very conscious of how designers present their ideas. You have to create an environment that makes people secure about what the process is in the first place. In other words, how to make people who are unfamiliar with design comfortable with a process that is inherently different from what they normally do. It is both about the design ideas and how you design conditions for those ideas to be well received.

When service designers enter into projects that seek to shape the public good, the ethical and political stakes of such work come clearly into relief. The outcome of a project can have profound impact on the everyday lives of people and the services they depend on. How do you understand the stakes of this work? What would designers entering into this field do well to consider?

In the public sector, the impact of service design can be profound. This may also happen in the private sector, but it is fundamentally different. In the private sector, one can choose, if they have the means. In the public sector, whatever you do, you will be affecting people who depend on these public services. When designers work for the public interest, there's an opportunity for setting up a standard of service excellence and providing quality, equitable services for all, no matter their income, race, gender, religion, or sexual orientation. You are setting a standard at the level of civil society. You are involved in saying, "This is how it should be." In this way, the stakes are quite high.

Where do you see the future opportunities arising for designers interested in creating transformative change through service design?

I think there are spaces of engaging with large questions of public interest. You can see new opportunities amongst various organizations and institutions facing big challenges to look at the problems they face seen through the lenses of what a designer can do. This is not to say designers can do this all alone, but there is a growing openness to exploring what design expertise can bring to the table.

What is some important advice for students interested in exploring public and collaborative services?

This work requires a humble attitude, and it is important to remain aware of where and how you are placed, or placing yourself, in this kind of work. To operate in space that often resists the kinds of speculative thinking that is characteristic of the design work, students must learn to interact with other disciplines, such as the social sciences, management, and public policy in order to communicate with policymakers and civil servants.

4.6
Learning features

Key points

- Services for public interest are about achieving societal welfare and include services offered by the public sector as well as services emerging from social innovation initiatives promoted by groups of individual citizens.
- Challenges for service design in the public sector are related to scale, regulations, organizational aspects, cultural barriers from the public, and the often risk-averse and conservative work culture in the public sector.
- Innovation labs inside or working very close to governments are a growing trend and offer an opportunity to champion service design projects.
- Social innovation initiatives may manifest through collaborative services, where service users are also members of the service-providing organization to which they contribute with their work. Collaborative services can also be used in the public sector.

Recap questions

- What are the main categories of applications of design in the public sector?
- Why is the point of view of civil servants critical to service design work in the public sector?
- What are the benefits and contributions that design-based innovation labs may bring to the public sector?
- What are the main characteristics and possible manifestations of collaborative services?

Activities

- Think of a public service that serves your neighborhood. Identify a challenge in which you could actually engage your community to improve the service for yourself and your neighbors. How can you take advantage of codesign processes or existing social innovations in your community?
- Think of a public service in a different neighborhood or community. Find a way to study the service, whether by interviewing a service provider or user, or by going to a prominent space and observing the interaction between users and providers or experiencing the service yourself. Create a new service blueprint highlighting the pain points and the areas in the service journey deserving change. What can you learn from your research that could help improve the service?

Glossary

- *Public sector*: Part of the economy controlled by the government; it is composed of the bodies that are responsible for offering public services for people, services that benefit all society. While public service provisions may vary in different countries, some basic areas are common to the vast majority such as infrastructure (roads, water systems, sewer, etc.), public security (police, military, fire department), as well as public education and health care.
- *Innovation labs*: Departments or units created within government or outside government but working close to government that use service design, design thinking, and social design to create new services and policies or redesign existing ones in innovative ways and improve the lives of citizens.
- *Social innovation*: Innovative initiatives that help solve a social problem, emerging normally from active citizens, individually or in groups, including nonprofit organizations. Social innovation initiatives creatively recombine existing assets (social capital, historical heritage, traditional craftsmanship, accessible advanced technology) in a way that benefits societal needs.
- *Collaborative services*: Services delivered with the collaboration of final users, who become an intrinsic part of the service system. Collaborative services include cooperative models, membership-based systems, and community-supported agriculture schemes and include both formal and informal initiatives.

Recommended reading

Bason, Christian (2010). *Leading Public Sector Innovation. Co-Creating for a Better Society*. University of Chicago Press.

Service Design Network (2016). *Service Design Impact Report. Public Sector*. Service Design Network.

05 The politics of service design

5.1 Introduction

This chapter introduces crucial political aspects present in services that service designers need to acknowledge when approaching service design projects. They include labor relationships, environmental aspects, and the challenges of dealing with organizations' cultures.

The chapter starts by examining political and ethical aspects contained in service provisions and interactions—in particular, the concept of *emotional labor*, in which front-office staff members engage in face-to-face interactions with service users. Unpacking this concept reveals not only gender, race, and class questions present in service jobs but also labor-related aspects. This section also includes an analysis of theatrical aspects of services and presents theater-based techniques that can help designers deal with the complexity of relationships.

Next, we look into the issue of environmental sustainability in services, analyzing the link between climate change and services. On one hand, the chapter considers consumption and lifestyle aspects, arguing that services themselves can be considered a strategy to environmental sustainability. On the other hand, it looks into cleaner production models developed by product design and architecture, presenting guidelines, strategies, and practices to improve product and system eco-efficiency such as *life cycle analysis (LCA)* and the LEED certification.

The chapter also considers the issue of organizations' politics, since designing services often involves redesigning systems and organizations. It suggests that when designers start a project with an organization, they need to recognize existing organizational culture and practices and may use tools such as visual mapping as a participatory strategy to involve people in organizations.

The chapter concludes with an interview with Cameron Tonkinwise, professor of Design at University of New South, Australia, who offers critical perspectives on the role of service design as designing the future of work, the relationship between services, and issues of sustainability, among other insights.

Vivienne Westwood
virgin atlantic
Virgin

Fig 5.3 Glamour uniforms for Virgin Atlantic designed by fashion designer Vivienne Westwood.

5.2 The drama of services: emotional labor

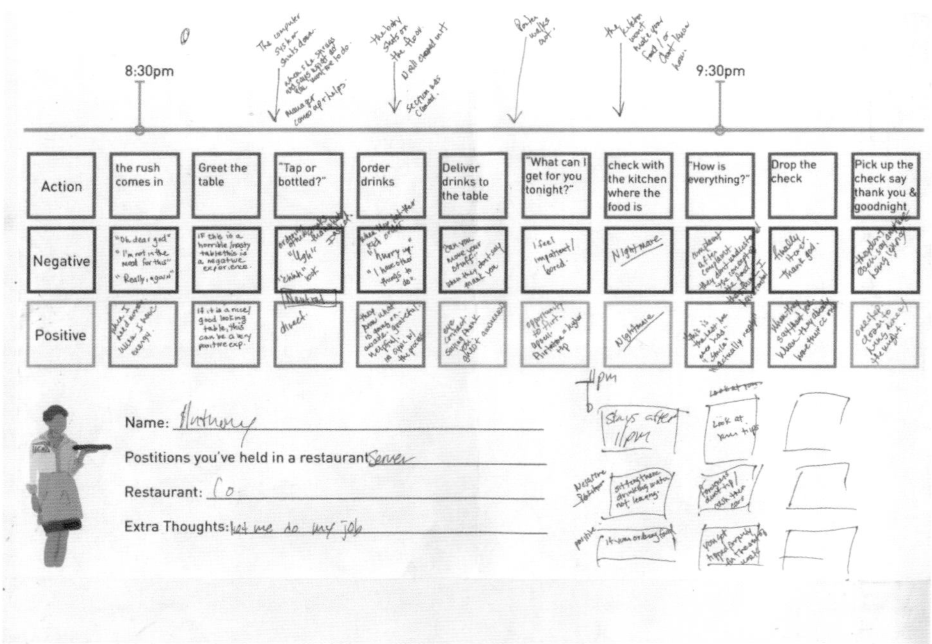

8:30pm
9:30pm
Action
Negative
Positive
the rush comes in
Greet the table
"Tap or bottled?"
order drinks
Deliver drinks to the table
"What can I get for you tonight?"
check with the kitchen where the food is
"How is everything?"
Drop the check
Pick up the check say thank you & goodnight
Name:
Postitions you've held in a restaurant:
Restaurant:
Extra Thoughts:

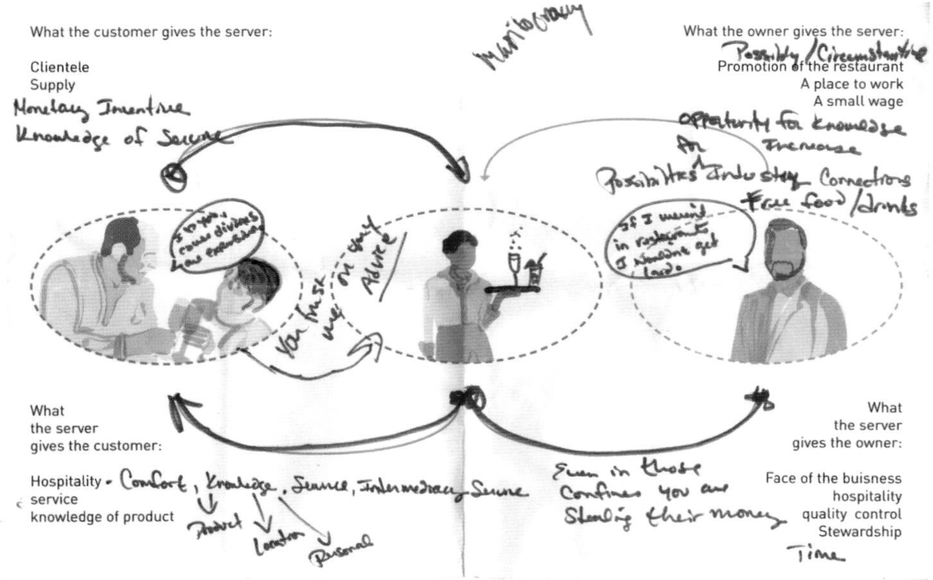

What the customer gives the server:
Clientele
Supply
What the owner gives the server:
Promotion of the restaurant
A place to work
A small wage
What the server gives the customer:
Hospitality
service
knowledge of product
What the server gives the owner:
Face of the buisness
hospitality
quality control
Stewardship

Figs 5.4 and 5.5 Tools for visualizing emotional labor with restaurant workers developed by service designer Siri Betts-Sonstegard. (Top) An emotional labor map is adapted from a journey map and in this case has been used as an interview tool. The designer interviewed restaurant workers to map out their emotional journey throughout a typical night shift. (Bottom) A power diagram, with the frontline restaurant worker at the center and his or her relationship with customers on one side and manager on the other.

Another approach to help capture emotions and power struggles in the service design process is through performativity. Theatrically derived methods can be useful both in research and design ideation for more nuanced and in-depth insight about complex emotional factors. The assumption is that participating in or enacting service interactions may allow us to better see conflicts and frictions as well as help service workers envision possible strategies for change. Drama techniques can help service workers when stepping into the often thorny politics of service relationships. Drama-related techniques used in service design include *bodystorming*, Focus Troups, and the Forum Theater method. See Chapter 9 for a description.

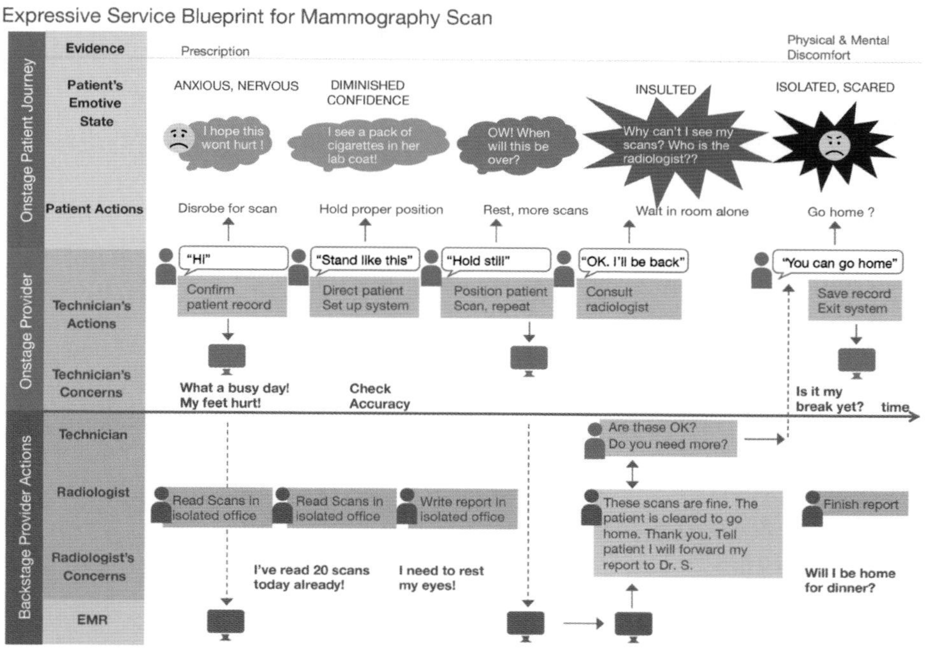
Expressive Service Blueprint for Mammography Scan
Onstage Patient Journey
Onstage Provider
Backstage Provider Actions
Evidence
Patient's Emotive State
Patient Actions
Technician's Actions
Technician's Concerns
Technician
Radiologist
Radiologist's Concerns
EMR
Prescription
Physical & Mental Discomfort
ANXIOUS, NERVOUS
DIMINISHED CONFIDENCE
INSULTED
ISOLATED, SCARED
I hope this wont hurt !
I see a pack of cigarettes in her lab coat!
OW! When will this be over?
Why can't I see my scans? Who is the radiologist??
Disrobe for scan
Hold proper position
Rest, more scans
Wait in room alone
Go home ?
"Hi"
"Stand like this"
"Hold still"
"OK. I'll be back"
"You can go home"
Confirm patient record
Direct patient Set up system
Position patient Scan, repeat
Consult radiologist
Save record Exit system
What a busy day! My feet hurt!
Check Accuracy
Is it my break yet?
time
Are these OK? Do you need more?
Read Scans in isolated office
Read Scans in isolated office
Write report in isolated office
These scans are fine. The patient is cleared to go home. Thank you. Tell patient I will forward my report to Dr. S.
Finish report
I've read 20 scans today already!
I need to rest my eyes!
Will I be home for dinner?

Fig 5.6 Expressive service blueprint by Susan Spraragen here exemplified with the journey of a mammography. The patient feels anxiety before having a scan and is even more insulted and upset after the scan. No one along the journey told the patient she was okay and that is why she could go home. The radiologist is backstage; the patient has no direct interactions with him or her. This tool allows designers to figure out how to provide a service in a more mutually productive fashion so that the patient leaves informed, confident, and respected, thus building trust in the service.

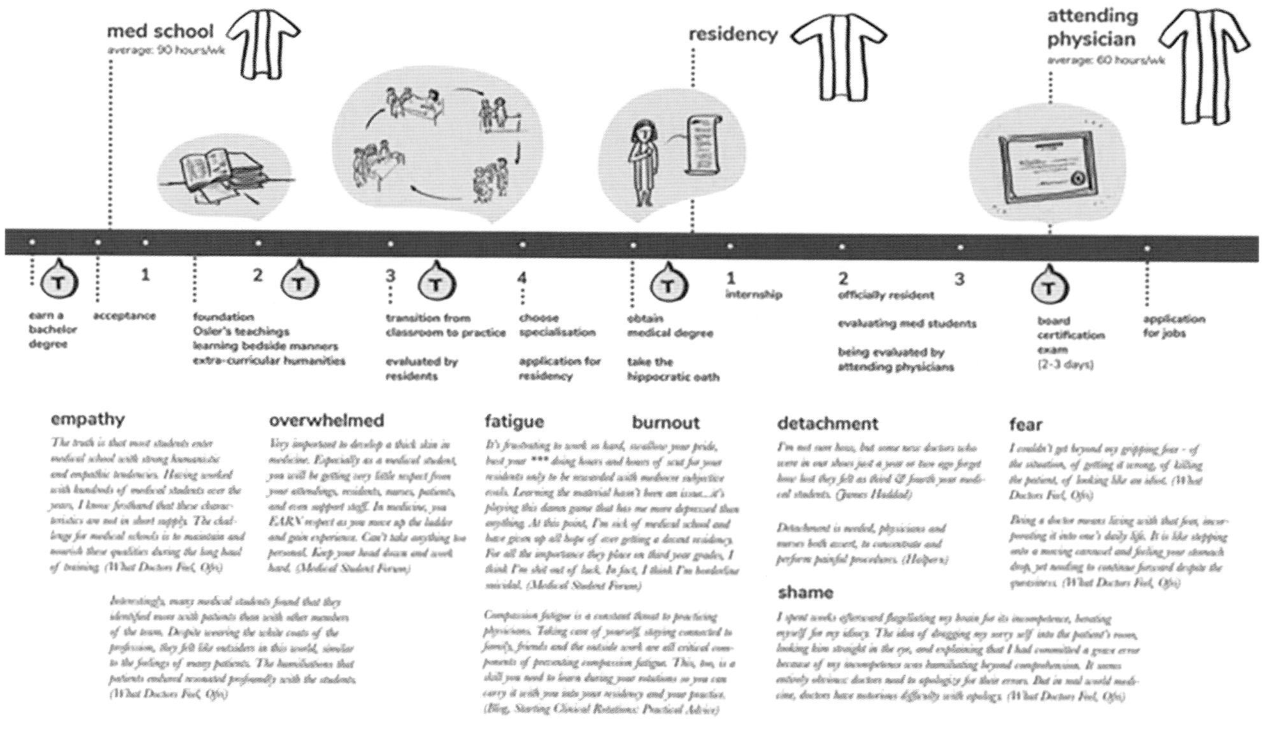
med school
average: 90 hours/wk
residency
attending physician
average: 60 hours/wk
earn a bachelor degree
acceptance
1
foundation
Osler's teachings
learning bedside manners
extra-curricular humanities
2
3
transition from classroom to practice
evaluated by residents
4
choose specialisation
application for residency
obtain medical degree
take the hippocratic oath
1
internship
2
officially resident
evaluating med students
being evaluated by attending physicians
3
board certification exam
(2-3 days)
application for jobs
empathy
overwhelmed
fatigue
burnout
detachment
fear
shame

Fig 5.7 The journey shows the emotional journey of a medical student as she goes through the residency period after earning a bachelor's degree. The journey map focuses on the issue of empathy at the beginning of doctors' careers, and the risk of losing it, as young doctors get immersed in the intense workloads typical of the medial profession. Project by Sophie Riendeau, Ankita Roy and Juyeon Lee.

5.3 Environmental sustainability of services

Just like labor relationships, the issue of environmental sustainability in services can get quite political because the discourse of sustainability is in itself a complex and often elusive one. It relates to many different factors and aspects in an interconnected web of political, financial, economic, and sociocultural forces. For example, while climate-related disasters have already proved to affect the poor in a disproportionate way, they haven't necessarily translated into prevention and remediation policies.

The link between climate change and services needs further clarification. How are environmental aspects considered when designing for services? Is there such a thing as sustainable services? But also, can services themselves be the strategy to environmental sustainability, as a means of reducing material consumption?

At the heart of the environmental questions lies the logic of industrial production—on which our whole economic systems are based—largely based on principles that disregard the finitude of global resources and the capacity of the planet to absorb the related impact. If we look at consumer areas such as fashion or electronics, the logic is that of short life spans and quick obsolescence. More and more products are made faster, distributed to larger areas, sold at cheaper prices, and planned to be replaced quicker. The need for a broader paradigm shift is clear, and it should consider both production and consumption patterns. Can we, as consumers, imagine living a better life consuming fewer resources and producing less emissions? The question to be asked is related to our perception of well-being and lifestyle: what are the things we need and why? Do we need a product, or do we really need to fulfill a certain function or solve a specific problem, regardless of product ownership?

Design is definitively part of the problem. As a community of practice, designers maintain that design can be particularly influential in affecting decisions that impact our environment and quality of life. Design associations, councils, and educational institutions have largely embraced an idea of design that accounts for environmental protection as well as related social aspects. The code of professional ethics proposed by the International Council of Societies of Industrial Design (ICSISD) outlines ethical guidelines for practitioners, including the need for designers to protect the earth's ecosystem and adopt principles of environmental stewardship.

In practice, the design community has developed and adopted guidelines, strategies, and practices to try to improve product and system eco-efficiency and contribute to cleaner production models. Criteria and guidelines for environmentally friendly design have been developed and adopted in tandem with new legislation and public awareness, responding to active pressure from advocacy and political groups, and the scientific and design communities.

Strategies for cleaner production include system life optimization (designing products that allow for parts to be replaced, to avoid early replacement), reduction of transportation/distribution (with local supply and consumption chains), reduction of material resources, minimization and reuse of waste, conservation, and biocompatibility/toxic reduction.

One important approach designers have adopted toward reducing environmental impact of products is *life cycle design (LCD)*, also known as eco-design. LCD considers the whole life cycle of a given product, from "cradle to grave," normally split in five main phases:

- preproduction, including raw material extraction and material processing
- production, component manufacturing, assembly, and packaging
- distribution, comprising all the distribution branches and purchasing
- use, including installation and use, service upgrading, and maintenance
- disposal, which might involve recycling, reuse, composting, incineration, or landfill

The analysis of a product life cycle can be done through quantitative methods and help reveal the main causes for the environmental impact associated with specific products. These causes are often counterintuitive; for example, most people tend to think that disposal at the end of a product life cycle is responsible for the main environmental impact, while in fact the use phase is normally the greatest villain, for example, through electricity consumption.

5.3 Environmental sustainability of services

METHOD	HOW IT WORKS
Life Cycle Assessment or LCA	The LCA method involves quantifying materials, energy and emissions involved in the whole life cycle of a given product. The result of an LCA analysis helps inform the decision-making process toward the redesign of products and processes according to more eco-efficient standards. LCA software uses data from context-specific databases as input for the quantification of each component and process involved. Both production and consumption are bound to context specific factors. For example, producing a car in a factory in a locality using mainly hydro-electric generated power is different from another similar factory in a place where the energy base is coal. The same goes for the use phase of the car: how long is it going to last will depend on a series of contextual factors, such as roads conditions. LCA tools are today only partially integrated in design or production processes. One main challenge with LCA tools is that the amount and range of data needed in such complex assessments are not only difficult to obtain but simply non-existent in many cases. The whole process may become extremely time-consuming and expensive.
Criteria card decks and checklists	There are several designer-friendly toolkits such as The OKALA Practitioner Guide by ISDA (The Industrial Designers Society of America) that help designers integrating sustainability criteria in the design and evaluation process of projects of products, services and communication systems. Some of them propose a hybrid of eco-efficiency criteria integrating physical and system-level aspects. Some toolkits comprise of card decks or checklists to be used as auxiliary brainstorm tools to help spot opportunities to improve sustainability in initial phases of project development. Others toolkits use artifacts such as matrix and questionnaires to help assessing existing systems or a project being developed, and are useful in later development phases of projects.
LEED certification	In the context of architecture, the LEED certification is an increasingly popular program to certify building projects. It makes use of different sets of environmental criteria that translate into points. Certain number of points will achieve different levels of certification. Rating systems are defined according to project types, such as buildings, homes or maintenance. Each project type uses a different set of criteria or credit categories issuing points, such as materials and resources used, water and energy efficiency among others. Some of the credit categories cater specifically to service industries such as hospitality, health care or education. The program also includes more systemic categories such as neighborhood-scale projects, with criteria including walking distance between houses and grocery store, integration of transportation systems among others.

The truth is, there is no universal tool to help service designers integrate environmental aspects into their processes. So what can we do? Service designers can and should make use of approaches and tools developed for product design and architecture to improve sustainability of the physical components of the service.

What else? As stated earlier, the crux of environmental aspects of services—and one of the reasons that designing services can be a political choice—is that in many cases services per se are considered an environmental strategy. We mentioned in Chapter 1 the successful model of car sharing and product service systems (PSS). Recent studies suggest that there are already 500,000 fewer individually owned cars on the road due to car sharing in the United States. Reductions in terms of carbon emissions as well as traffic congestion are associated with such services. In addition, the fact that car-sharing systems moved from a marginal niche model into a desirable urban lifestyle in a relatively short time frame is an indicator that the public is ready to accept consumption models based on services replacing individual ownership of products. This space should be the new playground for service designers.

Fig 5.8 Methods for measuring environmental impact in product design and architecture.

Design for:
1
Innovation
2
Reduced Material Impacts
3
Manufacturing Innovation
4
Reduced Distribution Impacts
5
Reduced Behavior and Use Impacts
6
System Longevity
7
Transitional Systems
8
Optimized End-of-Life

Fig 5.9 The Okala Ecodesign Strategy Wheel helps designers define eco-design strategies according to the stages of the life cycle of a given product. (Authors: Steve Belletire, Louise St. Pierre, Philip White)

5.4
Services as systems and the issue of organizations' politics

Another politically charged aspect affecting service design practice is the delicate topic of organizations' politics.

Services are largely based on several parts coming together. In practice, services are supported by systems composed of different organizations (providers, representatives, receivers, back-end providers) that exchange stuff with each other, whether material (products and infrastructure), immaterial (knowledge, information, communication), or financial and relational. Some organizations are core to a service, whereas others are additional, such as external providers.

For example, the core system of a stand-alone restaurant is composed of its physical space either owned or rented from a third party, municipal entities for permits and inspections, all the utility companies providing the necessary infrastructure, all the human resources involved, including the kitchen staff with all its hierarchical roles as well as frontline servers bridging kitchen and floor, and a host. This system also includes external service providers, namely the providers of food, beverages, and other consumables that cater the restaurant on a weekly basis, as well as furniture and equipment that need to be acquired or leased and constantly replaced. Other external subsystems might include an online booking system, accountant and legal services, public relations and marketing, interior design, communication design, web design and domain, and insurance and financial services. The users—in this case, restaurant patrons—are also an integral part of the service system.

The "system restaurant" therefore is the sum of all the components of the internal system of organizations and exchanges plus the external supporting organizations. Coordinating and balancing systems and their organizations present challenges related to business aspects, cross-sector/department coordination, or multichannel management and delivery, but also cultural ones. Each organization and, in some cases, each department inside the same organization has its own set of internal practices, cultures, and policies.

For users to experience services holistically, organizations need to break internal barriers, which in some cases might be in contrast with their very business model or organizational legacy. Organizations may also need to recalibrate their relations to external systems if something is not working. For example, a seafood restaurant will need to replace its fish provider if the provider fails to deliver fish according to the restaurant's needs.

Service designers need to acknowledge that designing services often involves redesigning systems or redesigning the organizations themselves. Each private company, public organization, or nonprofit has its own organizational ethos that might be more or less codified into rules, protocols, and processes. What designers need to understand is that when they step into an organization, they are not stepping into a void space, but a legacy and culture are already in place. People in organizations often spend a lot of time working to improve the existing services. Public sector agencies, for example, have long histories of design and redesign of their services, bound to policies and regulations, and have responded to changing administrations over time.

For this reason, concepts such as *change* and *disruption*, so dear to designers, may not sound like such good news to many people inside organizations. When designers start working on a project with an organization, they need to do so carefully, recognizing what's already in place, often based on delicate relationships and balances.

Service designers need to recognize *design legacies* and *design agendas* already present in organizations whether they are good or bad, efficient or not. And in doing so, they need to develop productive dialogues with the people inside different parts of the organization to see things from their perspective and define together which changes are needed and what are the possible ways to implement them. What are the practical tools to facilitate service designers' work with organizations?

Service designers have developed several tools for mapping systems. System mapping tools are useful to provide a bird's-eye view of an entire system of actors, flows, and subsystems. Variations of system maps include service ecology maps or stakeholders' maps. The service blueprint is also useful, especially to verify temporal chains between actors and subsystems.

But most importantly, tools to visualize systems can be used as tools for collective participation. A key aspect of the work of service designers is to be the vehicles for these organizations' self-reflection and learning processes, to unearth common understanding of core organizational purpose. Service designers commonly propose and facilitate workshops with an organization's staff, involving people from different departments and divisions. Such situations can be messy, contentious, and awkward. In this context, empathy and an overall capacity to *listen* and conduct productive debates are essential elements of a service designer's skill set.

5.5 Interview with Cameron Tonkinwise

Cameron Tonkinwise is professor of Design at University of New South Wales Art and Design in Sydney, Australia.

What do you understand to be some of the main political implications of designing for services?

I think service designers are designing the future of work. Right now work is undergoing a lot of flux due to new technologies and shifting economic relations. Determining what people do when they are not just living, that's increasingly falling into the realm of service designers. They're at the front line of defining the future of work.

Service designers are also designing employees and customers. It's the skill of directing customers to ask for, and receive, services in the right way, so that the whole service interaction creates value in an efficient, productive, and pleasurable way.

What's happening is companies, to some extent, are outsourcing from employees to customers, so customers are kind of becoming unpaid employees that have to do a lot of work in order to then arrive and move through the service in the right way. There is a politics to this.

A highly skilled service designer will make that seem both desirable and pleasurable, make the customer feel like they have autonomy in customization, but on the other hand it's leading to the general sense of being harried in our society at the moment.

Human-to-human interaction is underscored by emotional labor. The success or failure of a service is often dependent on the quality of various kinds of social engagements between people. How do you understand the role of emotion in the designing of services?

The essence of all service design is the idea of renting a friend. What you are doing is asking a stranger to act friendly towards you and advise you with some honesty and authenticity in order that the service maximizes value for you. And so you are always asking employees to do two things.

One is the idea of shedding your moods and baggage and literally putting on the costume or mask of being the service provider. You're then being asked to speak, move, and be in a particular way in a particular place in time.

Service design is about getting people to abandon themselves and adopt a role. There's a kind of emotional labor involved in somebody assuming the role of service provider. You ask them to not merely be an automaton following a script in a role, but instead to have the capacity to improvise on behalf of someone who is a complete stranger. That's part of emotional labor.

Another component is when you have to place in your mind the gap between the role that the manager and the service designer is instructing you to take, and the attempt to be a person to a person and therefore customize and bring some humanness to the interaction. This can be very stressful—where should the cut-off point of that human interaction be?

How can design deal with this complexity and account for all these fluid relationships when designing or redesigning services?

It's very important, given the politics of design, to understand that service design happens in a series of stages. It's a multistage process. There needs to be periods in which the service is trialed and allowed to mature, but different from other types of designing, here you stay with the problem for longer. Service designs have to deal with this kind of fluidity of the tension between a role and an improvisation, or a service system and customization of that service.

Why is it important for designers to maintain an awareness of issues of power, class, and gender when designing new service provisions?

The history of power is the history of different types of service provision. That is, getting people to serve other people and not just to serve the capitalist in manufacture, but to encourage somebody to serve a client on behalf of the capitalist. In many ways, the entire history of capitalism is the history of compelling people to work and provide service.

Getting service workers to do their work is more than getting workers to lend their body in terms of labor. It demands emotional labor as well. To compel somebody to do that is not only about money, it's not only getting them to do it for as little money as possible. The most significant history of service provision is actually that of getting people, as customers, to do service for no money, and that's where the issues of gender and race come in as well.

I think it's important that service designers recognize that they are part of that compulsion process, that they create meaning, and that the meanings they create are part of the compelling process.

It is difficult to fully understand the experience of another person. Yet, ordering experience is precisely the goal of service design. What are the ways in which designers might increase empathy between themselves and the people they design for?

My answer to this question is not empathy, but a return to qualitative interviewing. That is using processes that validate verbal self-accounts and the capacity of people to articulate how they feel about their practice, which in this case is a service.

It's amazing, from my experience, how little training designers, despite the flurry of design ethnography, get in interviewing. In particularly long form, semi-structured, unstructured interview. It's a real skill that takes a long time to learn, and no one teaches it in design school.

What is the role of social context in design for services?

A sustainable future requires finding ways to meet particular needs with multiple satisfiers, or one satisfier satisfying multiple needs. I think social context is a way of saying to a designer of services, "What are the various needs?"

For example, an employee is working because they need money, but may need some developmental capacities or need to feel a sense of autonomy. They need to feel like they're having some social engagements, either with their fellow workers or with customers.

So how do you create services in which they can do this multiple satisfier? Any company is not just creating value for its customers, it's creating value for its employees. I think it's valid to talk about the context in this kind of way. What are all the possibilities of satisfying multiple needs through one's service offering?

How do you understand the relationship between services and issues of sustainability?

Society has become unsustainably materials intense because we replaced people with products. Returning to service economies is a shift out of that kind of materials-intense way of delivering freedom and well-being. Services play a really important role in returning us to people-based, rather than ownership-based, distribution of resources. When you move from a product to a person, you're generally moving from a fossil-fueled economy to renewable economy.

Service economies also tend to be local. There are digital platforms and outsourced phone-in situations, but there's a way in which a lot of service economies require a kind of face-to-face contact.

Another advantage in terms of decreasing materials intensity is that by having businesses retain ownership to products and offer services instead, they have investment structures that allow them to maintain goods in a much better way than households. One of the problems then is transport logistics. Either the service has to come to you, or you have to come to the service. That's why service provision is better in a city than in a suburb. The cost factors work much better because transport provisions drop down enormously.

No service exists in a vacuum. Beyond the situated context of the front-end provision, services are enabled, facilitated, and are an extension of particular kinds of organizational structures. Such structures are composed of various hierarchies and power relationships. The relations that comprise a given organization may be uneven or inequitable, and, thus, represent the interests of some over others. Do designers have the agency to address such issues with the organizations they work with or for? If so, is it their responsibility to wield their agency as a means to influence more equitable outcomes?

In general, designers still get hired under particular contracts to deliver particular performance outcomes on particular time frames, and all of those constrain their capacity to have agency. However, it's important to recognize that service design is already recognized as part of what it means to do change management. It brings a changing worldview into business. Service designers have been called in because there is, I think, a general crisis in value generation at the moment. In this way, they have enormous agency.

This is why service designers are getting bought up by large management consultancies. They are desperately looking for service designers to restructure their entire organization so they can be more customer-value generating.

Service design outcomes have a great potential to affect the lives of people. These effects may be positive, negative, or even a mixture of both. However, despite the potential to impact people's lives, there is currently no formal regulation or code of conduct that sets clear ethical guidelines for designers in this field. Similar to codes of conduct and professional oaths in law and medicine, what might a Hippocratic oath for services design comprise of?

Service designers should never be overseeing a decrease in wages or a decrease in overall livelihood. If a service designer is being brought in to create the system that allows outsourcing to an independent contractor who no longer is getting health care, you should refuse the job. If your job is service designing something that is going to take existing employees, make them redundant, and rehired as zero-hours contract workers, then you should consider if that is a contract worth taking.

So, yes, you can't ensure the profitability flows to the workers from the result of your actions. But you certainly should not be overseeing or contributing to something that is decreasing frontline workers' livability.

5.6 Learning features

Key points

- Service frontline workers often embody behaviors and values of the organization when they interact with users, using their own emotions in the service delivery, configuring what is defined as emotional labor, which, while an asset for the organization, is not necessarily accounted for or compensated.
- Because women account for the majority of frontline service jobs in several service industries such as hospitality and care, their emotional labor is often related to outdated social expectations of women (e.g., natural empathy, docile attitude).
- The link between climate change and services can be related to both production and consumption aspects. Life cycle analysis and LEED Certification can help improve the environmental sustainability of the production aspects, affecting physical artifacts and the build environment side of services. Approaches such as product service systems (PSS) represent service-based sustainable consumption models.
- As designers work with systems and organizations, typical design mindsets related to innovation and disruption need to be approached carefully, employing a system-thinking approach as well as considering existing design legacies already present in organizations.

Recap questions

- What are the main aspects related to labor relationships within services?
- How are issues of gender and power present in service deliveries?
- What are the main approaches that service designers can use to verify and improve eco-efficiency related to the material evidence of services?
- What is the core aspect of sustainability in relation to services?
- What are the main aspects to be observed when entering organizations?
- What are the main tools for mapping systems, and how are they most effectively used within organizations?

Activities

- Research emotional labor occurring in a restaurant on your university campus. Using a *power diagram* or a *journey map*, observe the interactions between staff and patrons, and try to identify the moments when emotional labor happens. If you have the opportunity, interview the restaurant staff (make sure you have their explicit permission). Ask about relationships with management, the kitchen, and the customers, and how they coordinate the work with several customers at the same time. Try to employ *active listening* (see glossary) to understand how they might embody the restaurant ethos and brand and how much emotional labor is present in their work.

- Research a restaurant on your university campus from a systems perspective. Map out "system restaurant" using a system map. Start by identifying its core system, including human resources (kitchen staff, servers, cashiers), its physical space, furniture and equipment, and systems involved in its operation (payment, booking, online presence). Add third-party providers and any other aspect of the system restaurant. Talk to the manager and staff if possible (make sure you have their explicit consent). Identify opportunities for improvement and interventions in the service system. Define a consultation process if you were to develop the concept further. For example, how would you codesign with staff?

Glossary

- *Emotional labor*: The psychological effort of service workers that some scholars argue are commercialized into a service.
- *Servicescapes*: The entire physical setting of a given face-to-face service interaction. This includes the architecture, interior design, environmental graphics, sign systems, decoration, atmospherics, and all elements that have an impact on the physical experience.
- *Bodystorming*: Enacted experiences of a service interaction that use props and sets. In bodystorming techniques, participants experience the prototype, which allows for more vivid analysis of ideas than simply looking at it from outside.
- *Life cycle design (LCD)*: Also known as eco-design, design that considers the whole life cycle of a given product, from "cradle to grave."
- *Life cycle analysis (LCA)*: The main method of LCD; involves quantifying materials, energy, and emissions involved in the whole life cycle of a given product.
- *Active listening*: The ability to listen to someone with empathy, without letting your own personal assumptions and biases get in the way. Empathy means being able to understand another person's experiences, emotions, and conditions from her or his perspective.

Recommended reading

Hochschild, Arlie Russel (2003). *The Managed Heart: Commercialization of Human Feeling*, 2nd ed. University of California Press.

Meadows, Donella (2008). *Thinking in Systems: A Primer*. Chelsea Green Publishing Company.

06 Designing for services

6.1 Introduction

This chapter positions service design within the design universe, affirming it as a legitimate design practice; introduces its principles; analyzes the service design practice; and maps out the community service design.

Service design is now a credible design practice, with design firms around the globe practicing it with clients across different industries. It is also an established discipline with academic studies and doctoral theses helping to analyze and codify its ways in the present but also imagining its possible futures. Schools around the world are teaching service design courses for both young and seasoned learners. It wasn't always like this. Through project after project, designers demonstrated the kind of benefit they could bring through service design. It took some time for the design community to embrace this practice, and it also took some time for nondesigners working with services to accept designers' contributions. In fact, this is all still happening.

Thanks to pioneer practitioners and thought leaders, a strong community was formed around service design. Far from uniform or unified, its strength has been in great part due to its flexibility and plurality. This chapter makes a case for service design as new kind of design practice, building on the foundational aspects of design and linking them to core principles of the service design work, including its people-centeredness, the centrality of participation and codesign, the vital importance of visual narratives, the role of material aspects of services, and the holistic/systemic nature of service design.

Next, the chapter uses project examples to discuss different kinds of projects that service designers work on, what kind of benefit they might result in, and finally the kinds of output and typical deliverables of service design projects.

The interview with service design researcher and author Daniela Sangiorgi offers reflections about service design core principles, considering the arc of evolution of service design, among other key insights.

In addition, the process of prototyping services is often a collaborative activity, involving a diversity of stakeholders. See Chapter 10 for approaches and techniques.

Core principle 5: Service design is holistic

Holistic means considering something as a whole, combining its different parts into systems. It stands for integration, interconnectedness, and harmony. How do we achieve a systemic approach in services, and is it even possible?

Services are complex and multidimensional. They can be experienced through multiple channels, and channels can have origins in different parts of a given organization. Think about companies that have both face-to-face and online presences, such as banks. How do we expect to have comparable experiences and benefits whether we are in person in a branch, talking to the call center on the phone, or making a transfer through an online system? Consider also large organizations that operate through some channels dedicated to internal logistics and other channels dedicated to interacting with users.

A key challenge in designing services is therefore how to integrate the system, process, and touchpoints in a consistent and holistic way. Being holistic involves making sure that users experience the service delivery in a consistent way, regardless of the channel they are using; it also involves internal consistency with seamless integration of the different back-office operations.

Basic layers of integration to be considered include making sure that users receive a consistent message and functionality across different channels; that different departments of the same organization talk to each other using a common language; and also that the organization's relationship with its own workers, suppliers, and its social, economic, and cultural context is consistent and reliable.

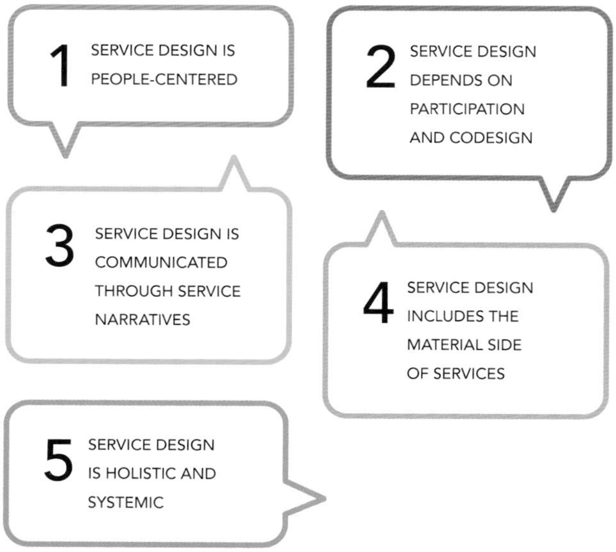
1 SERVICE DESIGN IS PEOPLE-CENTERED
2 SERVICE DESIGN DEPENDS ON PARTICIPATION AND CODESIGN
3 SERVICE DESIGN IS COMMUNICATED THROUGH SERVICE NARRATIVES
4 SERVICE DESIGN INCLUDES THE MATERIAL SIDE OF SERVICES
5 SERVICE DESIGN IS HOLISTIC AND SYSTEMIC

Fig 6.3 Core principles of service design, adapted from Schneider and Stickdorn.

6.4 What kind of project and what kind of benefit?

Let's dive into the practice of service design and see what kinds of problems service design projects are responding to; what kinds of ideas, solutions, and insights practitioners are coming up with; and what kinds of methods and approaches are being used to develop them.

The chapters in Part II are all about projects with in-depth case studies. For now, let's take a sneak peek into five projects, selected from award-winning service design firms. They can offer a broad overview of project typologies and briefs, and illustrate what kinds of output and impact can be expected from service design.

Example 1

The problem	The result	The process	Who did it
How to provide better services to visitors in one of Australia's busiest libraries	The development of a Future State Service with a suite of thirty projects to be implemented over the years, including redesigning the welcome zone, equipping front-office staff with mobile equipment, and initiating a pilot for a single customer service point	Researching current service delivery, resulting in a series of rich visual journey maps; engaging with hundreds of staff across the organization; conducting workshops, interviews, and live prototypes	Client: State Library Victory (Australia) Project by: Meld Studios

Example 2

The problem	The result	The process	Who did it
How to reduce the waiting time for high-risk women to schedule breast cancer preventive exams in the largest hospital in Scandinavia	A streamlined new procedure for breast cancer, part of the New Breast Diagnostics Centre, where the time for patients to get a diagnostic was reduced by 90 percent	Workshop with forty employees from different sectors of the hospital, mapping together the patient experience, interviews with patients, doctors, nurses, and service scenario cocreation	Client: Oslo University Hospital (Norway) Project by: Designit

Example 3

The problem	The result	The process	Who did it
How to streamline public services, helping citizens do things like book a wedding ceremony, request a death certificate, or update a driver's license without getting lost in the process	Implementation of a three-month "live prototype" of a public services one-stop-shop, as a way to capture citizens' perception of public services	The design and production of a temporary physical space complete with new branding, furniture, digital touchpoints, and staff training	Client: Victoria State Government (Australia) Project by: Studio Thick

Example 4

The problem	The result	The process	Who did it
How to improve the passenger platform experience when boarding trains	A mobile app and a 200-meter long LED screen above the train platform displaying real-time information about the arriving train and location of train doors	Analyzing the existing customer journey and identifying pain points; developing working prototypes of new services; implementing a pilot and getting user feedback.	Client: Netherlands Railways (NS) and ProRail (The Netherlands) Project by: Edenspiekermann and STBY

Example 5

The problem	The result	The process	Who did it
How to improve mental health and well-being in young people using their preferred media (Internet, social media, and mobile technologies), thus affecting a major public health care issue	A new online platform, a social media campaign, and a toolkit to help youth-related workers, policy makers, planners, and service providers interact with youngsters in more effective and meaningful ways	Working with young people aged thirteen to twenty-one to identify what kind of digital tools could help improve mental well-being, both their own and their peers'	Client: NHS Greater Glasgow & Clyde (UK) Project by: Snook

6.4 What kind of project and what kind of benefit?

DAY 1:
The patient visits her GP who then sends a referral for further diagnostics at the hospital. Patients are given a brochure clearly explaining next steps, along with a phone number to call with any questions.

DAY 02:
All new referrals are assessed daily and patients are called up immediatly to book an appointment. Less urgent cases and check-ups after recovery are funneled to private clinics.

DAY 03:
The patient attends the appointment at the hospital, with all her examinations within one day. At the end of that day the radiologist gives her a preliminary answer on the spot.

DAY 04:
The next day, in a routine-based morning meeting, a multi-disciplinary team iscusses the patients. The same afternoon, the patient can return for her final diagnosis and treatment plan.

Fig 6.4 and 6.5 Designit journey map for Oslo hospital.

Looking at the projects described in the preceding table, we can see that typical deliverables of service design projects reflect the diversity of project briefs and objectives but can be roughly categorized as follows:

- **Analytical**. Analytical outputs can be documents that synthesize findings from research—for example, visual reports from observation and shadowing users and staff, reports from surveys, reports of interviews with project stakeholders, or sets of *personas* that represent main user groups. Journey maps and service blueprints are also used to aggregate data from research. This category also accounts for evaluation reports prepared after pilot implementation.
- **Recommendations**. Projects in which the main outputs are insights about new processes, practices, and strategies for organizations to implement are materialized through recommendation reports. Reports may include visual descriptions, service blueprints for implementation of protocols and organizational flows, or other visual and descriptive materials to support and disseminate recommendations. In some cases, the recommendation package includes sets of projects and features to be implemented over the course of several years, informing the future of the organization's investment and work.

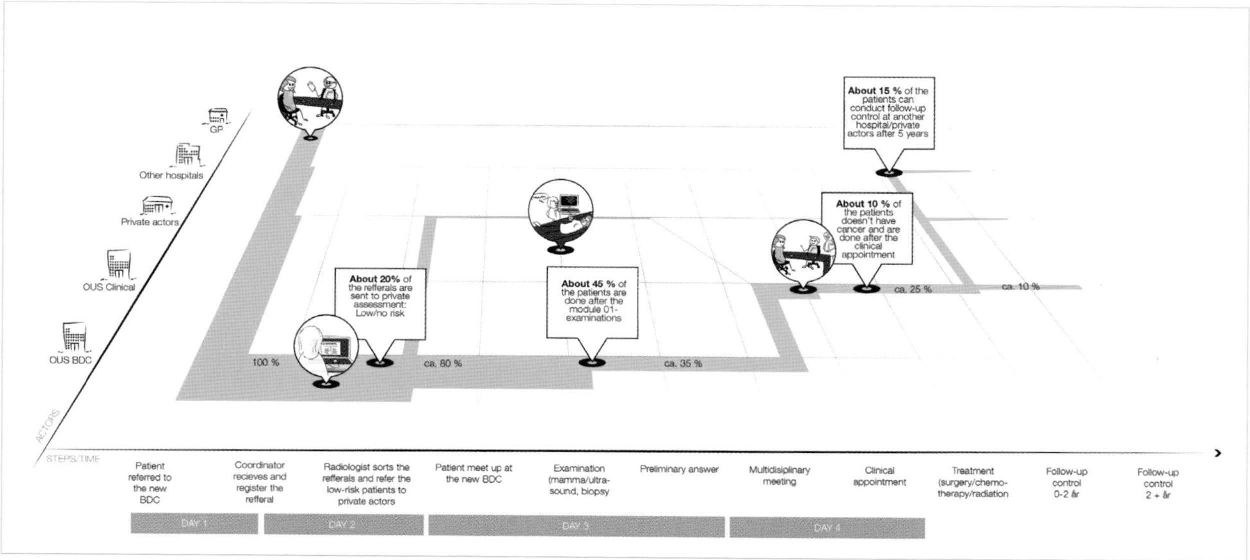
GP
Other hospitals
Private actors
OUS Clinical
OUS BDC
ACTORS
STEPS/TIME
About 20% of the refferals are sent to private assessment: Low/no risk
About 45 % of the patients are done after the module 01- examinations
About 15 % of the patients can conduct follow-up control at another hospital/private actors after 5 years
About 10 % of the patients doesn't have cancer and are done after the clinical appointment
100 %
ca. 80 %
ca. 35 %
ca. 25 %
ca. 10 %
Patient referred to the new BDC
Coordinator recieves and register the refferal
Radiologist sorts the refferals and refer the low-risk patients to private actors
Patient meet up at the new BDC
Examination (mamma/ultra-sound, biopsy
Preliminary answer
Multidisiplinary meeting
Clinical appointment
Treatment (surgery/chemo-therapy/radiation
Follow-up control 0-2 år
Follow-up control 2 + år
DAY 1
DAY 2
DAY 3
DAY 4

6.4 What kind of project and what kind of benefit?

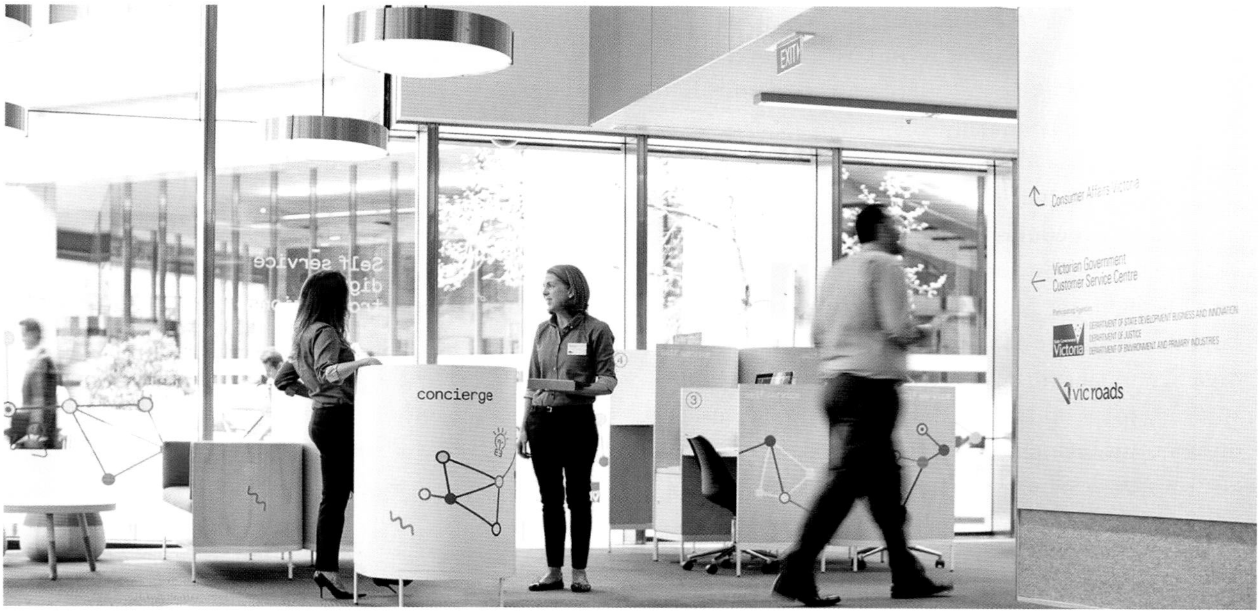
EXIT
Self service
concierge
Consumer Affairs Victoria
Victorian Government
Customer Service Centre
DEPARTMENT OF STATE DEVELOPMENT BUSINESS AND INNOVATION
DEPARTMENT OF JUSTICE
DEPARTMENT OF ENVIRONMENT AND PRIMARY INDUSTRIES
Victoria
vicroads

Fig 6.6 Temporary one-stop-shop for government services in Victoria, Australia.

- **Experiential and learning outputs leading to organizational change.** In some cases, service designers are asked to conduct creative sessions or other educational activities so that staff and even users (for example, patients of clinics and hospitals) can experience new practices and adopt them into their contexts. The main takeaway in these cases is the learning experience itself. Several client organizations talk about some kind of transformation of their work and even organizational culture as a result of engaging with service designers. The portfolio of many service design firms includes offering creative workshops for organizations.
- **New service experiences materialized through touchpoints and servicescapes, journeys, and protocols.** Service designers may design touchpoints of services and, in some cases, produce these touchpoints ready for distribution (communication materials, digital interfaces). Some firms have the internal capacity to develop apps and produce printed material. In other cases, service designers will deliver specs (specification documents) for building and executing touchpoints or recommend other professional designers (architects; interior, light, and product designers; interface designers; illustrators; video makers; and other applied artists). Other kinds of outputs in this category include service blueprints or journey maps describing user experiences and touchpoints as well as back-office processes and materials.

6.5
The service design community

Let's look at the people behind service design and the main outlets that gather practitioners, researchers, teachers, and students.

In the past ten to fifteen years, the service design community worldwide has grown into a diverse and rich network of practitioners and researchers, educators and students, as well as enthusiastic clients across an array of sectors and industries. Several service design firms have emerged anew, and many existing design firms have included service design as a vital capability. Also, government offices and agencies, health-care organizations, financial institutions, and others have hired service designers and created service design teams in-house. Schools and universities have been training generations of service designers, and researchers have been studying and codifying the service design practice.

With the blooming of a practice and discipline, a number of initiatives and specialized communities have branched out with outstanding enthusiasm and dynamism. Here's a brief overview of the main groups of the service design community and other key resources.

- **The Service Design Network**
  The Service Design Network was established in 2004 and since then has emerged as the main resource in the field, defining the professional identity of service design. Operating on a membership basis, it aggregates professionals, academic institutions, and public and private sector industries through three main outlets: the *Touchpoint Journal*, a peer-reviewed quarterly magazine; global and national conferences; and national chapters that aggregate local communities of practice on a country and city level.

- **ServDes Conference**
  As service design evolved into a discipline being researched and taught in universities and research centers, ServDes, or the Service Design and Innovation research group, emerged as a dedicated academic group attracting academic researchers, practitioners, and industry representatives. Its conferences are a venue for the exchange of original knowledge in service design, working with a peer-reviewed system to review papers.

Fig 6.7 Service Design Jam Berlin.

- **Service Design Jam**
  Created in 2011, the Service Design Jam is a global event that takes place in one single weekend every year, with teams around the world all working on the same service design challenge. The jam challenge is launched on the first day of the event by a central team, and self-organized teams in cities around the world work through the weekend in a collaborative spirit. The Service Design Jam is quite a successful initiative among practitioners, students, and service design enthusiasts worldwide.

- **DESIS Network**
  Launched in 2009 as a network of labs within design schools, the mission of DESIS (Design for Social Innovation and Sustainability) Network is to amplify the potential of social innovation as a driver of sustainable change through design. Service design is not always explicit in the main DESIS Network narrative, but the social innovations recognized by DESIS as emerging and sustainable ways of living to be modeled after are essentially service-based initiatives, such as cohousing, community-supported agriculture, community gardens, neighborhood care, or time banks.

- **Service design blogosphere and social media**
  Because service design is a new discipline deeply embedded in practice, practitioners, students, researchers, and other aficionados have established an active blogosphere as an important vector for knowledge dissemination and exchange. Other web-based communities have sprouted up through social media, such as LinkedIn groups and Twitter hash tags.

- **Service design firms' newsletters**
  Firms such as Engine, Live|Work, and many others share their processes and projects through their websites and distribute newsletters with the latest details from their work.

- **Repositories of tools and bibliography lists**
  Repositories of tools such as http://www.servicedesigntools.org/ have been instrumental to diffuse methods, approaches, and tools among professional and students. Bibliography lists such as http://www.servicedesignbooks.org/ have been consistently aggregating publications relevant to service design and offering annotated bibliographies.

- **Service design awards**
  Awards are an important thermometer of practice, serving as a comparative showcase of the best projects designed and implemented every year. Noteworthy awards in service design include Core 77 Awards (service design category), active since 2011, and the Service Design Network Service Design Awards created in 2015.

- **Service design educational sphere**
  Starting with a handful of courses and graduate theses in a handful of design schools, the landscape of service design education has evolved considerably over the years. From undergraduate programs to master's programs up to doctorate level as well as executive education and certificate courses, there are several options to learn service design around the world. The Service Design network website (www.service-design-network.org/) has a comprehensive directory of service design schools.

6.6 Interview with Daniela Sangiorgi

Daniela Sangiorgi is Associate Professor Politecnico di Milano and coauthor of *Designing for Services* (Gower).

Can you offer your personal understanding of what constitutes service design?

Service design is a field of practice that began to emerge twenty years ago. In the beginning, it was kind of an academic study, then gradually became more practice driven. In the area of service innovation approaches, it's introducing a mode of thinking that comes from a designerly way of innovating. This mode is very people centered and is informed by a collaborative wave of insight and idea development using visual and mental tools to inform the design elements of a service. So it is quite experience-centered, but it also touches on more organizational dimensions as well.

Why does the creation of services need designers? What is the value that designers bring?

I think it's a mix of the ability [to] translate insights from people and their behaviors into ideas and solutions that also have aesthetic qualities. Service designers have an ability to design around needs and the actual capabilities of people. So, it's somehow a mix of bringing a people-centered approach, but also an ability to translate that in terms of tangible, or intelligible, creations. For example, new service ideas or concepts, or different ways of interacting with a service. The attention to people and experience results in services not only driven by technology or not by markets, but by user experience.

What is the relationship of design thinking to service design?

Design thinking is used more when you want to translate a concept design for management to other fields. It's working to generalize some of the qualities or ways of thinking of designers into different contexts. For example, if you want managers to be more able to act like designers, then you talk about design thinking. So, I can see a relationship in terms of introducing design within organizations. However, design thinking has been somewhat isolated from actual design practice, that is professionals who have been trained as designers. Design thinking is in many ways an abstraction of what design practice actually is. While you might lose a lot in this translation, it can be a useful way to allow managers, or marketing people, to better understand design, and maybe be able to communicate or use it better.

At its core, service design is concerned with the ordering of various kinds of social interactions. This requires being attuned to the needs and habits of people. User-centered design approaches are often critical to a successful service design project. To what extent is service design a user-centered practice?

More than user-centered, we say human- or people-centered, because it's more about understanding social interactions rather than simply thinking about users. In other words, it has to do with the understanding of interaction between different kinds of people that are involved in a service provision. This is the core. Without it, it's not service design. Without that deeper understanding of interactions, behaviors, habits, and needs, it can't be defined as design.

Beyond including the perspective of users in a design process, cocreation is also a fundamental aspect of what it means to do service design. In which moments during the design process is cocreation crucial to facilitating better design outcomes?

Cocreation can mean a few different things. If you want to consider cocreation as when people can be brought into the design process, then it really depends on the project. Different projects may need [a] different level of inclusion. If you are in a social kind of project which requires the work to be more representative of different groups and individuals, then you need to guarantee a higher level of inclusion in the process. If you are in an organization, then there might be a different degree of inclusion. I think inclusion and cocreation should be present in all stages of an iterative process. The biggest question is more who to involve, why, and how. These questions are important because it's very difficult to be representative. The decisions you make about who gets to participate can have great impact on your project.

Why is an understanding of systems and organizational structures crucial to effectively design services? How can designers develop their skills of thinking systemically?

This really depends on the kind of service. Services are provided within systems or organizations. Without understanding what these systems are, it's impossible to design a service. This would be like designing for manufacturing without understanding production processes or materials properly. You might design something that is not feasible or is too expensive. Organizations are the material for service design.

With regards to how designers can better think systematically, generally this [is] done through developing on their ability to navigate complexity by studying systems. And so [it] would be like anthropology for me: how do you immerse yourself in systems and be able to get inside and visualize the complexity, interactions, and so on? By understanding systems, it's possible to understand how different parts are interrelated, so whenever there is a change in one place, this can have an effect on someone or something else. This is where the concept of inclusion and participation is fundamental.

One practice is to immerse people into systems as an experiential practice, which then gets represented through visualization. Another way to understand is more from a procedural perspective. So, this means looking at systems more as machines, understanding the mechanics in terms of processes and operations and how this is related to a traditional service delivery order.

What are some tools for making tangible complex systems of people and things visible in a design process?

There are different tools that have different ways [of] sort of presenting system. Some are more machine-like, like a blueprinting; some are more emerging based on a thermal or biological metaphor. For example, thinking of a system in terms of an [ecology] or environment.

I think the tools also depend on what is your aim or issue. If you are in an exploratory phase where you may be trying to gain a sense of an ecology, you might use systems mapping. If you are in a specification space, where you need to relate experience with different stages of a service provision, then your tool might look more like a service blueprint.

Prototyping an idea in traditional design fields often means making an idea physical. One can build out a model or a rough prototype and see the product of that labor in front of them. To prototype a service requires a much more expansive approach, often having to orchestrate an assemblage of materials, people, and social interactions. What is the role of the prototype in the service design context?

One way is to consider what is the finite experience. What can you do that helps you simulate that experience with the service and allows people to give you feedback on the interaction. That is more kind of a quick approach to gaining insight. If you are [interested] in developing a working prototype, that means you really are trying to see how the technology works in an organization. This then would require a deeper collaboration with the clients. In this case you might create smaller prototypes of some proposed organizational practices where you engage with the prototype to simulate some of the processes.

I think for students, what's important is thinking of a prototype as a means to gain experiential insight into the service you are proposing.

Over the past ten years, there has been an explosion of interest in service design. This includes not only new professional organizations, conferences, and programs, but also many more service designers coming out of design schools. How have you seen the field grow, and where do you think it will go in the future?

I think there will be more specialization. Service designers will likely develop their own practice in different ways depending on where they specialize. You can see this already with many design companies that [have] been working specifically in the public sector, or in areas of social or behavioral change, as well as in digital technology. There might be more integration with what's called business consultancy, but also entering into a more entrepreneurial space. In this case creating their own business.

I think services will probably mix into this new evolution or become more embedded in organization and management as a kind of new solution. I see this as a move far away from traditional service design practice that is primarily concerned with service interaction design experience.

6.7 Learning features

Key points

- Design is about having ideas by envisioning preferred futures, defining new relationships when transferring new ideas into reality, visualizing and communicating and sharing ideas, and delivering well-being to people.
- Core principles of service design:
    1. Service design is people-centered.
    2. Service design depends on participation and codesign.
    3. Service design is communicated through service narratives.
    4. Service design includes the material side of services.
    5. Service design is holistic/systemic.
- Typical deliverables of service design projects can be analytical (interviews, reports); recommendations (for new strategies, processes, practices); experiential and learning outputs leading to organizational change; and new service experiences materialized through touchpoints and servicescapes, journeys, and protocols.
- The service design community is diverse, composed of practitioners, academics, researchers, and students.

Recap questions

- What are the basic definitions of design?
- What are the core principles of service design?
- Why is service design people-centered rather than user-centered?
- What kinds of projects are done by service designers through what kinds of deliverables?
- What kind of impact can be expected from service projects?
- What are areas of application in which you would like to see more service design projects and why?

Activities

Working individually or in teams, investigate the landscape of service design practice. Possible activities:

- Prepare a directory of service design firms in your city, region, or country.
- Research one particular service design firm and analyze its projects and approaches. What kinds of projects does the firm do and who are its clients? What are its approach and methods? What is its definition of service design? Who works there, and what are the skills of team members?

- Produce a service design documentary. Reach out to a service designer and interview her or him in person or by phone or Skype; videorecord if possible. Ask the service designer prompt questions about her or his definition of service design, projects and clients, processes, methods and tools, and opinion about the service design practice.
- Map out the main conversations happening using the Twitter #servicedesign. Are there any controversies? Produce a debate. Take a side.

Glossary

- *User-centered design*: A design approach and philosophy that emerged to ensure that the needs of final users were addressed in the design of new products and technology. Methods include ethnographic research (interviews, observation, shadowing) and generative methods (cocreation workshops and prototypes).
- *Participatory design and codesign*: Design approaches that recognize people as partners of a project, by involving them throughout the design process through workshops, interviews, consultations, meetings, and conversations, preferably as sustained engagements and constant dialogue.
- *Holistic*: In services, holistic means considering the service as a whole or as a system, composed of different integrated components. A holistic service assures that users experience the service delivery in a consistent way and that there is seamless integration of the different back-office operations.
- *Service narratives*: Visual narratives or stories such as journey maps that represent services over time, as experienced by users, staff, and other stakeholders.
- *Material evidence*: Artifacts or *touchpoints* that enable a certain experience in a service journey, directly or indirectly. It includes brand elements, signage, objects, but also colors and other sensorial aspects.

Recommended reading

Meroni, A., and Sangiorgi, D. (2011). *Design for Services*. Gower.

Stickdorn, M., and Schneider, J. (2010). *This Is Service Design Thinking. Basics - Tools - Cases*. BIS Publishers

Part II
The Service Design Process

07 Starting the service design process

7.1 Introduction

In this chapter, we explore how the service design process begins. The brief is a key piece in the beginning of a service design project. However, due to the holistic and systemic characteristics of the service design approach, the initial briefing produced by the client needs to be revisited and reformulated through quite a long process. Therefore, it is critical to plan for enough time and resources at the beginning of the process to revisit the initial client brief. This chapter describes the role of project briefs, how to define their parameters, and how they can be negotiated between clients and designers.

Service design is a holistic, systemic, and strategic process. It involves a high degree of research and discovery as well as ideation, prototyping, and proposal generation. As a result, for a client to engage in the service design journey requires a degree of commitment and buy-in, which service designers themselves may assist in producing. In this chapter, we consider effective ways to communicate the value of service design to clients.

In addition to constructing good project briefs and communicating service design value to clients, we explore some typologies showing how the service design process might take shape. In doing so, you learn about the various creative and analytical parts that comprise a service design approach.

Fig 7.1 Some of the outcomes of the project: maps with the different bus routes.

7.2 Case Study: APAM Bus Company Mantua, Italy, by Intersezioni Design Integrated

APAM is a public transportation company in Mantua, Italy, serving both urban and interurban areas. APAM's CEO initially contacted the Milan-based product and service design agency Intersezioni Design Integrated asking for a redesign of the company's website. The concern was that, as a communication tool, the website was broken.

After initial meetings, however, it became clear that the issues with the website were only the tip of the iceberg. It became clear to the Intersezioni team that APAM's service offering and company's values were not in alignment. Confusion among end users was prevalent due to ineffective communication strategies, resulting in inconsistent service experiences. A simple redesign of APAM's website would not solve the larger problem the company faced. As a result, Intersezioni redirected the client toward a broader brief, one that spoke to the needs of the communities APAM serviced. Intersezioni managed to convince the CEO to change the initial brief entirely and embark on a long discovery process. This investigation centered on the company's presentation to final users, as well as its communication with workers and internal stakeholders. The website was eventually done after three years of project development.

The design process involved a long discovery phase in which the design team examined the organization in detail to understand its departments, staff, and services, as well as existing aesthetic and communication strategies. At the same time, the team engaged in research with the users of the company's services, the many passengers traveling through APAM's service region. Through this investigation, the team was able to map out APAM's services in detail, including the various touchpoints and visual aspects. This process of service mapping informed the definition of the initial project guidelines.

The next step in the process involved codesign activities with key individuals in the company. These activities resulted in a deeper understanding of the current state of affairs within the company. Most importantly, they helped validate and identify design opportunities as well as set project guidelines.

It was only after this prolonged discovery phase that the real design brief emerged. From here, the team was able to transform a long learning process into a creative interpretation of needs and opportunities and then into concrete project guidelines.

The project guidelines were translated into a final document containing a new brand identity, a plan for its application at various communication touchpoints, and a range of newly redesigned service provisions.

7.2

7.3

7.4

7.5

A.P.A.M.
FERMATA
A RICHIESTA
A.P.A.M.
FERMATA
A RICHIESTA

7.6

7.7

Figs 7.2 through 7.7 Images from the research within the organization, its staff, and users.

Figs 7.8 and 7.9 Mapping of existing services and definition of initial guidelines.

Figs 7.10 and 7.11 Activities during the codesign phase.

Figs 7.12 through 7.15 Project guidelines, or the "real" design brief translated into a book with design principles and all the learning from the research phase, like a snapshot of the organization as a whole.

Fig 7.16 Final design touchpoints supporting the new and improved services.

7.8

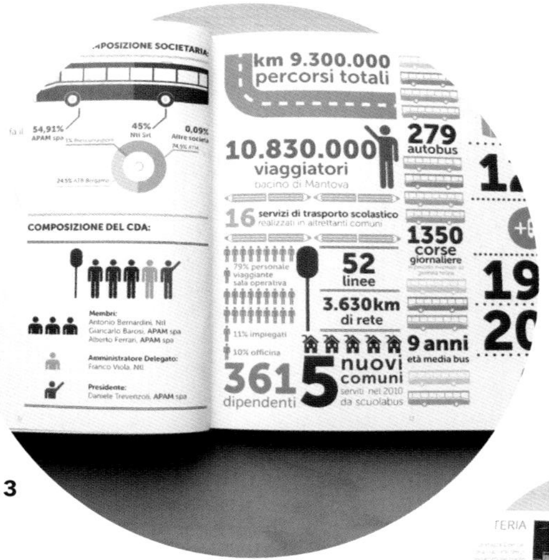

km 9.300.000
percorsi totali
10.830.000
viaggiatori
bacino di Mantova
279
autobus
16 servizi di trasporto scolastico
realizzati in altrettanti comuni
52
linee
3.630km
di rete
1350
corse
giornaliere
9 anni
età media bus
361
dipendenti
5 nuovi
comuni
serviti nel 2010
da scuolabus
COMPOSIZIONE DEL CDA:
Membri:
Amministratore Delegato:
Presidente:

7.13

28.000
visite utenti
in biglietteria

7.14

7.9

7.15

7.10

LINEE GUIDA
IDENTITA' VISIVA
DI APAM 2009
IMMAGINE COORDINATA E LOGHI

7.12

7.11

7.16

7.3 Interview with Alessandro Confalonieri, Intersezioni

Alessandro Confalonieri is director of Intersezioni Design Integrated in Milan, Italy.

Intersezioni's project for APAM Bus Company Mantua started with a very small brief from the client, who initially asked for a new website, and then it grew into a broader project with results affecting both users and the company as a whole. What is the role of designers in reframing project briefs?

The fact is, most of the time companies aren't entirely clear on what they need. They know they need to change something, but don't know the what and how. APAM's CEO was very different from the usual public sector manager and was very eager to explore new ideas and willing to promote positive change. He approached us initially with a "classic brief": a request for a website. However, we quickly understood that a new APAM website would not be the answer to their real needs.

What was the process of discovering and formulating the "real" brief?

We engaged in long conversations with the company to better understand what were the real needs. At Intersezioni, we understand that in many cases the need for design is not always clear to companies. If seeing the value of design is not immediate, a longer process needs to be established to make it visible. With APAM, we proposed a brainstorm workshop in our studio to help us find out more about the larger context in which the project exists. By the end of this session, we were able to convey to the CEO that solely investing in [the] website would not serve their larger needs and would end up being money spent for nothing.

How did you get to the conclusion that the original brief needed to be reformulated?

We realized that APAM was a service company that needed a profound restructuring, as its then current offerings were all over the place. For example, its urban and interurban services were often mixed together in a way that created unnecessary confusion for clients. Signage was hard to read, and information was not clearly communicated. Like many public companies in Italy, APAM was not looked upon favorably by local residents. A change was needed in both the client perception of the company as well as how the company communicated its services. Luckily, the CEO was highly invested in promoting necessary organizational changes.

What was it like to design a broader brief/proposal from scratch?

Well, we asked for one week to work on a proposal, for which we charged very little because we were committed with getting this project. Our goal was to prove the value of design first, while also establishing the grounds for setting in place a longer, research-driven design process. Our proposal was formulated around one very tangible result: the production of a proposal presented as a book. The book contained two main elements: first, the proposal for a new visual identity, and second, a series of new service concepts, each of which requiring some level of organizational change. We figured that a printed book was both accessible and tangible as a tool to communicate ideas to a board composed mostly of people in their sixties and seventies. They are very old school!

Can you describe the research process for producing the outcomes presented in the book?

We conducted two months of research where we asked for direct access to the company. We had meetings with all the important stakeholders and made use of questionnaires and interviews. A road map began to emerge slowly, pointing towards possible directions for change. We presented our findings in a meeting, using a straightforward PowerPoint presentation showing the problems we identified as well as the hidden needs and opportunities. This also included reviewing previous research done by the company. Then we facilitated structured workshops to learn more and test the company's assumptions. We invited participants to map out the perceptions of how the company functioned, giving us a clear view of how they saw their service operating. This was the starting point for creating guidelines for the company's organizational change that essentially turned into the brief. So in short, our approach was first to understand the company, its people and chain of production, engage with people through interviews and structured workshops, and then define the real brief itself, that synthesizes the company's unmet needs.

Can you describe more aspects of the participatory approach? How did people react to your research and activities? What was the process of engaging people and building trust like?

The CEO liked our participatory approach, and used these engagements as opportunities to explore his own ideas for the company. From our side, we appreciated working with people from different parts of the company. Typical of a public sector company, the staff is really good but often times find themselves in a dormant kind of state, not necessarily attuned to innovation. Public sector politics also plays a role in setting moods and relationships amongst staff. In the first session, some staff participants did not welcome our ideas at all. Our activity was interpreted as a top-down imposition from the CEO. It was a slow process of gaining trust; only after one year the staff started to understand who we were and started to like the way that we were working and became very cooperative.

In the process of defining the brief, and then in later project phases, how did you address the user side of the service?

Bringing in the user perspective was a key component of our process. We started by going to APAM's ticket office and experiencing the user journey ourselves. Albeit located next to the main train station, it was hard for nonlocals to find the ticket office. We noticed how visual and spatial clues were off-putting to customers. For example, the doors were half closed and there was a myriad of signs blocking the window so customers couldn't see inside. Inside the ticket office, the customers' area was full of old signs all over the place, in contrast with the interior part of the office where the staff stays that was really neat and nice. This contrast was very telling about the sense of belonging and care the staff had in relation to their own spaces which didn't transfer to the customer area. The result was a poor and often random user experience. We then talked to the staff about the meaning of welcoming people in a better way and how giving clear and correct information to customers results in them not bothering you anymore!

What was the process of implementing the concepts that you produced in the book?

After the board meeting, they gave us the "go ahead." We then sat down with the CEO and started to plan what order things were going to be implemented over the course of the next three years. We created a road map for concept implementation plus a budget with implementation costs. This approach matched well the CEO's plans for the company; implementation in phases was a good choice for them in economic terms. We started by implementing the new visual identity and the following step was implementing the school bus service.

Is the mission of organizational change inherent to service design?

I believe that, as a designer, you can't simply approach a company and say: "I have an idea, and my idea is better than what you've been doing for years." In our process we are involved in constant conversations with staff. We design in constant consultation with staff, giving them a sense of power and ownership that helps get them to the point where the ideas finally start to clink in their minds. It was a really beautiful process. I think service design is about that: you need to create a path within a company and the community you are working with. There is a lot of education that happens alongside the design process. The challenge is how to communicate to companies the value of service design through these educational elements.

7.4 Case study analysis

Defining the Brief

The case of Intersezioni's work with APAM illustrates how service design briefs are often the product of initial research into a client's organization and service needs. In this case, the design team was offered a brief limited in scope to the company website. Through Intersezioni's research-driven process, it then became clear that a more systemic solution was needed. To arrive at the true brief, the design team engaged with company leadership and staff as well as users, learning about their perceptions of the APAM service. In codesign workshops, the team, along with members of APAM, mapped existing services and gained crucial insights into gaps and opportunities for service design interventions, thus creating the initial guides for a new project brief. As we have learned, service design is inherently systemic and collaborative. In the preceding description, we can see how these systemic and collaborative elements figure into the earliest stages of a project where the brief itself is the product of in-depth contextual research and an idea validation process.

Defining the Designer-Client Relationship

As exemplified in the preceding case study, it is quite common for a client to approach designers with a very limited scope of the issues they face. Their close proximity to the problem can make it hard to see the bigger picture. Service design is well positioned in its holistic approach to reframe problems to arrive at a proposal or brief with the greatest value impact. However, it is often necessary to educate clients who may not be aware of the value service design can bring in discovering and addressing the true issue. This is part of the reason that the definition of the designer-client relationship is crucial to the success of a project.

The case of the APAM Bus Company highlights some effective strategies for defining the designer-client relationship. Intersezioni was able to identify individuals with institutional clout, in this case the CEO, who were sympathetic to innovation and change. This opened the door for the favorable reception of suggestions from the design team that diverged from the initial project brief. Intersezioni was also successful at lobbying for an enhanced window of time to create a proposal that, rather than pushing a radical new agenda for the project, sold the client on the value of service design as a process, thus establishing the grounds for a more substantial research and discovery phase. By getting the clients to commit to these more modest goals, the team was able create a space for getting to know the client organization better, while simultaneously proving the value of the service design approach. As a result, the design team was eventually able to secure support for a wide-reaching, long-term process for overhauling APAM's service system and offerings.

It is also important to note the potential of codesign workshops, as exemplified in the preceding case, for defining the relationship between the designer and the client as well. From the earliest stages, Intersezioni included staff and management in collaborative workshop sessions. This helped to set the stage for a collective service design journey in which the client would invest time and expertise to the outcome, not just their budget. These kinds of relationships are important when designing for services, since your proposals will likely require organizational change as much as the implementation of new service provisions.

Defining a process and a sequence of activities

Intersezioni's process alternates research and discovery with convergent thinking and creative synthesis. The pivoting from a learning mindset into a creative one is a movement of the service design process from problem setting to problem solving. The key to this passage is pivoting from understanding realities and conditions, seeing the opportunities and gaps, and proposing new ways to tap into identified opportunities and overcome existing gaps.

Within this general framework, Intersezioni conducted a unique version of a typical service design process through the following sequence of phases/activities: researching (within organization and with users); mapping existing services; defining initial guidelines; codesigning with the organization; validating research and initial guidelines; and defining final project guidelines (the "real" design brief), the design development, and initial implementation. Building on typical service design processes, Intersezioni's process in this project responded to the unique conditions of the client organization.

7.5 Methods and tools

The following guide introduces key approaches, methods, and tools to help you set a service design process to structure your project as well as define a service design brief.

Charting the service design process

The service design process is a journey in itself. While design agencies have developed and adopted their own frameworks and rules of engagement with clients, each project is unique and based on subjective factors and variables such as trust and alignment of values and language between client and designer, ability of the designer to make sense of project context, and ability to capture the politics of the organization.

That said, the typical engagement between client organizations and designers involves a contract that lays out the phases and describes the expected outcomes of the project.

Typically, any service design project starts with a research/discovery phase in which designers immerse themselves in the project and search out problems, look for opportunities, and gain a general perspective. The next step is determining the project parameters based on research findings and, from there, start the ideation process, which involves codesign with the organization and its final customers and users. The next step involves exploring possible concepts, testing them through early prototyping, and finally defining one main concept for development and implementation.

The *double diamond* design process described by the Design Council UK and adopted by several service agencies is essentially based on two "diamonds," each one alternates a divergent and convergent phase:

First diamond

- *Discover*: In this phase, designers focus on gaining insight into the problem and then delving into the people and their context as well as existing services.

- *Define*: This phase is about translating insights into an area to focus on and then defining design directions and a clear problem space.

Second diamond

- *Develop*: In this phase, designers develop potential solutions, generating and testing new service concepts.

- *Deliver*: This phase focuses on delivering solutions and specifications for implementation.

The main aspect about this process is how they alternate from an open, divergent mode and pivot into a focused synthesis. In the first part of the double diamond, the Discover process should result in a set of opportunities and gaps that will help guide the Define process, which is based on the creative exploration of ideas that can tap into the identified opportunities and gaps. The "real brief" emerges through the consideration of these ideas. From there, a new divergent part of the process starts with the development of these ideas into robust concepts through prototyping and codesign with staff and users. A main concept should emerge from this process, leading to the final step of the double diamond being developed into an implementation of final solutions.

A revamped version of the double diamond has been recently described offering more detail on the activities comprised in each diamond. In this model, the first Discover phase starts with the client brief, that is meant to be "ripped" and expanded through primary and secondary research, followed by analysis and synthesis of the research findings into themes, opportunity areas and finally the definition of the final brief at the end of the first diamond. The second diamond starts off with ideation activities and the second half is dedicated to cycles of prototyping and testing of ideas until a final solution is defined.

Such models are useful tools to help designers structure their process and work as a shareable tool for negotiations with clients and other project stakeholders. It can definitively be used to help structure contracts and organize project milestones. The unique conditions of each project will dictate how the process will unfold in real life, however.

The following images offer different examples of processes used by service designers.

Fig 7.17 The double diamond model of the design process. The brief is defined only after research (Discover) and analysis (Define) phases.

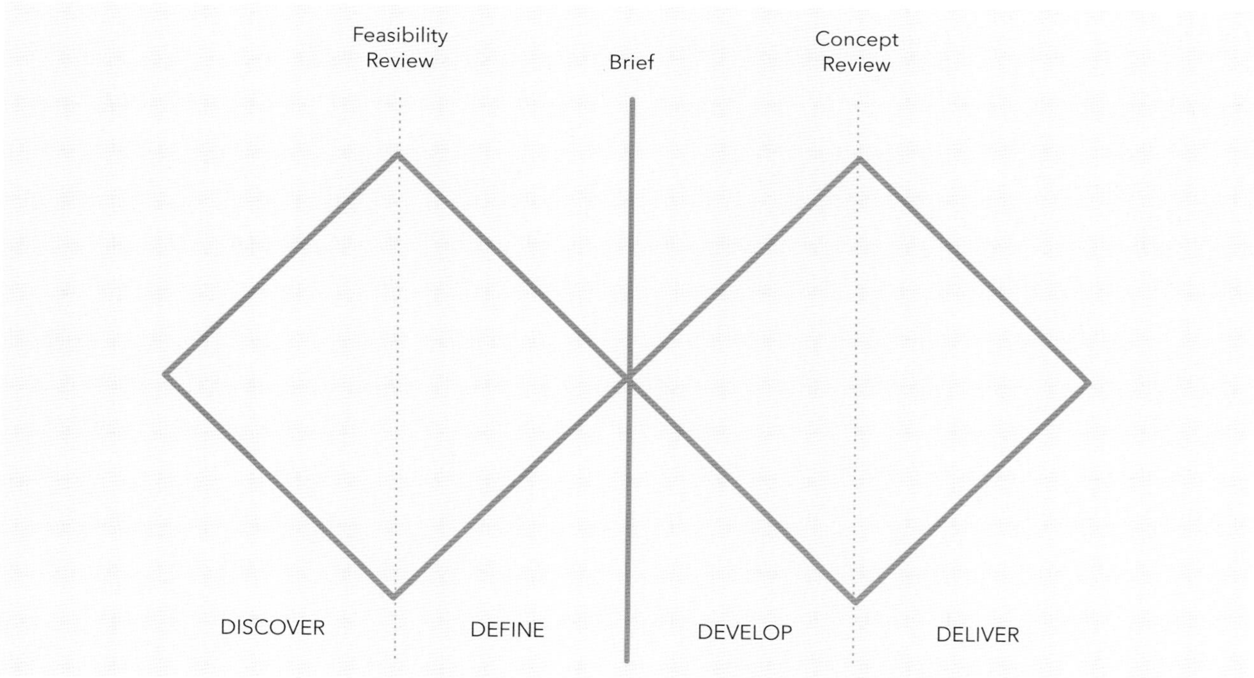
Feasibility Review
Brief
Concept Review
DISCOVER
DEFINE
DEVELOP
DELIVER

A revamped version of the double diamond has been recently described, offering more detail on the activities belonging in each diamond. In this model, the first Discover phase starts with the client brief, which is meant to be "ripped" and expanded through primary and secondary research, followed by analysis and synthesis of the research findings into themes, opportunity areas, and finally the definition of the final brief at the end of the first diamond. The second diamond starts off with ideation activities, and the second half is dedicated to cycles of prototyping and testing of ideas until a final solution is defined.

Such models help designers structure their process and work as shareable tools for negotiations with clients and other project stakeholders. They can definitively be used to help structure contracts and organize project milestones. The unique conditions of each project will dictate how the process will unfold in real life, however.

Fig 7.18 Dan Nessler's revamped double diamond. Note the final brief between the two diamonds is suggested as HMW ("how might we") questions. HMW questions are prompt questions that might help formulate the main question that defines the brief.

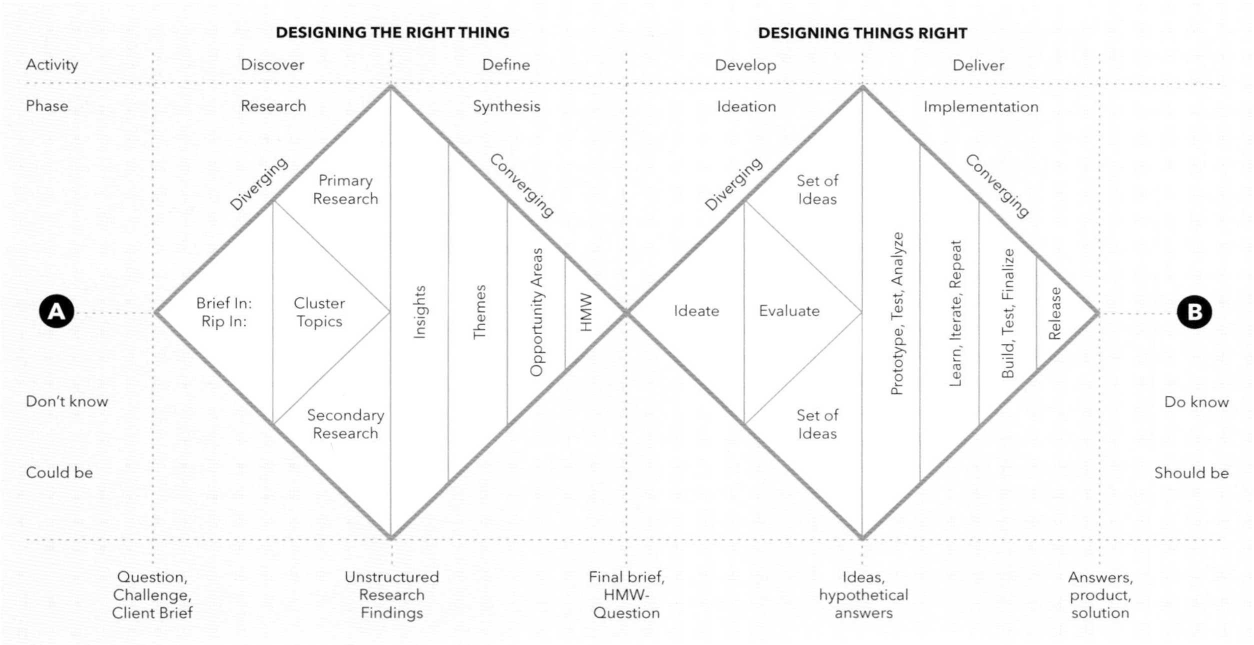
DESIGNING THE RIGHT THING
DESIGNING THINGS RIGHT
Activity
Discover
Define
Develop
Deliver
Phase
Research
Synthesis
Ideation
Implementation
Diverging
Primary Research
Converging
Diverging
Set of Ideas
Converging
A
Brief In: Rip In:
Cluster Topics
Insights
Themes
Opportunity Areas
HMW
Ideate
Evaluate
Prototype, Test, Analyze
Learn, Iterate, Repeat
Build, Test, Finalize
Release
B
Don't know
Secondary Research
Set of Ideas
Do know
Could be
Should be
Question, Challenge, Client Brief
Unstructured Research Findings
Final brief, HMW-Question
Ideas, hypothetical answers
Answers, product, solution

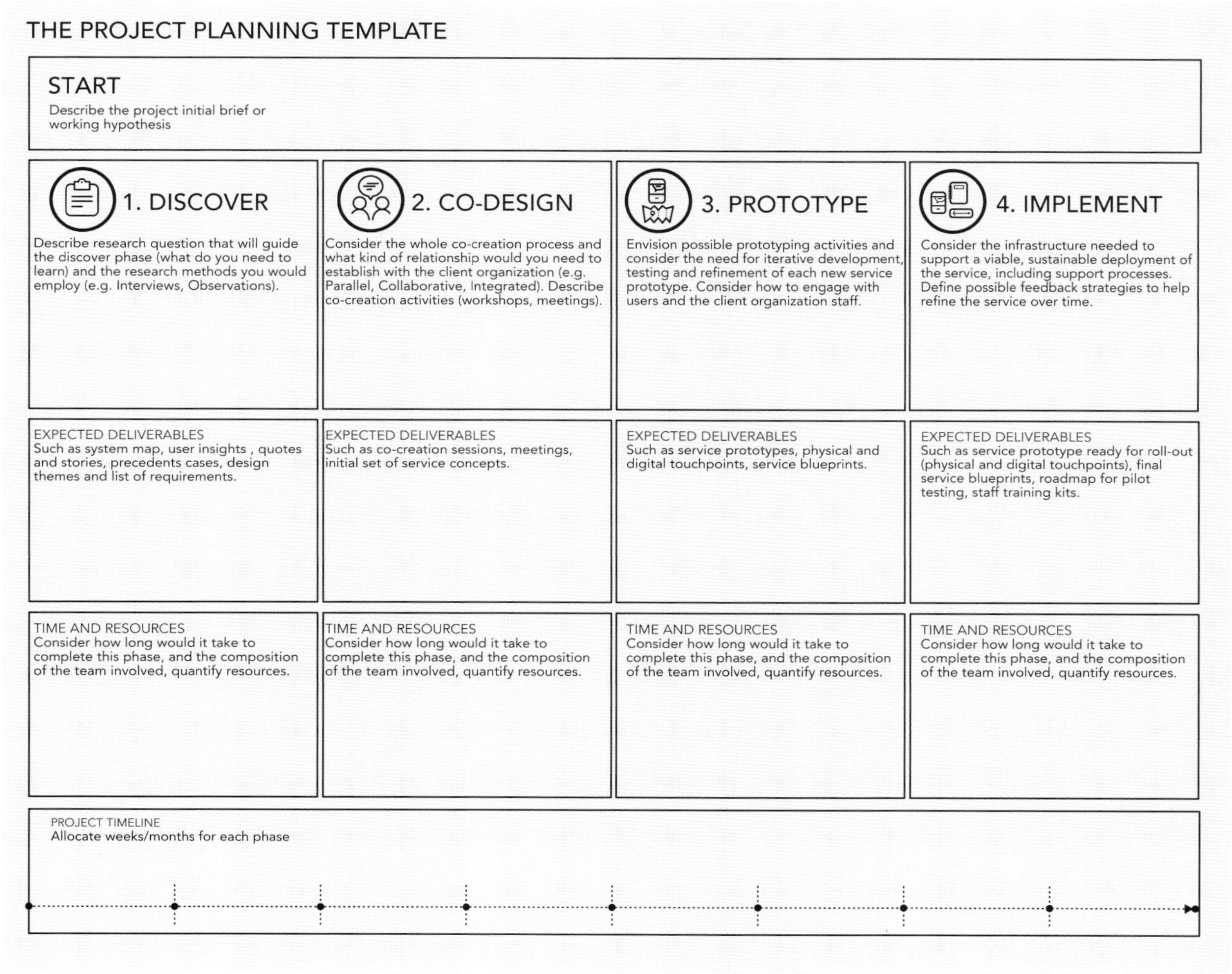
THE PROJECT PLANNING TEMPLATE
START
Describe the project initial brief or working hypothesis
1. DISCOVER
Describe research question that will guide the discover phase (what do you need to learn) and the research methods you would employ (e.g. Interviews, Observations).
2. CO-DESIGN
Consider the whole co-creation process and what kind of relationship would you need to establish with the client organization (e.g. Parallel, Collaborative, Integrated). Describe co-creation activities (workshops, meetings).
3. PROTOTYPE
Envision possible prototyping activities and consider the need for iterative development, testing and refinement of each new service prototype. Consider how to engage with users and the client organization staff.
4. IMPLEMENT
Consider the infrastructure needed to support a viable, sustainable deployment of the service, including support processes. Define possible feedback strategies to help refine the service over time.
EXPECTED DELIVERABLES
Such as system map, user insights , quotes and stories, precedents cases, design themes and list of requirements.
EXPECTED DELIVERABLES
Such as co-creation sessions, meetings, initial set of service concepts.
EXPECTED DELIVERABLES
Such as service prototypes, physical and digital touchpoints, service blueprints.
EXPECTED DELIVERABLES
Such as service prototype ready for roll-out (physical and digital touchpoints), final service blueprints, roadmap for pilot testing, staff training kits.
TIME AND RESOURCES
Consider how long would it take to complete this phase, and the composition of the team involved, quantify resources.
TIME AND RESOURCES
Consider how long would it take to complete this phase, and the composition of the team involved, quantify resources.
TIME AND RESOURCES
Consider how long would it take to complete this phase, and the composition of the team involved, quantify resources.
TIME AND RESOURCES
Consider how long would it take to complete this phase, and the composition of the team involved, quantify resources.
PROJECT TIMELINE
Allocate weeks/months for each phase

Fig 7.24 Project planning template

08 Research and analysis

Equestrian Experience: Get to know a horse
Host Planning
Civics 101: the ins & outs of Canadian Politics
European Languages & Culture Badge
Taster Orientation Experience

8.10

100s of Mind–Growing Experiences
Want to go deeper or wider?
Grid
List
Map
Aboriginal Mother Centre
Learn about floor hockey
Weave Your Own Fabric
Speaking up in Victoria
Gardening with Madame Beespeaker
Make Jewelry

8.9

DESCRIBE 3 THINGS THAT YOU TOUCHED AT YOUR EXPERIENCE.
DESCRIBE 3 THINGS THAT YOU TOUCHED AT YOUR SELECTED ACTIVITY

8.11

Figs 8.7 to 8.11 Touchpoints of the pilot Kudoz project (zine, website, game).

8.3 Interview with Sarah Schulman, InWithForward

The research conducted for the Burnaby Starter Project involved long stretches of highly immersive fieldwork over an extended period of time. What did this immersive research look like in practice?

For us, it is important to build meaningful relationships with people in order for them to open up and share what is really going on with them—the keys to good insights. What we're trying to design for is people's lives, not just a single interaction point. To do this, we really need to understand the whole of people's lives, the rhythm of their days. In this project, we moved to Burnaby and lived inside a social housing complex to conduct ethnographic research within the space we were trying to understand and build relationships.

Ethnography is about spending lots of time in people's context, across their context, to understand the world from their perspective. It is also useful in identifying disconnects between what people say, what people do, what people think, and what they feel.

Our ethnographic work is really a blend of unstructured observations, hanging out with people, shadowing them over the course of an entire day, and often several days at a time, as well as more prompted conversations where we are bringing in projective talking tools in order to gather their reaction to a thing.

What were some other methods beyond ethnography that you used in the research phase of the Burnaby Starter Project?

In Burnaby, we used a set of stories that were loosely based on people we've met in other projects which we used to elicit insights from the people we are currently working with. We also used cards of different types of services that we might create or support. In this project, we had a set of forty "made-up" services, supports, and networks. After doing this work for ten years, we actually have a large bank of real stories. They're not fictional personas. They are based on our experience and research. The fact that the personas are based on real people that we're credibly able to speak about as ethnographers and design researchers works to create rich dialogue between us and those we work with.

Another specific tool we use is "segmentation." We make stickers with all of the people we've done ethnographic fieldwork with. We'll then take over a room and take our ten favorite theories that we've read in articles and our stickers from the people we've met and have a fun debate about where we might place people, why we would place them in those categories, and the logic behind those placements. The idea is that we don't know what patterns or interests will emerge.

Can you describe how you analyze and synthesize insights gained through the research process?

Our first step is taking all of our observations, photos, video, and other material from the field and begin to write stories with it. We then create photo stories, synthesized videos, or podcasts from that as well. Before moving to analysis, we like to return them to people first. It's a more ethical approach and often adds another layer of data, or triangulation on top of things.

We then get to a process of generating a series of themes and "What if" statements. Our goal here is to look for opportunities for things to be different in people's lives. "What if this thing changed in their environment?" or "what if they had access to something like this?" or "what if in the past there had been a different intervention, or a different interaction point?" What we are doing is simultaneously looking past, present, and future in our "what if" statements.

Then we use a lot of social science theory. This is where we move from being researchers and designers to also trying to incorporate a lot of social science research, particularly around behavior change, and what we know actually contributes to people changing what they think, or say, or feel, or do.

Can you say more about how you incorporate social science theory into your work?

In our work, we draw from various social scientific theories culled from books and journals and run them through the actual stories that are being uncovered in our field work. We ask ourselves, for example, "if stigma was the framework for understanding this story, what would it tell us, and what kinds of solutions would we develop with that framework in mind?"

We do this with at least five or six different theories so that we're generating a range of ideas based on all these different theoretical models. We then try and share that back visually in some way. I think reading things like long documents and academic articles and learning how to extract information from them is very generative and a source of creativity. You can see it as a kind of brainstorming tool.

So writing and reading are very important to your research process?

Often one of the first things we do is engage in a process of writing. More specifically, writing long-form narratives of the folks that we meet. We make great efforts to try and embody their voice using their direct quotes and the way in which they talk, or correct themselves, so that they really do come through in the writing. It's so important to be able to visualize information, and to use photos and other media to share what's happening for somebody, but it's equally important to learn how to write a great paragraph, one which can capture somebody's voice in an authentic way. And that's also what builds really good analytic skills is when you're forced to put together a point of view, a cohesive statement, about what's happening and not get lost just in a lovely photo or picture.

InWithForward emphasizes a multidisciplinary approach in its service design projects using methods and theories from a variety of different places. Can you talk about the role of multidisciplinarity in service design research?

In the case of the Burnaby Starter Project, we had an initial team of six people. This consisted of myself, a trained sociologist, two service designers, a graphic designer, and two secondees from the existing service system. One had the background in community development and the other a background in human resourcing and management. So, we were a blend of all of those different things.

For us, it's really important to have at least half of our team come from the existing service system and working with us full time. Designers are often great at having ways to move through a process, but often lack the kind of historical or philosophical context of things that have been tried before. We need that depth of knowledge and expertise. This is why we read articles from different disciplines and want to work alongside folks that have been in a particular field for ten, twenty, thirty years. They have those historical reference points. They know what's been tried and what hasn't worked. At the same time, we're trying to take a fresh approach on it. It's a really interesting dance. We are critical of the existing service system, and we're asking our secondees to have a very critical lens on the work they've done in the past as well. We emphasize that we need newer, alternative ways of doing things, while at the same time, understanding the depth of the know-how that is there.

In the Burnaby Project, you're dealing with very sensitive issues, like social isolation, poverty, disability, etc., which brings your research into contact with vulnerable communities. What are the ethical considerations that service designers and researchers must make in doing this kind of work?

Ethical consideration is always really tricky because we're trying to get authentic glimpses and data about people, and sometimes, when you reveal too much about your intent or what you're doing, people change their behavior. In our work, we move in a light touch way where we begin to build relationships and have conversations that start with verbal consent. We identify who we're working with, explain what our organization is about, and then ask for permission verbally to have a conversation. As we get deeper, we present a kind of consent form that explains how we plan to use this data and that we would really like to share the stories back with them. On our consent forms, we have a have a whole slew of options where people can pick to say, "I don't want my name used," or "I want you to change all geographic details," etc. We try and give people a lot of choice about how we represent them in the story. In the Burnaby Project, we had a lot of different versions of consent forms in very clear language with pictorial representations of what we're doing. We also try to have service providers in their life also explain it if there were confusions, which there often was.

8.4 Case study analysis

Let's look into the main learnings one can extract from the Burnaby Starter Project.

Defining the central inquiry

You'll notice that the Burnaby Starter Project starts by defining a broad/wicked problem. In this case, the InWithForward team devised a central question to guide their approach: "How can we support people to not just live in a community, but to flourish as part of a community?" This is quite a broad inquiry, and part of the designer's job is being able to make or create sense out of ambiguous and often contradictory situations. As the engagement with the community of people and organizations relevant to the inquiry evolves, we can see the key themes and concerns that focus our thinking around the problem at hand: community, support, and inclusion. These themes are a good way to ensure that your investigation has a sense of direction based on a specific interest. By integrating the initial question with a focus on a specific community (in the case of the Burnaby Project, individuals with specific disabilities), the team had a clear sense of which people they needed to find to conduct their research.

Landscape analysis

In a given project, you may find that the topic you are exploring has been explored by other practitioners and scholars in the past. This pre-existing base of knowledge can inform your work. A landscape analysis of secondary data such as reports, white papers, academic publications, statistical reports, results from surveys and market research, as well as "big data" analytics showing behavior trends can help give you the historical and contextual knowledge you might need during the design process. The Burnaby Starter Project is a good example of how a landscape analysis can identify useful material that can inform the research and design process.

In addition to problem framing in the initial stages of research, the results of landscape analysis were also used in the Burnaby Starter Project to help refine the insights the team gained during fieldwork. The team used outside theories to "test" against the things they had learned from working with individuals and service providers. In service design, it can be productive to draw from outside scholarship and other fields of expertise in order to support, challenge, or enhance the insights we gather and ideas we produce.

Observation through engagement

You'll notice that a sizable portion of the research conducted during the Burnaby Starter Project was spent in the field within social housing developments and among service provider organizations. The team didn't just study potential users or conduct site visits. The team lived within the community they were seeking to learn about, thus bringing the larger issues they sought to understand to life. They employed a range of observational methods such as contextual interviews and both fly-on-the-wall and participant styles of ethnographic research. By immersing themselves in this way, the team gained greater access to individuals with whom trust-based relationships could be formed. In spending time and building relationships, the team was able to have a degree of access that proved invaluable in the understanding of the current service system and how it might be improved. The outcome of this process is a more empathetic, people-centered view of the issues InWithForward sought to address.

In addition to time spent among housing residents, the team spent time talking with and shadowing service providers. By both talking with service providers and examining their organizations in everyday practice, the team was able to identify gaps in what providers hoped to achieve and what they were actually doing. The space between what people and organizations say and what they do in practice can be very insightful and generative of potential ideas and concepts.

For data analysis, the team employed techniques such as clustering of ideas and definition of themes and patterns, and from there, they extracted a definition of principles that guided the further development of the project. These principles were instrumental in bridging research and ideation.

8.5 Methods and tools

Following is an annotated index of the key methods and tools used in service design research.

Research planning and strategy

Each project requires a specific research strategy, with design ethnography being a major component of service design research. In broader terms, the design ethnography research process, according to AIGA (*An Ethnography Primer*), is based on the six following steps.

Step 1 is defining a research strategy, which consists of clearly defining the main problem at stake; in practice, this translates into defining a main research question. Often the initial research question may be somewhat fictitious and evolve as the research progresses. For that reason, the research question should be revised periodically throughout the whole project.

1	2	3	4	5	6
Define the problem	**Find the people**	**Plan an approach**	**Collect data**	**Synthesize data and interpret gaps and opportunities**	**Share insights and recommendations**
Identify specific issues and questions	Look for those who can provide critical understanding about these questions	Define methods and materials for observing and interacting with respondents	Through field work involving observations, interviews, informal interactions and probes	Collate data, finding patterns, themes and interpret them as design principles, personas embodying typical users, and list opportunities for intervention	Create visual narratives that can inform clients, partner organizations, user groups and other stakeholders

Fig 8.12 The design ethnography research process, according to AIGA's six steps.

Fig 8.13 Examples of materials in a research toolkit.

Step 2 is finding the key people who can help you understand the questions. They can be users, providers, managers, or experts. Step 3 is about planning the research approach—in the case of the Burnaby Project, full immersion. Step 4 is about collecting data; in the case of the Burnaby Project, the full immersion approach used tools such as observation, contextual interview techniques, and shadowing. Steps 5 and 6 represent a transition between an analytical mindset into a creative mindset. Step 5 is about making sense of the data collected. It might involve a few long sessions with the whole team and some critical analysis of how findings may translate into design principles and identification of opportunities for design intervention. Step 6 is about communicating insights and opportunities to a larger audience through visual narratives, to inform project stakeholders and allow decision making on what to do next.

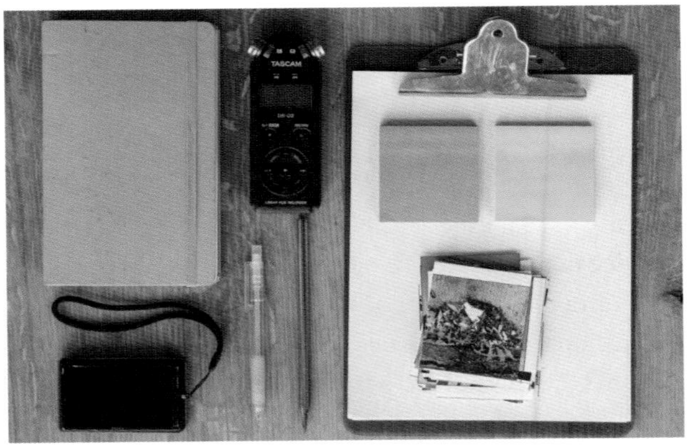
TASCAM

A key aspect of defining a research strategy is allocating time and resources for each task (who will carry out the work, how many hours need to budgeted, is travel involved), and reaching out and coordinating with people who can be key to understanding a given context and situation (reaching out to key people, building trust, and agreeing on activities). The preparation of a research plan and its materials should involve careful consideration.

Conducting landscape analysis

Landscape analysis involves secondary data, expert inputs, theoretical frameworks, and precedents. Secondary data include reports, white papers, academic papers, statistical reports, results from surveys and market research, and results from "big data" analytics showing behavior trends. Theoretical frameworks such as behavioral insights or historical analysis can help provide a rational structure for the research phase and beyond. Experts in the field who are not directly involved as project stakeholders may have critical information that could help designers gain important insights and perspectives. Also useful would be analyses of similar offerings, analyses of other organizations operating in the same fields or analogous case studies, and initiatives that may inform the current conditions.

No project starts from zero. And often, a project proposal is built on the success or failure of previous initiatives. After entering a new problem space, service design teams first try to cover the horizons and understand the main indicators, history, conditions, and previous experiences relevant to the context. Understanding the landscape of a project is not a finite task within the process, however. This discovery process continues as a parallel action throughout the project development by revisiting the research question and the project goals.

Secondary data may come from a myriad of sources. Research centers, census data, and governmental and other official documentation are the most reliable sources for data. Reading reports, theoretical texts, and other written sources and collating critical learnings and frameworks from them are important but not necessarily popular tasks for designers. Precedent analysis is often done through case studies containing descriptive information and visuals.

Observation

Observation techniques involve attentive looking and systematic recording of phenomena in a given context and include people, artifacts, environments, events, behaviors, and interactions.

Observation techniques are used to reveal behavioral patterns or physical flows so that broader relationships (between people and people, people and artifacts, people and the environment) and motivations behind certain interactions are disclosed. It is commonly recognized that what people say they do might not correspond exactly to what they actually do because we tend to idealize our own actions. Observations are essential to reveal broader cultural and social contexts.

In the fly-on-the-wall technique, the researcher watches activities as an unobtrusive and unnoticed observer, to avoid people changing their behavior if they were aware of being observed.

As in any observation activity, an ethic approach is key. Respect is paramount, avoid judging, be empathic. The empathetic mindset involves being respectful for the other person's behavior and neutralizing your own reactions, refraining from quick interpretations.

THE NEW STORE

The AEIOU framework helps structure observations according to components:

- Activities: What people do, pathways to accomplish something
- Environments: Dimensions, proportions, materials, light, atmosphere, *servicescape*
- Interactions: People with people, people with objects, people with environments
- Objects: Artifacts/*touchpoints*, physical and digital, static and mobile
- Users: People's behaviors, emotions, motivations, values, relationships, needs

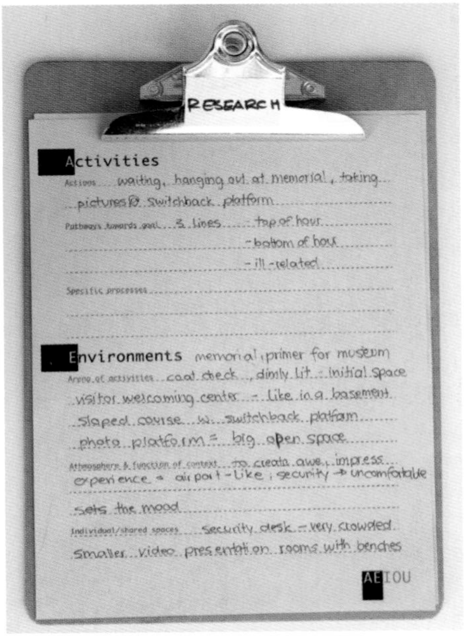
RESEARCH
Activities
Environments
AEIOU

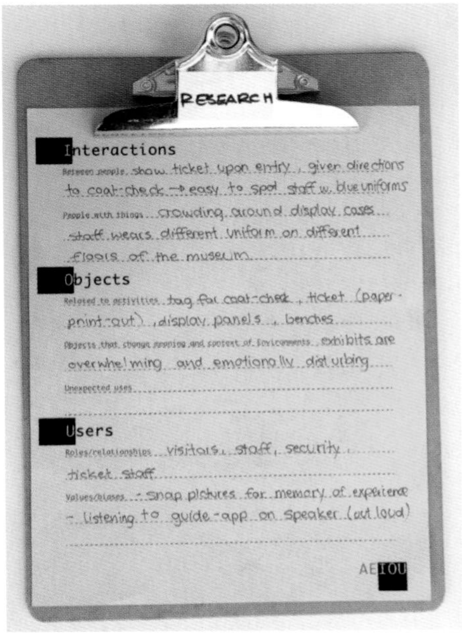
RESEARCH
Interactions
Objects
Users
AEIOU

Figs 8.14 to 8.16 AEIOU sheets, to support an observation activity.

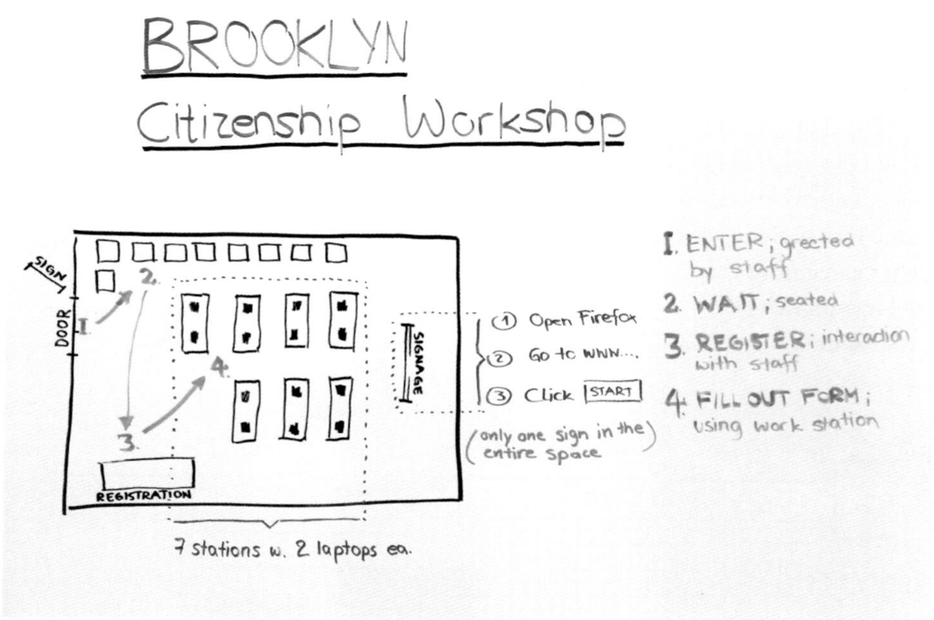
BROOKLYN
Citizenship Workshop
SIGN
DOOR
REGISTRATION
SIGNAGE
① Open Firefox
② Go to WWW....
③ Click START
(only one sign in the entire space)
7 stations w. 2 laptops ea.
I. ENTER; greeted by staff
2. WAIT; seated
3. REGISTER; interaction with staff
4. FILL OUT FORM; using work station

Fig 8.17 Behavioral mapping sketch of a citizenship service in a Brooklyn public library.

Behavioral mapping is a place-centered observation approach. The researcher watches and makes sketches, noting how people move in space; and looks for patterns in relation to spaces, noting how people come and go and what they do.

Interviews

Talking to people and conducting a close observation of people as they go through experiences are effective ways for learning how people do what they do and why they do it. Research activities also help the researcher gain perspective on the daily lives of users and staff and their social cultural contexts.

Designers tend to use qualitative rather than quantitative research methods. Methods such as questionnaires and surveys that are generally used to obtain quantitative data can be extremely difficult to structure and conduct properly, with the risk of producing invalid and biased results. Because of that, designers are discouraged from using quantitative data and from investing their time in surveys. If there is an unquestionable need for quantitative data, it is better to use prevalidated surveys and adapt the research to the one that best fits the interests of the project.

The best approach for designers is to rely on a qualitative research approach through personal interviews. Contextual interviews are generally open-ended, often guided by a few points that the researcher prepares in advance to help steer the conversation. The main idea of contextual interviews is to spend time with the person in her or his own "territory" (e.g., home, workplace, neighborhood) to reveal the participant's behaviors, motivations, and values. In this way, the researcher can capture the participant's full story on a deeper human level. Empathy and active listening are essential approaches to interviewing. Empathy involves first listening to a person and trying to understand her or his emotional and cognitive patterns—in other words, how the person feels and why. And from there, the researcher can try walking in the other person's shoes and in this way anticipate how she or he would think and react in a future situation.

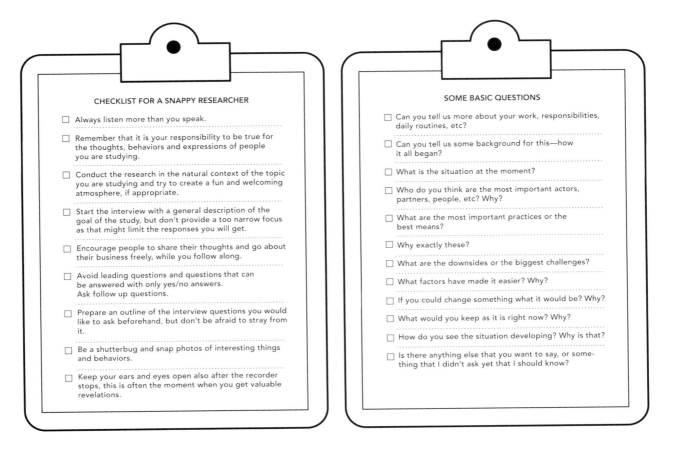

CHECKLIST FOR A SNAPPY RESEARCHER

- ☐ Always listen more than you speak.
- ☐ Remember that it is your responsibility to be true for the thoughts, behaviors and expressions of people you are studying.
- ☐ Conduct the research in the natural context of the topic you are studying and try to create a fun and welcoming atmosphere, if appropriate.
- ☐ Start the interview with a general description of the goal of the study, but don't provide a too narrow focus as that might limit the responses you will get.
- ☐ Encourage people to share their thoughts and go about their business freely, while you follow along.
- ☐ Avoid leading questions and questions that can be answered with only yes/no answers. Ask follow up questions.
- ☐ Prepare an outline of the interview questions you would like to ask beforehand, but don't be afraid to stray from it.
- ☐ Be a shutterbug and snap photos of interesting things and behaviors.
- ☐ Keep your ears and eyes open also after the recorder stops, this is often the moment when you get valuable revelations.

SOME BASIC QUESTIONS

- ☐ Can you tell us more about your work, responsibilities, daily routines, etc?
- ☐ Can you tell us some background for this—how it all began?
- ☐ What is the situation at the moment?
- ☐ Who do you think are the most important actors, partners, people, etc? Why?
- ☐ What are the most important practices or the best means?
- ☐ Why exactly these?
- ☐ What are the downsides or the biggest challenges?
- ☐ What factors have made it easier? Why?
- ☐ If you could change something what it would be? Why?
- ☐ What would you keep as it is right now? Why?
- ☐ How do you see the situation developing? Why is that?
- ☐ Is there anything else that you want to say, or something that I didn't ask yet that I should know?

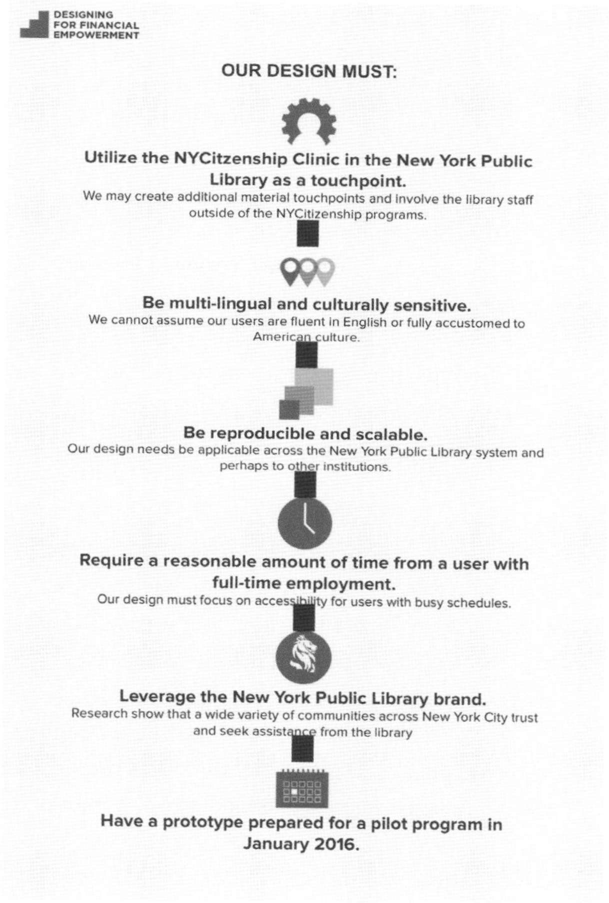
DESIGNING
FOR FINANCIAL
EMPOWERMENT
OUR DESIGN MUST:
Utilize the NYCitzenship Clinic in the New York Public Library as a touchpoint.
We may create additional material touchpoints and involve the library staff outside of the NYCitizenship programs.
Be multi-lingual and culturally sensitive.
We cannot assume our users are fluent in English or fully accustomed to American culture.
Be reproducible and scalable.
Our design needs be applicable across the New York Public Library system and perhaps to other institutions.
Require a reasonable amount of time from a user with full-time employment.
Our design must focus on accessibility for users with busy schedules.
Leverage the New York Public Library brand.
Research show that a wide variety of communities across New York City trust and seek assistance from the library
Have a prototype prepared for a pilot program in January 2016.

Fig 8.26 Sample list of requirements. Initial research involved interviews, observations, and mapping of typical journeys, conducted by different themes.

8.6 Learning features

Activities

In-context design ethnography

- Working in pairs, plan a visit to a local museum, where you will observe or shadow each other. Start your research by defining your research approach and research toolkit (e.g., notebook and color pens, use a smartphone for pictures and video). Start your research from a distance: observe how your teammate acts and note his or her reactions along the experience. Note specific interactions with staff, fellow visitors, and the whole service infrastructure of the museum.
- In the next step, become more interactive: Ask careful questions about why your teammate did one thing and not another. What moments were especially enjoyable or challenging? Refrain from any judgment: just listen. During and after your time together, take notes, attach photos, and transcribe memorable quotes regarding the service interactions. Make sure to ask permission before taking pictures or recording video that includes other people.
- Finally, synthesize the data you collected through your observations and interview. Create your user's journey map using the template.
- Sort your findings to develop a series of insights: What are the pain points, or what is entirely missing in the service that you observed? What positive moments could be further amplified by service improvement? Use these insights to define design principles and/or a list of requirements to inform future design development.

Recommended reading

Remis, N., and the Adaptive Path Team at Capital One (2016). *A Guide to Service Blueprinting.* Adaptive Path.

Crouch, C., and Pearce, J. (2012). *Doing Research in Design*. Bloomsbury Academic.

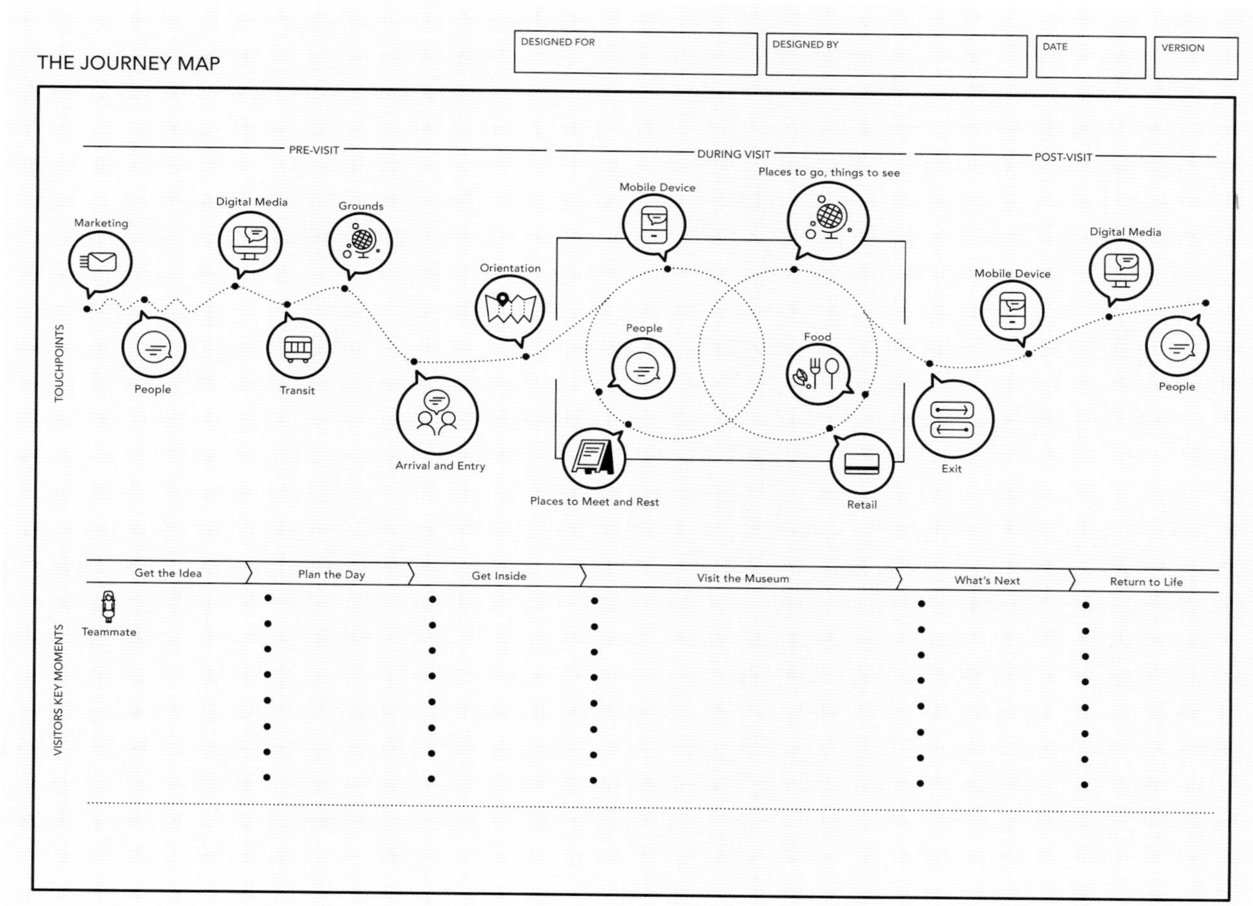
THE JOURNEY MAP
DESIGNED FOR
DESIGNED BY
DATE
VERSION
PRE-VISIT
DURING VISIT
POST-VISIT
TOUCHPOINTS
Marketing
People
Digital Media
Transit
Grounds
Arrival and Entry
Orientation
Mobile Device
Places to go, things to see
People
Food
Places to Meet and Rest
Retail
Exit
Mobile Device
Digital Media
People
VISITORS KEY MOMENTS
Get the Idea
Plan the Day
Get Inside
Visit the Museum
What's Next
Return to Life
Teammate

Fig 8.27 Journey map template.

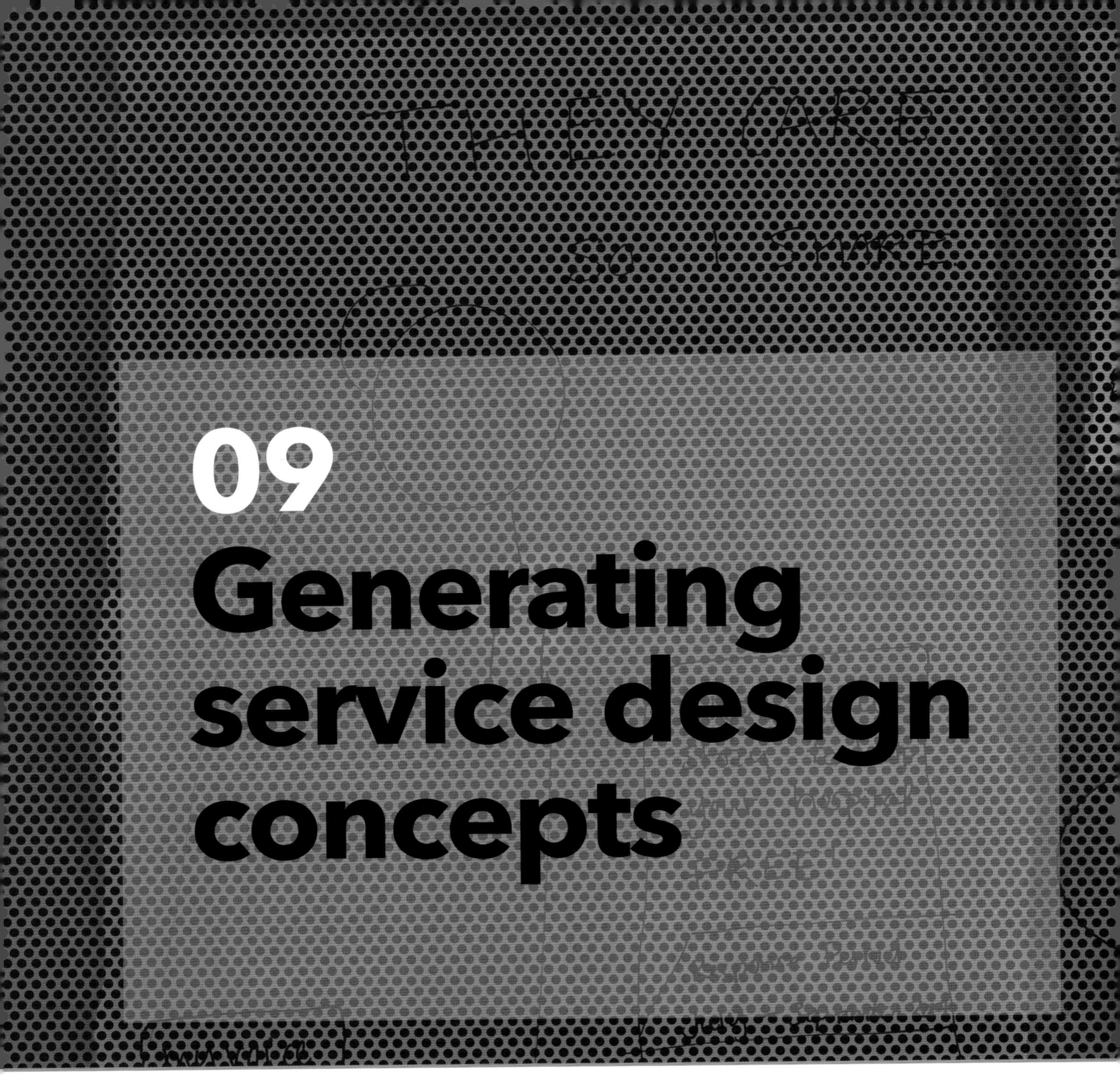
THEY CARE
SO I SHARE

09 Generating service design concepts

9.6

9.7

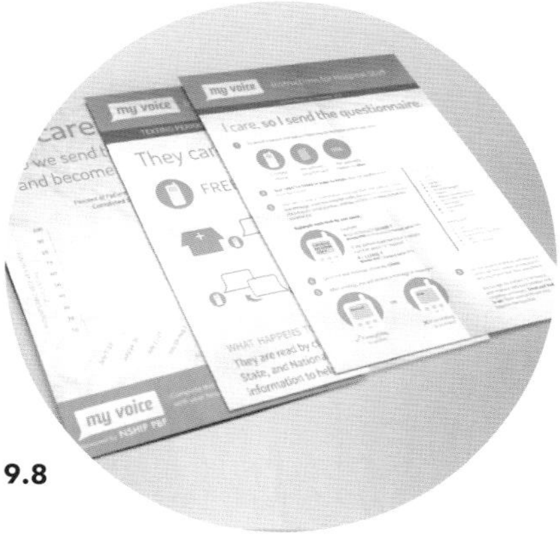
my voice
I care, so I send the questionnaire.
my voice

9.8

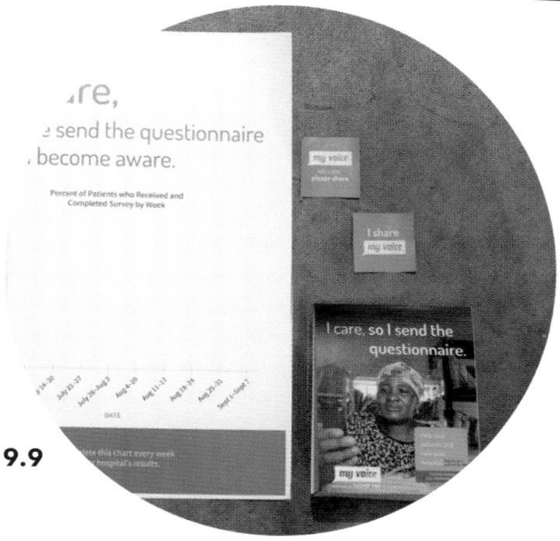
send the questionnaire
become aware.
Percent of Patients who Received and Completed Survey by Week
I share
my voice
I care, so I send the questionnaire.
my voice

9.9

so I share
Was the hospital equipment clean?
Reply 1 for yes or 2 for no to 55999.
1
Share your voice to help your hospital
FREE!

9.10

9.11

9.12

Figs 9.8 to 9.10 Final communication touchpoints.

Figs 9.11 and 9.12 User test and staff training session.

9.3 Interview with the Reboot team: Nonso Jideofor, Panthea Lee, & Adam Talsma

Nonso Jideofor was program coordinator for this project, managing stakeholder engagement. Panthea Lee, Reboot's cofounder and principal, served as technical advisor and lead designer. Adam Talsma, country manager of Reboot's Nigeria office, was the project manager.

How was the transition from the research phase to idea generation?

The research was fundamental to the ideas. There isn't a lot of available information about what citizens in rural Nigeria think, or about their access to technology and health care. The World Bank was eager to leverage mobile phones as a key communications channel for this project, given its broad penetration in this context, but there were major open questions including the viability of technology and choice of language. In the case of language, for instance, we found that while a majority of citizens in the region spoke Hausa, most could not read or write it as they were taught in English-language schools. So, we needed a firm research foundation to generate viable ideas.

Our research, idea generation, and design are contiguous, immersive processes. We based our research and design team in Wamba, where we were working. This was vital: It allowed us to conduct deep ethnography as well as build truly deep relationships. Since our team lived there (and didn't just come in for a short research sprint), we were able to not just hear about people's beliefs and actions, we could actually observe them in practice and over time. It also demonstrated our team's level of commitment to local citizens, health officials, and government executives that we weren't just there for a few days or weeks of consultation; it showed that we were really there to work shoulder-to-shoulder, through the entire design process.

We quickly learned that people had some very legitimate complaints about the health-care system. This made us think: Is there some way to design how we collect feedback from citizens—for example, through question design—that would also help frontline service workers and policymakers? Thus, the research led us to two tracks of idea generation. One focused on citizens (the community users) and how they were going to input feedback. The other focused on government actors (the institutional users) and how they could be motivated to support a feedback system and use it to improve services.

9.3 Interview with the Reboot team: Nonso Jideofor, Panthea Lee, and Adam Talsma

Were there any specific frameworks that you adopted in the project that drove the idea generation?

We had two! One was a World Bank social accountability framework describing how systematic and direct feedback from citizens to policymakers and implementers could help them improve programs' designs—and reallocate resources to make them happen.

The other was an internal "institutional integration" framework we developed to think about how to generate political interest in citizen feedback when governments have no political or legal responsibility for it. For this framework, we mapped all the layers of government in the service delivery chain—from the nurses in the clinics all the way up to the national health program administrators in Abuja. For actors at each layer, we needed to understand their (i) motivations (personal and professional); (ii) their constraints (personal and professional); and (iii) the processes (formal and informal) they used day-to-day.

We conducted research with individuals at each of the layers of the service delivery chain to understand these factors, then synthesized user personas for guiding the design of the system.

We also sought to identify specific individuals that, for one reason or another, could help champion this new process within the layers of government institutions.

Whenever you're introducing something new into government, at the outset, you have to work with those individuals that can help champion the process. It also helps to decrease the barriers to adoption as much as you can. The best way to do that is to build off of and integrate into existing processes—so that you're only asking people to make incremental changes on what they currently do. This framework helped us generate ideas and concepts that were tailored to leverage points in the existing system.

What were some of the useful tools or methods your team employed during the idea generation phase of My Voice?

One of our key tools during idea generation was process mapping, which helps identify and understand institutional leverage points (building on our institutional integration framework). Once we understood the motivations, constraints, and existing processes, we needed to identify specific institutional entry points.

For example, we identified one state-level program administrator who wanted to demonstrate success to national policymakers and international donors, in order to scale a program across his state. This was a great example of motivation: If this citizen feedback initiative could help the administrator's ambitions, he could be motivated to champion it. To meet his ambitions, we needed to understand how program scaling decisions were made. So we mapped the entire decision process, identifying specific tools and fora used (such as quarterly executive meetings). We were then able to design the outputs of the citizen feedback initiative to appeal to this administrator, and to easily integrate within existing tools and fora.

Another key tool was prototyping, which we used not only for design, but also stakeholder engagement. Once we had some ideas, we developed mock-ups, both of products and of processes, to show our government counterparts. For example, we showed designs of the government reporting dashboard, as well as guides for how to deal with challenging feedback.

We'd say: "Hey, if we get citizens to input on X, Y, or Z aspect of primary health services, these are the types of things that might be coming back to you." Government stakeholders would respond, "Oh. This is actually really useful," and tell us tweaks to make them even more useful. We were actually very close to workable solutions with our early prototypes, because we'd done such careful work on institutional research and stakeholder engagement. But this prototyping served as another stakeholder engagement tool, earning buy-in over the process and ownership over the final products.

How do you take such a diverse set of stakeholders who normally would never be in contact with one another—bureaucrats, politicians, health-care providers, citizens—and bring them together to create new ideas?

First, it's important to consider if and when it even makes sense to bring people together to create new ideas. Cocreation has become such a buzzword now, but there are only certain scenarios where it makes sense, and even then, the interactions have to be carefully designed. Unfortunately, they usually aren't; we've seen too many cocreation exercises end up a disaster.

If and when you do bring together people who don't normally come in contact with each other, it is important for everyone to first understand each other as humans with common values and goals. One way we do this is getting people to tell stories around a common theme, to build empathy. In Wamba, we chose prompts to unite people around aspirations or challenges, such as, "When was a time the health-care system really failed you?" It brought up sad stories, as you can imagine, but sharing these personal experiences helped us identify the hopes and fears that bind us.

Still, there are often big challenges to bringing together diverse stakeholders–there are power dynamics to reckon with, social and political pressures on behavior in the presence of those outside our tribe, and the mechanics of workshop participation. We don't try to put people together if the scenario makes it impossible to address these. No matter how much empathy building you do, you're not going to be able to erase all the baggage people carry into a workshop.

In these cases, we codesign asynchronously. We did a lot of that with My Voice: going to groups individually in research, design, and prototyping. Going to citizens, to the ward development committee, to the traditional leaders, to the frontline workers, to the facility managers, and to the policymakers. We didn't try to force people in the same room when they weren't ready for it just for the sake of cocreation optics.

Can you talk a bit about the challenges of idea generation in very specific cultural contexts that are perhaps very different from your own?

One big part of the challenge is that you have to be willing to break apart your own process, or to not follow process at all. You have to be adaptable, especially when you're working with public policy. And that takes a deep sense of humility.

We designers get it drilled into us that there are specific processes to follow, which will lead to specific outcomes. In a formal research process, you don't always know how to ask for what you don't know.

A workshop, for example, might have to be completely turned upside down. Participating in the types of workshops we might be familiar with is a professional skill in Western, rich countries–you move at a certain pace, ask everyone to use Post-its, and then you have your outcomes. That can be really detrimental, particularly if you're working in areas where there's been a lot of NGO activity. People are often highly skeptical of yet another intervention. You may be the tenth person to come around in the last three years, wanting to improve their community.

We won't get into all the ways that model is hugely problematic; the bottom line is, the poor and the marginalized are already significantly disempowered. Using a certain design approach that they may struggle to participate in, and that doesn't consider how best to empower them and draw out their expertise, can be further disempowering. Taking the time to talk to people at their own pace, in ways that respect and celebrate their knowledge, is important. This may require you to turn your own process on its head.

9.4 Case study analysis

In the My Voice Project, the design team faced the challenge of translating vast contextual insights gathered through research and interactions with multiple stakeholders into a new service concept. Their ideation process involved the challenges that commonly arise from complex contextual constraints. The team deployed codesign processes based on collaborative workshop sessions as well as rounds of consultations with stakeholders and user testing. In particular, they conducted asynchronous codesign sessions and consultations separately with citizens, the ward development committee, traditional leaders, frontline workers, facility managers, and policymakers. They chose this approach to avoid dealing with interactions that could turn out to be challenging given the historic dynamics between the different groups of stakeholders that prevailed before the workshop. The team considered this to be the best approach to create new long-lasting ideas.

As in many service design projects, the creative exploration of new ideas and possibilities is anchored in quite restricted spaces. Nevertheless, new and good ideas do emerge and flourish. For many, the secret lies in the constant balance between creative sprints and collaborations with key people while allowing for inward-looking inspiration (e.g., interventions that have been done in the same context previously) and outward-looking inspiration (e.g., analogous cases from different contexts, different industries).

The ideation phase typically picks up the outcomes from the research and discovery phases and uses them to inform creative synthesis, e.g., a new concept. This is hardly a linear process, but as discussed in Chapter 7, the relationship and contract with clients makes it necessary to structure a project into linear phases and sequential deliverables.

Two of the main challenges of ideation are first how to balance creativity with feasibility and project constraints, and second how to manage the people who should participate in the creative process as codesigners and cocreators. No two projects are the same in how they deal with these challenges, and as usual in design processes, there are no preconceived formulas for how to have good ideas.

9.5 Methods and tools

The following pages offer some typical approaches and techniques for first pivot from the research findings into idea generation, tools, and techniques for generating ideas and developing them into concepts.

Bridging research and ideation

One critical component of the service design process is pivoting from understanding a current situation to moving into imagining a preferred future. This is a crucial moment in the design process, and a design team can plan for one or more sessions to allow for this passage, although it may be revisited at several moments throughout the project development.

Practitioners describe this moment in different ways—for example, pivoting or bridging the gap between (research) analysis and (creative) synthesis. The essence of bridging is capturing all the main learnings so far, defining opportunity areas, while allowing for a creative mindset to set in. The challenge is twofold: on one hand, you need to capture the most important issues and constraints related to the project revealed through research. On the other hand, you need to channel creativity into those specific issues rather than embarking on a free flow of ideas.

Some designers suggest synthesizing main patterns and themes that emerged from research into one main story, using personas and describing their journey and emotional states. The story can then be used as the brainstorm leading question.

Another approach is using "*how might we*" (or *HMW*) questions that help formulate the final project brief. "How might we" questions can be formulated by focusing on improving an identified problem ("how might we reduce queue lines?") and linking it to a specific persona's point of view (a mother with small children), avoiding however questions that lead to answers that are either too narrow or too broad.

How to structure such a critical moment? Consider planning a session with team members, project stakeholders, and experts in the field. It might be helpful to surround yourself with the project materials by, for example, printing quotes, images, and other materials and pinning them up on walls.

In addition to "how might we" questions and the use of stories, you may consider conducting a guided conversation that allows for a mix of evidence and intuition and capture statements that might help formulate the final, or revised, brief (see Chapter 7 for brief points) as well as early ideas to be further developed.

Generating ideas and concepts: Brainstorming and codesign workshops

Brainstorming sessions aim at encouraging free creative flow rather than immediate feasibility. According to IDEO's *Field Guide to Human-Centered Design*, a typical brainstorming session should follow seven basic rules:

- Rule 1: *Defer judgment.* Avoid cutting people's ideas off before allowing them to evolve, and all participants should feel they can contribute (and not be intimidated by others).

- Rule 2: *Encourage wild ideas.* They might lead to desirable future scenarios without current constraints on technology, materials, etc.

- Rule 3: *Build on the idea of others.* Use the technique "yes, and ..." instead of "but."

- Rule 4: *Stay focused on the topic.* Keep the discussion on the initial brainstorming question to retain the purpose of what is trying to be accomplished.

- Rule 5: *One conversation at a time.* Full attention from all participants is critical in a shared session because it leads to more possibilities of making a creative leap.

- Rule 6: *Be visual.* Quick sketches can be more effective at conveying ideas.

- Rule 7: *Go for quantity.* Jotting ideas down quickly is a creative technique for capturing creative insights before a judgment can be made. In some cases, an hour-long session can generate up to 100 ideas.

Figs 9.13 and 9.14 Brainstorming sessions.

Brainstorming sessions can be informed by all kinds of stimuli. In particular, the sessions should start by reviewing the research findings, including design principles, themes, personas, or any predefined scenarios.

A brainstorming session normally starts by identifying a question. Facilitators need to define rules (time for each task, individual versus collective participation). The session might begin with a set time and number of ideas for individuals to generate, which is determined by the facilitator—for example, ten ideas in ten minutes. Participants write down and/or draw each idea on a Post-it note.

After the initial individual exercise, it makes sense to review the ideas collectively, cluster similar ideas, and then select and vote for the most promising ones. Teams can then develop the selected ideas further, giving them a title and subtitle, drawing the main touchpoints, and describing the main interactions, using a storyboard, for example. A brainstorming session might conclude with one or more ideas being developed into rough concepts, with initial visualizations or rapid prototypes of the main touchpoints and a list of their features, as well as visualizations and notes about the main interactions and their implications.

Following a brainstorming session, teams will carry out further development sessions, prototyping and testing/vetting with clients, stakeholders, and user groups.

Brainstorming and other types of codesign sessions are opportunities for the main stakeholders to collectively generate new ideas based on the different sets of expertise and perspectives of participants, as well as to build trust among them. It is a key moment for leveraging knowledge because, for many complex projects, different people who don't normally connect with each other may hold pieces of information.

Codesign and participatory design practices have a long tradition dating back to the 1960s. In service design, codesign workshops are a foundational part of the design process because they bring together the different groups of people who might be involved in a given service. Since service design projects tend to be complex, workshop participants are recruited from different parts of an organization as well as from outside the service-providing organization.

Here are a few guidelines for typical codesign session. Before the session:

- Invite participants who have expertise in different fields and different aspects of the service.

- Communicate the idea of the session carefully to invited participants. Consider that creative workshops can produce extraordinary moments for many people, a sort of back-to-childhood feeling that many associate with creative processes. In a way, this is true. Organizational hierarchies and constraints can make the free flow of ideas difficult or almost impossible in some cases. For this reason, a workshop needs to create the right kind of environment, one that is both exciting as well as something to be taken seriously.

- Ensure that the leading team conducted prior research and through that identified areas of problems, opportunities, or main themes. Each theme may generate a set of specific challenges that can be grouped according to the main stakeholder affected (e.g., citizen, provider, volunteer, or city). The team should present the pre-identified challenges using visual materials (e.g., cards, sheets) to easily communicate them to participants.

- Prepare in advance a set of stimulus materials, such as analogous cases or ideas taken from case studies from other contexts dealing with similar problems. These tools help create divergent thinking and stimulate new insights.

- Plan for a session longer than a meeting, typically half a day, or three to four hours. Consider carefully the space; it should be an immersive space with adequate equipment and furniture and ambiance. Favor a neutral space instead of the regular meeting room.

- Prepare materials in advance (drawing aids, worksheets) and pick the right tools (art supplies, Post-its, pens, cards, etc.).

- Plan the experience of participants by arranging food and coffee.

During the session:

- Start with general introductions. Use warm-up activities to help put people in the right mood.

- Have facilitators introduce the "rules of the game": the goals for the workshop, the general agenda, and the tools that will be used.

- Divide participants into prearranged teams and go through two or three ideation rounds. Each round can focus on one main challenge and involve both individual and collective idea generation.

- Let each team select and visualize the ideas generated in this session using preprinted worksheets or canvas. Teams can also make use of materials that might help participants feel comfortable with the creative process and visualization, such as prefabricated human figures, stencils, or LEGO toys.

- Have facilitators move into a collective final round so that each team can share ideas and insights, and final collective conclusions can be articulated and wrap the session.

- Have the team analyze the outcomes of the ideation session and develop them into a report containing a catalog of ideas, from which some can be selected for further development and pilot implementation.

- Start your session with collective and individual brainstorming to generate an initial set of ideas. Collect them on the prepared worksheets. Let each group discuss ideas, aggregate them, and form clusters.
- Participants may vote in the most interesting idea, give it a catchy name, and start defining its key interactions and touchpoints, including physical infrastructure and digital touchpoints. Teams may draw storyboard illustrations (four to six panels) that highlight the new service, its interactions, and its touchpoints.
- Once the ideas are visualized, it is time to get active! Write a script and distribute roles. Produce rough prototypes of touchpoints. Teams may choose between live enactment such as bodystorming or a desktop walkthrough using LEGO figures.

Use a template (workshop canvas) as a starting point for developing your own workshop canvas.

Recommended reading

Montgomery, E. P., and Woebken, C. (2016). *Extrapolation Factory. Operator's Manual: Publication version 1.0, includes 11 futures modeling tools.* CreateSpace Independent Publishing Platform.

IDEO.org (2015). *The Field Guide to Human-Centered Design*, 1st ed. IDEO.

THEY CARE
SO I SHARE

Fig 9.36 Template workshop canvas.

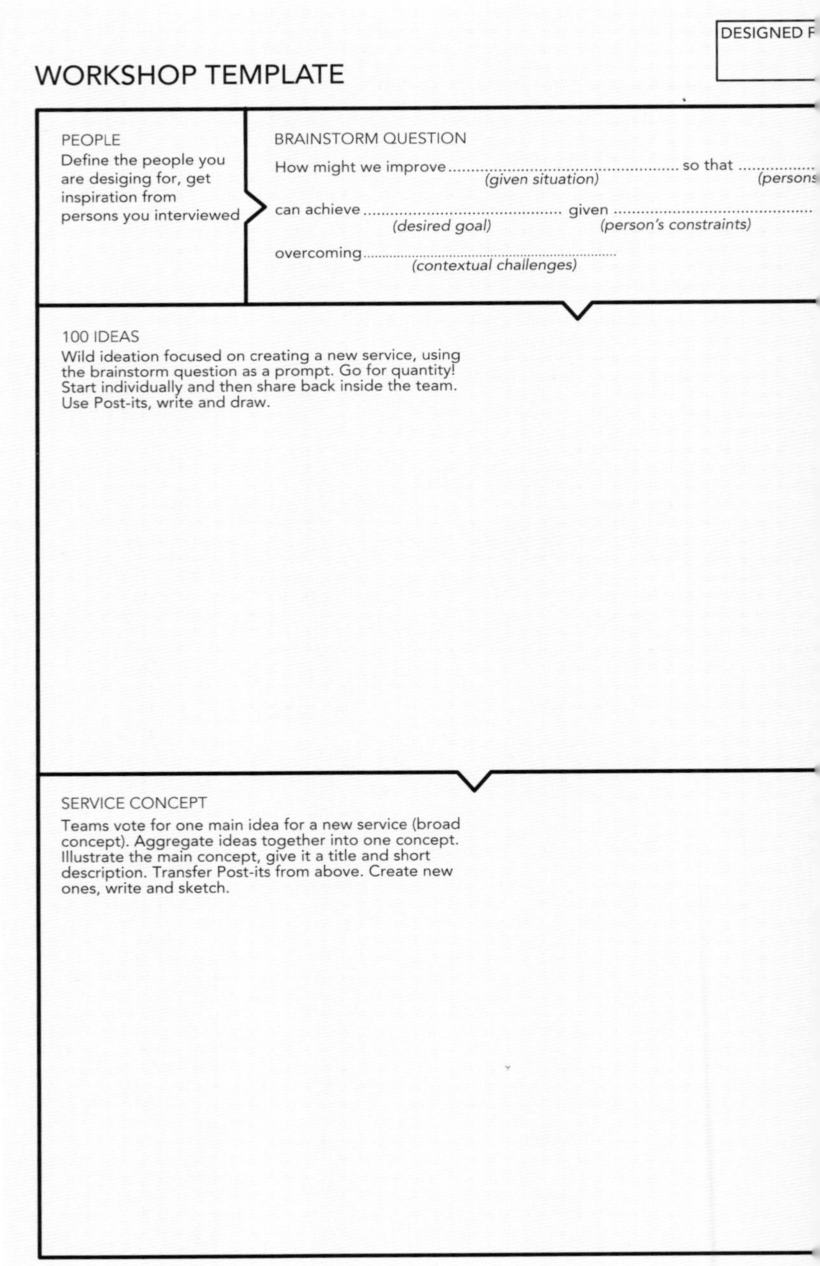
DESIGNED F
WORKSHOP TEMPLATE
PEOPLE
Define the people you are desiging for, get inspiration from persons you interviewed
BRAINSTORM QUESTION
How might we improve .... so that ....
(given situation)
(persons
can achieve .... given ....
(desired goal)
(person's constraints)
overcoming........
(contextual challenges)
100 IDEAS
Wild ideation focused on creating a new service, using the brainstorm question as a prompt. Go for quantity! Start individually and then share back inside the team. Use Post-its, write and draw.
SERVICE CONCEPT
Teams vote for one main idea for a new service (broad concept). Aggregate ideas together into one concept. Illustrate the main concept, give it a title and short description. Transfer Post-its from above. Create new ones, write and sketch.

DESIGNED BY | DATE | VERSION

OARD
he concept by telling teh story of its main
ons. Draw and write a storyboard showing
nents.

board as a script for enactement or
walkthrough using Lego toys.
d prototype the service touchpoints.

10 Prototyping, testing, iterating

During the People's Pharmacy project, how did you decide to move into the prototyping phase?

We identified that when customers were waiting to be served with their prescriptions, it was a passive time for them. They were sitting in one corner of the pharmacy waiting for their turn. Once they got to the prescription desk, they were served and were given the prescription.

With regard to the pharmacists, this time is when they learn a lot about the customers' needs. Yet, they have no way of going with the customer to show them products or services. They are stuck behind this desk.

Another thing we noticed is that there's a mix of different kinds of customers. Some of the customers, roughly speaking, have a lot of time to spend and they also want to talk a lot with the staff. Usually, this is the older customer base. Then there are a lot of younger customers. They are much more inclined to want faster service. We decided to blow this setup up and create two lines of pharmacy desks.

This raised the additional question of privacy. How do we design a safe zone in a way that protects people's privacy? This is something difficult to design just using AutoCAD or rendering the space design. Feeling privacy is really something that you experience bodily. We identified that there is a need to try this out somehow, and to practice and come up with the interactions and the kind of physical environments these interactions require.

Could you talk a little bit about how you use the prototype as a research tool in this project?

Designing is also very much a physical activity. In our design process, we always had some sort of physical aspect. We always create a space for our team where we put up all our information on the walls. Coming up with ideas is very much a physical process in itself.

Physical cardboard prototyping is a natural extension of this. Once we start getting early ideas and forming them into concepts, at some point we come to a stage where we really have to prototype the interactions, environments, and objects that allow for these interactions.

For example, the prescription desk. We had an idea for a stand-up desk where you meet the client in a different angle than the normal face to face. However, you don't know what this experience feels like unless you try it. We decided to build a few of these desks.

At our offices, we have a multipurpose gallery space where we can do prototyping and do events and stuff like this, so we simulated one part of the pharmacy in a very rough manner. We built three desks there so you could get a sense. We then simulated a prescription event. We had some artifacts there, and the designers were playing the customers.

Quite quickly we realized that, if you are handling pharmaceuticals, a round table is not a very good way to do that with two people. The things easily fall off the table and it's a bit clumsy. You don't know exactly where to position yourself. We changed the round desks to triangular desks. It formed the natural space for all the pharmaceuticals, the required papers, as well as the computer enrollment tools.

We also noticed while we were doing this, one of the sides of the triangles is exposed. We quickly just put a piece of cardboard on that one angle and created a much more private setting.

By doing it physically, you start realizing these things very naturally. They are difficult to learn only working on a computer.

You've mentioned that you set up some prototype materials in your studio space. Were you having specific events with different "users" at different times?

It was very event based, and we always prototyped with staff. When necessary, we also bring in the customers. With the pharmacy, we could prototype the privacy ourselves. We didn't need to involve customers for that.

How do employees participate in this phase? What does this process of inclusion actually look like?

During prototyping and user testing, the employees were involved in a training module where we asked, "What does this concept mean, how did we end up with these solutions, what kind of new ideas are they going to be?"

Then we asked them to create a customer journey. We had the initial customer journey already laid out as templates, but we wanted them to fill it out with the more detailed interactions because they are the experts in that.

We then divided them into groups to explore what happens when people enter the pharmacy, what happens during queueing, what happens during the prescription, and what happens at the end of the service interaction.
They sketched interactions and tried them out. We wanted to illustrate for them the whole model. That's how they internalize the service concept and gain a sense of ownership.

How did you go about facilitating and collecting feedback from the prototyping events? Were there specific methods or practices that you used to make what you learned help inform future design decisions?

We always document prototyping with photographs. Someone is always also taking notes. Additionally, the materials we use have a coating that can be drawn on that you can wipe off. You can also put Post-it notes on it. It's another way of documenting. We might draw an interface on the wall or a sign.

It's not just about getting feedback, but it's actually codesigning the environment or the objects while we're prototyping.

I think it's really important that prototyping tools invite people to participate. A prototype should be something that invites changing and doesn't look too finalized. That's why in prototyping we always use materials that you can rip apart, draw on, change, or modify. The materials should resemble material that people are used to handling. It's not just about inviting commentary. It's actually about inviting people to do something.

How did you come to a point in this project where you felt satisfied to move forward?

The whole design process is a process of creating a hypothesis. We test, validate, and iterate on that hypothesis until we are more and more sure. However, I don't believe in the idea that there is a certain point where you have some metrics that give a definitive answer to your question. You've just got to go step by step and continue. At some point, we came to agree with our clients that we were ready to move forward.

Part of a true codesign process should involve participation from frontline staff and users, as well as the leadership commissioning the project. However, accessing the frontline staff can be hindered by leadership's eagerness to participate in all phases of testing and prototyping. How should designers operate in negotiating the politics of codesign participation?

This relates to how designers hold power. We have the ability to make our clients take big decisions on investing resources. We have to design something that the frontline personnel can, and perhaps even want, to do. We also have to design something that brings benefits to the organization that invests in us and the design. I think it's very important for designers to understand how to get their ideas through, though. It's partly by having a wealth of both empathic and rational understanding of the context of the service. You achieve this only by collaborating with all kinds of stakeholders; by talking, by listening, by observing. This is the only way to gain this understanding.

10.4 Case study analysis

What are the main lessons learned from the prototyping approach in the YTA Pharmacy Project? By employing physical prototyping, the Hellon team was able to make ideas tangible, understand better their users and staff, and ultimately help them and the client organization make informed decisions. Prototyping affords a first pass into making an idea come to life, which is really critical in services, since so much depends on experiencing things with your body and senses, including sound and time, body movement and, as a consequence, people's emotional states and needs in a way that a drawing representation cannot match. It also affords staff involvement in a participatory way, allowing them to gain ownership of the new concepts in a way that two-dimensional representations cannot reach.

Prototyping events need to be properly planned, not only the material props and supports but also how the codesign will actually happen and how to document the whole session. It is crucial, for example, that artifacts don't look too finalized so that participants feel they shouldn't touch them. Instead, use materials that participants can rip apart, draw on, change, or modify.

While prototypes help making decisions, one shouldn't expect there will be a moment when everything is super clear. There's no way to be sure about decisions, but clients and designers should agree the moment when they feel confident enough to move forward with a concept.

Here are a few specific ways Hellon used prototyping in the People's Pharmacy Project.

Physical props

While services can be thought of as primarily about ordered social interactions and exchanges, servicescapes are almost always populated by a range of physical artifacts that help make the system work. In the example of the People's Pharmacy, desks, tables, and physical spaces were crucial in creating a service that was at once private, but also facilitated ease of movement throughout the retail space. Hellon's use of physical props such as cardboard prototypes served as a research tool for understanding the dynamics of how this service interaction could be produced from a physical and emotional perspective. Through the use of unpolished, low-fi, physical props, such as the prescription desk, the team was able to learn quickly about what design decisions would work best for their intended outcome. In the case of the People's Pharmacy, the team knew that the service, and the physical artifacts that populate it, needed to accommodate customers with very different needs. Key to achieving this goal was the acting out of the experience facilitated by the rough and dirty cardboard props. Physical props present a theory about what a future service might look like. Since the props are low-fi and unpolished, they are strong enough to suggest a service narrative tangible enough to imagine, yet still open to new insights, ideas, and modifications. The final outcome of the People's Pharmacy project took shape as a direct product of the insights gained through the process of prototyping with physical props.

10.5 Methods and tools

Participatory Prototype Cycles

The People's Pharmacy project highlights the value participation plays in prototyping service design concepts. Using a multipurpose gallery space in the Hellon studio provided an opportunity for life-sized physical prototypes to be engaged with and changed over time as new ideas emerged in collaboration between staff, customers, and the design team. The inclusion of multiple stakeholders in various prototyping events clearly demarcated space in the life of the project for enacting and embodying the future service environment. These moments are valuable for both testing and continuously improving ideas through the inclusion of nondesigners in the process. This process of learning through participation in the case of the People's Pharmacy was based on the interplay between making physical props, enacting service experiences, and then describing and critiquing those experiences alongside the team who can then incorporate those insights into future iterations of the service.

This section provides an annotated index of the key approaches, methods, and tools used in service design prototyping. We will now explore them, following the guide below.

Physical prototyping

Cardboard prototyping and physical props are key techniques used by Hellon, as shown in the People's Pharmacy case study. In another project, Hellon's team (then called Method) produced a hospital floor using a theater stage and cardboard furniture simulating different environments in a hospital. The main advantage of this kind of prototyping is that it creates empathic learning through its participatory nature, engaging users and staff in role playing so the experiences of patients can be simulated by nurses or other staff.

Physical props trigger storytelling by allowing us to *feel* experiences and thus helping us predict the future. Low-fi and low-tech props and elements are recommended over finished pieces because people engage better when the pieces don't look like final products.

Fig 10.17 Another example of cardboard prototyping by Hellon, in this case, a cardboard hospital set up in a black block theater.

Enactment can happen in cycles, allowing for continuous improvement and testing of different interaction approaches, for example. Elizabeth Sanders describes *Participatory Prototype Cycles* (PPC) as a framework for cocreated prototyping based on the interplay between making, telling, and enacting. It enables the development of artifacts through experimentation and embodiment, as it allows the capture of tacit knowledge from the participants, which is very necessary in service design.

Prototyping digital interactions: Low- and high-fi

For the most part, service designers are not necessarily the ones designing digital interfaces, platforms, or systems, especially their back end, such as writing the code behind them, even if these capacities are becoming increasingly diffused. But most likely, service designers will get involved in the front end or user-facing part of digital interfaces, platforms, or systems. For that reason, we will consider only prototyping (for digital interactions) without code.

The core aspect of digital interactions that are essential to those designing for services involves defining the outcomes they enable (e.g., a subscription, reservation, purchase, consultation) and how well they communicate these functions to the user through their visual and aesthetic appearance (e.g., their look and feel) and usability (e.g., if they are intuitive and easy to use, its sequence and coherence).

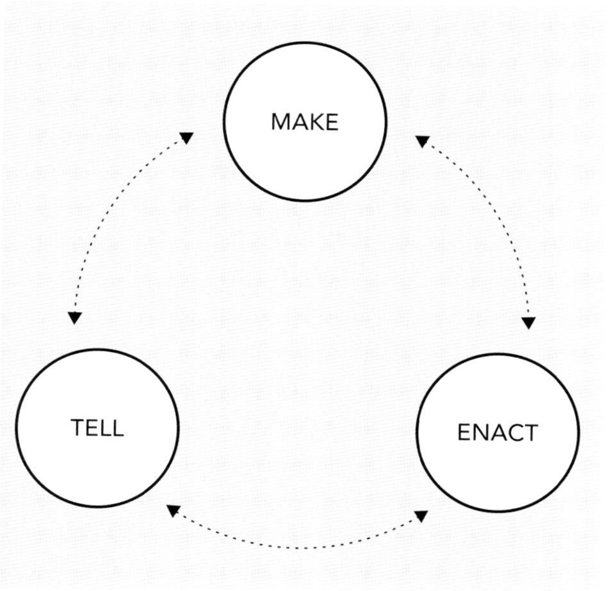
MAKE
TELL
ENACT

Fig 10.18 Elizabeth Sanders's Participatory Prototype Cycles (PPC) framework.

The main role of service designers is therefore being able to define what are the interactions contained in a service; what needs to happen in these interactions; what they enable; and how a digital platform, system, or interface behaves with a user.

The digital prototyping process starts by considering the nature of the desired interaction and what it affords: Is it a subscription, reservation, purchase, or consultation? Does it happen in mobile or stationary mode, or both? What are the main desired outcomes of these interactions? And which is the best media to achieve that, whether websites or mobile applications? What kind of user interface (UI) will it require? What kind of aesthetics makes more sense? Are sensing and connectivity involved, etc.?

Here are a few things to consider when choosing digital prototype techniques. First, ask what is the real intent of the prototype. It might vary from a demo tool to be discarded later or an actual piece with coding that can be reused in the final product. Second, ask who that prototype is for. Is it going to be user-tested, does it need to be shared, or does it need to be done in a collaborative way? Do you need low or high fidelity at this point? Finally, how familiar are you with the prototyping tools? Can you code, and how much time, effort, and resources can you afford?

10.5 Methods and tools

Many people favor starting the process with paper prototype techniques because they allow for quick explorations of desired interactions and are a great collaborative tool, easy for cocreation and teamwork. It remains a popular and versatile tool to date; anyone can do it. It is also a great collaborative tool, easy for cocreation and sharing. It allows for any kind of exploration of desired interactions.

The traditional kit for paper prototyping includes materials such as paper, transparencies, index cards, Post-it notes, and cardboard or foam board when prototyping the device. There are several downloadable kits with templates and stencils for user interface (UI) elements as well as software through which you can take pictures of paper prototypes and quickly convert them into interactive screens.

Either drawing by hand or using premade materials, paper prototyping is essentially a low-fidelity, nonaesthetic technique that focuses solely on information architecture and interaction sequences.

Start by defining a few elements and then playing with sequential interactions. One main consideration is understanding the changes of state; for example, clicking on a button opens a new screen or checking a box or selecting an option. The questions here are, How would the users know something has happened, and how can they go back or advance to the next step? This kind of thinking calls for experimentation, by writing in the paper prototype or using transparencies to go back and forth. The purpose is to simulate the interaction and determine the sequences and transitions.

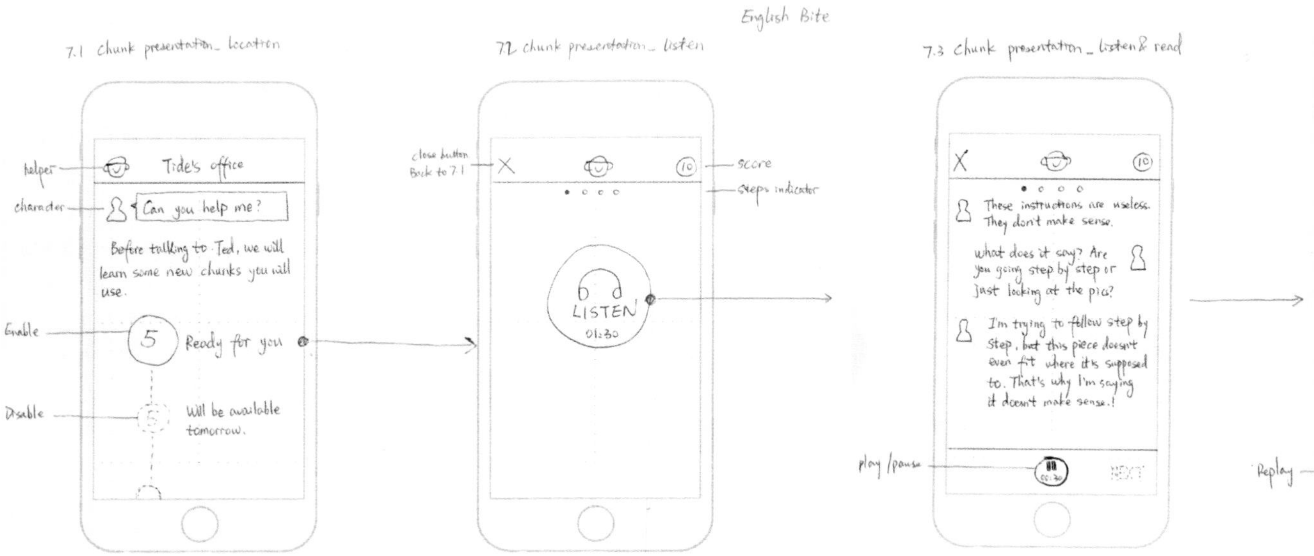
English Bite
helper
character
Can you help me?
Before talking to Ted, we will learn some new chunks you will use.
Enable
5
Ready for you
Disable
Will be available tomorrow.
score
steps indicator
LISTEN
01:30
These instructions are useless. They don't make sense.
play/pause
Replay

Fig 10.19 Handwritten paper prototyping using stencils.

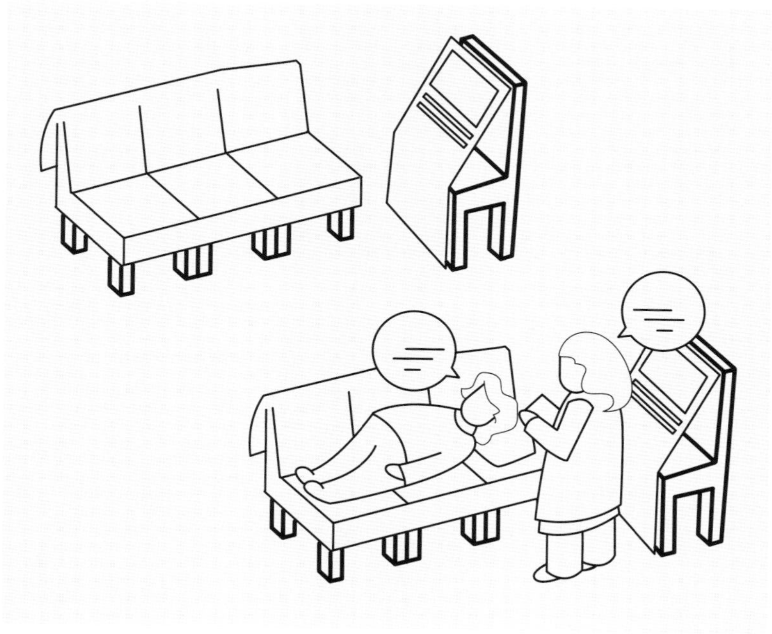

Fig 10.26 Interaction prototype setup.

11 Implementation and evaluation

USA
London 2012

11.3

11.5

Weightlifting
The athletes
Size isn't everything
19

11.6

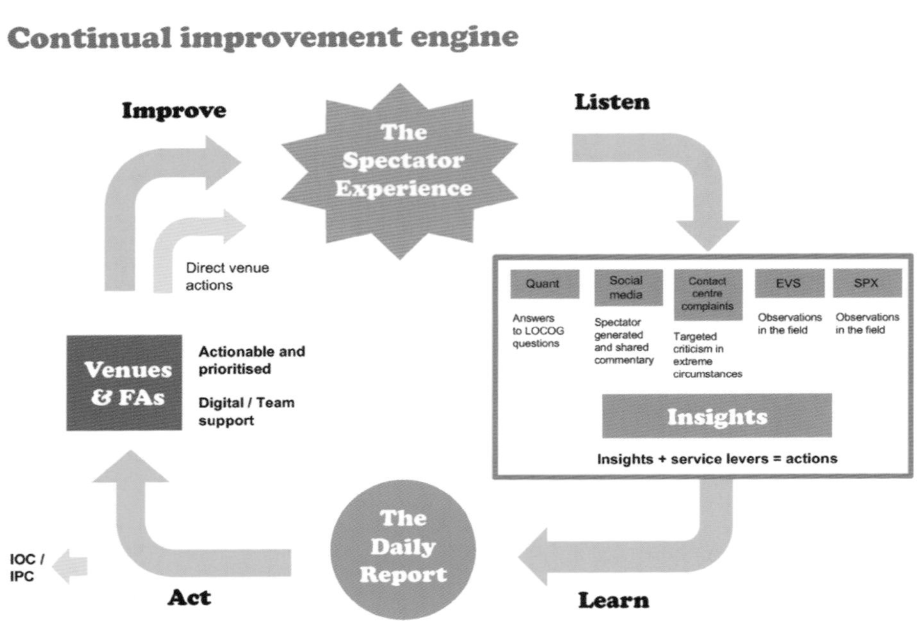
Continual improvement engine
Improve
The Spectator Experience
Listen
Direct venue actions
Quant
Answers to LOCOG questions
Social media
Spectator generated and shared commentary
Contact centre complaints
Targeted criticism in extreme circumstances
EVS
Observations in the field
SPX
Observations in the field
Insights
Insights + service levers = actions
Venues & FAs
Actionable and prioritised
Digital / Team support
IOC / IPC
Act
The Daily Report
Learn

Fig 11.7 The "continual improvement engine" of the management of the spectator experience, showing the different feedback sources generating daily reports that informed actions and priorities.

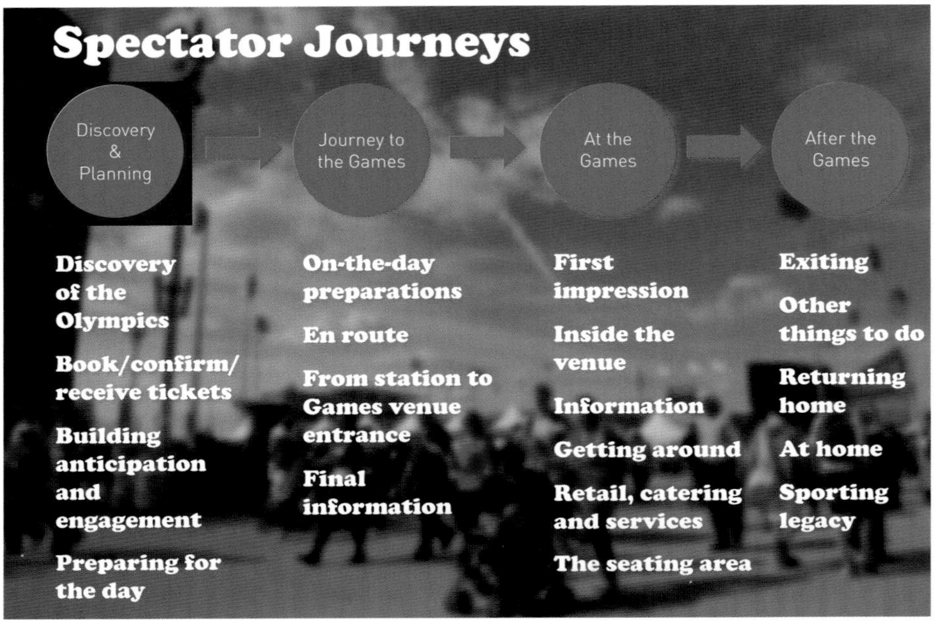
Spectator Journeys
Discovery & Planning
Journey to the Games
At the Games
After the Games
Discovery of the Olympics
Book/confirm/ receive tickets
Building anticipation and engagement
Preparing for the day
On-the-day preparations
En route
From station to Games venue entrance
Final information
First impression
Inside the venue
Information
Getting around
Retail, catering and services
The seating area
Exiting
Other things to do
Returning home
At home
Sporting legacy

Fig 11.8 Description of the spectator journey, considering planning, journey to the game venue, inside the venue, and after the games.

The team created a whole set of strategies to mitigate the waiting in queues. One idea was called "Magic Moments," a photo opportunity in which spectators could take a selfie holding a genuine Olympic torch. Queue entertainers were present in several places, called by radio by the staff on demand to specific places where big queues were forming. To prevent people stopping in places and blocking the flow, a band would start up, marching off into the park, and people would follow them quite naturally—a trick learned from Disneyworld. Activities for kids were created and animated by volunteers and other staff in areas around the stadiums, reducing the risk of overcrowding at some key points. Sports-related exhibitions were staged to educate spectators about the rules and regulations of specific sports. The atmosphere created was of a festival with lots of touchpoints all around town.

The team realized that, regardless of how well things were planned and prepared, there was no way to get everything right in an event of such scale, especially at the beginning. Their approach was to continuously enhance the spectator experience, monitoring the situation and implementing improvements on a daily basis. The main sources of data came from questionnaires, feedback on social media, and insights by the frontline staff, all generating daily reports revealing the things that were working or not working. The approach of daily improvement was critical because as the team leader Alex Nisbett realized, "every day—even the last day of the games—is going to be somebody's first impression, first experience."

They used quantitative data from questionnaires, asking operational questions across the different venues and hotspots, generating a spreadsheet. They learned basic things such as access to and quality of food and drink were poor or cleanliness of the toilets was an issue. The daily report was produced and circulated as a PowerPoint slide to stakeholders, who could then take action to improve the situation.

They also collected qualitative data by asking participants, "What one word sums up your experience?" and generated word clouds that changed every day. This approach proved to be a good barometer of the general feelings. Social media was monitored, although the team wouldn't engage in conversations. This source provided a great deal of feedback and was essential for continuous improvement along with the help of the spectators.

From this feedback, they were able to improve water provision, for example, by creating more fresh water stations and mobilizing all providers of water fountains in the country. By the time the Paralympics started—weeks after the Olympics— the whole organization felt comfortable and able to create more nuanced experiences.

11.3 Interview with Alex Nisbett

Alex Nisbett is Head of Design at Livework Studio, London. He is a member of the SDN management team and leading SDN's event board. Alex was Spectator Experience Project Manager at LOCOG, The London Organizing Committee of the Olympic and Paralympic Games.

Can you give a brief description of the nature of your involvement in the design of the spectator experience at the London 2012 Olympic and Paralympic Games?

London was the first Organizing Committee of the Olympic Games that specifically designed and delivered a spectator experience. No other host city had really thought about spectators and the experience that they were going to get to the degree London was going to. We were essentially writing the rule book for the spectator experience client group. We looked at the spectators and their whole journey from way before the games. For example, how people found out about the games, selected, and bought tickets as they traveled to the games. What we did explicitly was to focus on the experience at a venue level. What was happening if you were a ticket holder? What was happening on your game's day? That was where the focus was and that is where the focus was in refining the experience.

Can you give an example of this attention to the spectator experience?

Spectators would be required to turn up to venues almost three hours before their event starts, and research told us they might spend up to 40 percent of their day in queues. This is because of all the security, the event schedule, or having to walk for a long way to get to their seat. There was a bit of education needed, a bit of preparedness for the spectators. For example, "If I turn up to a venue two hours before my event, what I am going to do?" You're waiting around. What we sought to do is provide some entertainment and some education by helping people to understand a bit about the spot that they are looking for, what they are looking at. The goal was to get spectators to the right place at the right time, but in the right state of mind. If they are in the right state of mind, they are more likely to applaud when they need to applaud. That's what the broadcasters want. They want a perfect backdrop for the athletes. Also the business wants people to spend money on merchandising and catering. We call that high-performing spectators.

How do you match all the necessary moments with how people would normally behave? What about the tension between what you plan for and then what you end up having to do at the moment of the event?

If you think about the majority of and a lot of businesses that use service design to think about maximizing the experience and, therefore, the big business impact, they always think about positive things. Interestingly, at the Olympics, we were always focused on preventing the negatives, which gets you to the same conclusion but starts from a different point. We had a plan for a continual improvement loop, a tool we created because we knew it wouldn't be right on day one, day two, or day three and we had to review and keep reviewing in order to, again, build on what we learn. Our planning in the spectator experience team was based around, "How do you mitigate against certain factors, but do it in a way that's going to excite, engage, captivate, and inspire spectators?" Our team focused on solving problems, but in a way that delights. This is one of the big challenges that we face in service design, "How can I support what the business wants (generate value, speed up processes), but do it in a way that is useful and desirable for the patient, the passenger, or the spectator. That duality is where we know the real value of services is generated.

In regards to bridging business interests, spectator experience, with this idea of being responsive to a massive system that's unfolding in real time, were there specific practices that you used to evaluate how things were going as the games progressed?

I would say this idea of listening to your audience, learning from them, acting upon it, and then improving the experience. Then, of course, the next day you would do the same thing. Listen, watch, learn, act. That, to me, is an iterative loop. You build upon what you've learned, test, and see how it works. This includes listening and watching the behaviors of members of the public. We did research to understand what they were thinking and feeling before the games, and then we acted big time on what they were saying about their plans. We uncovered unmet needs. Then we iterated at the Games, that continued improvement loop. Each sport held a full competition test event, just like a pilot, about a year or so before games time, which also helped us identify improvements to the spectator experience.

How did you go about implementation of touchpoints while working in a complex system of multiple stakeholders and operational channels?

There are a number of capabilities which we had. The first factor was a very well organized organization. Every Olympic Games has a very clear playbook for each Functional Area, a user guide if you will, which supported the complex system. The spectator experience team enjoyed huge buy-in from the IOC who totally believed in what we were doing, and were 100 percent advocates for us. Experience within the team of managing complex large-scale events and situations was also critical, so very high levels of collaboration were as you might expect, evident in what is essentially a team sport.

Are there some examples you can share of a specific service implementation?

One example could be the ticketing system. It started with the premise that we didn't want any empty seats. In some previous games, in some sessions, the TV camera would pan up, and half the stadium would be "half empty." London didn't want that, and as a result the concept of the ticket lottery emerged to ensure no empty seats. You'd enter the lottery, with your preferences, but wouldn't know what tickets you'd receive. This meant that there's high chance that every ticket will be bought, but this did leave a level of uncertainty for the spectator in what sport they would see. For example, wanting to see the 100-meter final, but getting a ticket for weightlifting. Would that mean, "Oh, I'm disappointed. Do I want to try and change tickets? Will I bother to turn up? I will turn up, but I've got no idea what weightlifting is all about." We realized what the spectators might be going through and wanted to turn possible disappointment into a positive exploration or inspiration, "That looks like fun. Maybe I'd like to try that."

A little of what we did was a lot of education around "This is weightlifting. Here's an exhibition about the history of weightlifting, the different lifts and weight classes etc."

We sought to provide information that could help to understand what that sport is all about, so that when the spectator sits down in their seat, they'll know what good looks like. During the games, I took a lot of photographs of people and what they are doing. There's one picture of a spectator standing in front of an exhibition stand which we designed. The stand features a photo of an athlete lifting a bar above her head. Her hands are up in the air, and there's a picture of this guy staging in front of that mimicking her movement with his partner taking a picture of him. What we created was an opportunity for people to learn about the sport whilst they're queuing and waiting for the session to start and photo opportunities as lasting memories. This all helped create an atmosphere that was more electric, something that the weightlifters and broadcasters love.

You raise the issue of having institutional buy-in. Can you explain more about this? Is it something that must be lobbied for?

There's a few things. First, being able to succinctly express the vision. We created propositions for the experience at certain points along the spectator journey and how these supported venue operations. I needed to be able to succinctly express the value and benefit of the things we proposed. You're also thinking about the money. How much bang for buck can we get? How much do we need to spend here? What's the cost going to be to mitigate the risks? Do we really need this thing, or can we get away without that? In other words, being able to make things appear concrete or tangible is an extremely valuable lesson to learn, because you can say, "Believe me, we need to do this. Spectators are going to be queueing up for an average 40 percent of their day. We need to give them other things to do." or "There's going to be a huge pinch point here, because people are going to want to stop and take a selfie of themselves against the Olympic stadium and the first thing they will be faced with is a huge bottleneck." The real lobbying was when we were able to make things tangible and real. The mitigation of risks, which we did, and building a comprehensive business case, was the language that leadership understood. Once we realized our objectives and how we'd achieve them, we couched everything as a risk to be mitigated, rather than simply an experience to be improved; we would be ruthless in talking their language to get the buy-in.

How, as a service designer, would you coordinate conversations with different actors that, ultimately, you need to talk to and gain approval from, for example, in the case of the Olympics, big business, sport federations, the military, transportation services, etc.?

The model that was used was about having teams and forums where these concerns, concepts, thoughts, mitigations could be shared at such a level, with such a group of people that everybody can form a shared opinion, and then develop individual working groups to refine the details. There were a lot of committees. There was a lot of working collaboratively. What we did, in many respects, was to come in and add our voice of the spectator into that existing framework. I found myself speaking with the sport federations, technicians, broadcasters, architects, lots of different agencies. What service design's taught me is that you could be talking with patients who are suffering from high cholesterol one minute and the next you're talking to somebody from government or somebody from an airline or somebody who's more used to renting out dumper trucks. You get used to having conversations with lots of different actors and understanding what their role might be in the delivery of the service, and what their role is in helping provide their users with a great experience.

One final question might be about the beginning. How do you even start a project of this scale?

The (obvious) thing about the Olympics is its scale. You have to break it down into small and manageable chunks. That's what we had to do because we were a tiny team. It's important, also, to think about where are you going to make maximum impact. Our idea of Brilliant Basics and Magic Moments was quite a powerful one in this respect. Get the basics right. Make sure that people can fill up their water bottles. Make sure that people know what time they have to sit down. Make sure that people know where to go to. Make sure that if people get into trouble, they can be helped. Those are the basics. The Magic Moments, being able to take a picture with a mascot, having your picture taken with the Olympic torch, getting an autograph of an athlete, those are things that really, really make it. Breaking it down and understanding what's useful and what's not, what's valuable, what's super valuable! Then enjoy every single minute of it.

11.4 Case study analysis

Road maps

Due to the complexity of an event like the Olympics, the design team framed much of their ideas around the concept of mitigating risk. Each design decision was seen by the organizing committee through the lens of potential risk. To implement service concepts, the spectator experience team created risk register maps prior to the event. These maps illustrated in precise and tangible ways how each design decision would work, as well as how it would achieve the larger goal of facilitating the flow of spectators and avoiding troublesome bottlenecks. These modes of communication between design team and organizing committee were crucial tools for the adoption of service concepts.

Feedback strategies

In this case study, successful implementation and "continuous enhancement" of services relied on the use of effective feedback strategies that focused on people's experience. Implementation requires a degree of responsiveness, whereby changes can be made to the service as you learn what is working and what needs to be improved. In the case of the London Olympics, real-time information about the spectators' experience was collected through a "continual improvement loop," which aided the team's ability to act in a responsive manner. Here, we see how implementation and evaluation merge into a continuous process of doing, learning, and improving, which is guided by feedback from a range of sources (i.e., spectators, staff). The tools for collecting feedback were multiple, leveraging a variety of qualitative and quantitative information streams (questionnaires, social media, staff feedback), which culminated in daily reports. These reports made communication of insights across a diverse set of stakeholders easy and accessible (i.e., use of PowerPoint slides). This practice of evaluation and communication helped guide decisions to alter aspects of the service experience.

Clear value proposition

The case of the London Olympics highlights the importance of a clear value proposition in the successful implementation of a new service design. The heart of the value proposition was the idea of Brilliant Basics and Magic Moments. The focus of each idea was straightforward and clear, tying positive experience to efficient, pleasurable, and enriching services (e.g., manageable queues, easy-to-find water, informative exhibits, strategically designed selfie opportunities, kids' activities).

In addition to the concrete spectator's experience, the team was able to translate their ideas into a comprehensive business case in order to strategically communicate with stakeholders in their own language. This required the team to frame ideas strongly in terms of risk mitigation, in addition to improving spectator experience. By doing so, the team was able to increase buy-in and acceptance of their ideas.

11.5 Methods and tools

The following methods and tools provide examples of how to bridge the creative generative phases and prototyping leading to implementation through pilots and road maps, how to integrate business modeling into the service design process, how to integrate feedback strategies, and how to consider assessment in service design projects.

Pilots and road maps

Pilots are real-life, small-scale controlled implementations of service designs. They involve real people, staff, and users in actual venues. Pilots are critical mechanisms for bridging prototyping and scaled implementations. They allow testing of new service concepts and their *touchpoints*, and collect information on what works and what doesn't.

While live prototypes are normally one-off high-fidelity tests in real-life conditions, pilots consist of several rounds, rolling out over weeks or months. Therefore, pilots allow for the evolution of designed service features with modifications applied at each round of testing. In projects involving multiple channels and *touchpoints*, pilots are even more useful because they can test different touchpoints and channels at different moments and at a different pace, making coordination more manageable. Planning the logistics for a pilot is therefore crucial as different parts of the same organization are mobilized.

To get to the stage of conducting a pilot, the service design team would have already been through several rounds of approvals and modifications with the client organization and have gotten the buy-in from decision makers and leaders at the management level, as well as conducted preliminary testing and consultation with frontline staff and users. A service design concept ready for piloting normally involves producing a family of touchpoints ready to be deployed, aided by specification materials such as the service blueprint and other descriptive materials that might include written documents explaining the materials and the way they should be used.

Once these materials have been approved, a location for the pilot needs to be identified and might involve bringing new people and new partners onboard. Establishing clear evaluation goals for the pilot as well as a comparative baseline is important, for example:

- Primary project goal (quantitative): Determine whether the pilot has an impact on the number of users who go through the new service, by comparing data from the pilot to data from another site.

- Secondary project goal (qualitative): Determine whether the pilot helps users understand the new added value of the service.

- Identify what changes, if any, can be made to the pilot: to (1) increase the number of users and (2) improve their understanding of the impact of the new offering on their individual lives and needs.

The design team, in consultation with project stakeholders, should define key questions and potential details to measure. The next step is crafting and vetting a detailed plan that describes activities and roles across time. The plan should encompass regular check-in evaluations of participants and facilitators. The design team should expect to make small improvements and modifications to the designs throughout the pilot.

Road maps are documents that are crafted after the pilot phase; they describe how to roll out a new service into broader implementation. This document might involve a year-long (or longer) calendar mapping out activities and milestones. It might be easier to break down streams of actions into different tracks, starting with the near future (one month away) and building the following months. A different strategy is *backcasting*, starting from an end goal one year from now, and reconstructing backward to the present, with the needed steps and major milestones in between. It is recommended to pair the road map with a resource assessment (see below) and an assessment of the role of staff throughout the road map.

Business implications: The Business Model Canvas

The *Business Model Canvas* is a tool that helps break down the complexity of business elements, understanding feasibility and modeling how a concept can make sense as a business, and how sustainable it might be. According to Osterwalder and Pigneur, creators of the Business Model Canvas (2010), a "business model describes the rationale of how an organization creates, delivers, and captures value." For new service concepts, it helps designers and organizations make a business case for the new service, and it can be used in participatory ways.

At the center of the canvas is the *value proposition*: the benefits of a service to its customers/users and how it creates quantitative (price, speed) or qualitative (experience, aesthetic) value for them. The value proposition is, in fact, the heart and meaning of a service and is the starting point for its business development. The service needs to deliver a value that potential clients perceive as worth its cost of production plus whatever margins are needed, whether related to

- *Partners*, including suppliers, strategic alliances, and providers of outsourced or shared infrastructure

- *Key resources* (whether physical such as brick-and-mortar spaces; financial, either cash, credit, intellectual including brand, proprietary knowledge, partnerships, or databases; or human, related to all the people involved and their skills)

- All the *Activities* that need to take place to make the service function, including production activities for setting up a new service (e.g., design and build a new physical space; design a web platform, produce information materials), activities for maintaining its regular functioning and constant troubleshooting and improvement (e.g., management of materials, distribution of information materials, training and knowledge management), as well as those related to developing and maintaining platforms and networks (for example, eBay or PayPal, which bridge customers and third parties)

The next question is whether the new service value proposition is coherent and meaningful to specific *customer segments*: the people your service wants to reach. Does the service get the job done, that

Fig 11.9 Example of a five-month pilot plan in a service design project. Pilots might involve several rounds of tests and consultations with users, staff, and third-party experts and consultants.

TIME FRAME	SERVICE DESIGN TEAM	CLIENT ORGANIZATION: CENTRAL MANAGEMENT	CLIENT ORGANIZATION: BRANCH	CLIENT ORGANIZATION: BRANCH
Month 1	• Create a "pre" evaluation form/ questionnaire for users to complete before they engage in service • Create a "post" evaluation form/ questionnaire for users to complete after they engage in service • Create an evaluation form/questionnaire for staff who perform service • Schedule times to administer evaluation forms/questionnaires	• Collaborate and provide feedback on content and structure of forms • Liaise with branch for scheduling	• Schedule times for Service Design team to administer evaluations	• Consult on evaluation design and process • Feedback on content and structure of forms
Month 2	• Administer 1st round of evaluation forms • Compile form results with additional data staff • Conduct analysis of data and survey results, pose suggested changes to the pilot program to address areas where the pilot can be improved	• Logistical assistance for administration of eval forms, as needed • Liaise with branch to collect data	• Collect and provide data. • Complete evaluation form	• Consult on best practices for quantitative and qualitative data analysis
Month 3	• Make adjustments to the pilot based on results of round #1 • Re-administer evaluation forms for 2nd round of evaluation • Conduct analysis from round #2 results	• Collaborate on determining adjustments to the pilot • Liaise with branch to update on adjustments and schedule for 2nd round	• Schedule times for Service Design team to administer evaluations • Collect and provide data • Complete evaluation form	• Feedback on proposed adjustments
Month 4	• Make adjustments to the pilot based on results of round #2 • Re-administer evaluation forms for 3rd round of evaluation • Conduct analysis from round #3 results	• Collaborate on determining adjustments to the pilot • Liaise with branch to update on adjustments and schedule for 3rd round	• Schedule times for Service Design team to administer evaluations • Collect and provide data • Complete evaluation form	• Feedback on proposed adjustments
Month 5	• Final summary of learnings	• Make decisions on how to proceed	• Schedule times for Service Design team to administer evaluations • Collect and provide data • Complete evaluation form	• Consult on how to best present overall learnings

is, solve the problem of these specific groups of customers/users? Are the right *channels* being used to communicate with them? Are the physical or digital channels the right ones for this audience? And are the right *customer relationships* being built and supported throughout the service journey? Do they need personal assistance or self-service automated service?

While flexible, the Business Model Canvas centers on financial aspects only. Other values and models can't be captured through this tool—for example, social and environmental aspects and scopes. The *Social Business Model Canvas* borrows the structure of the Business Model Canvas and adapts it to ventures that center on social value proposition, such as nonprofit organizations or even for-profits that have a social mission.

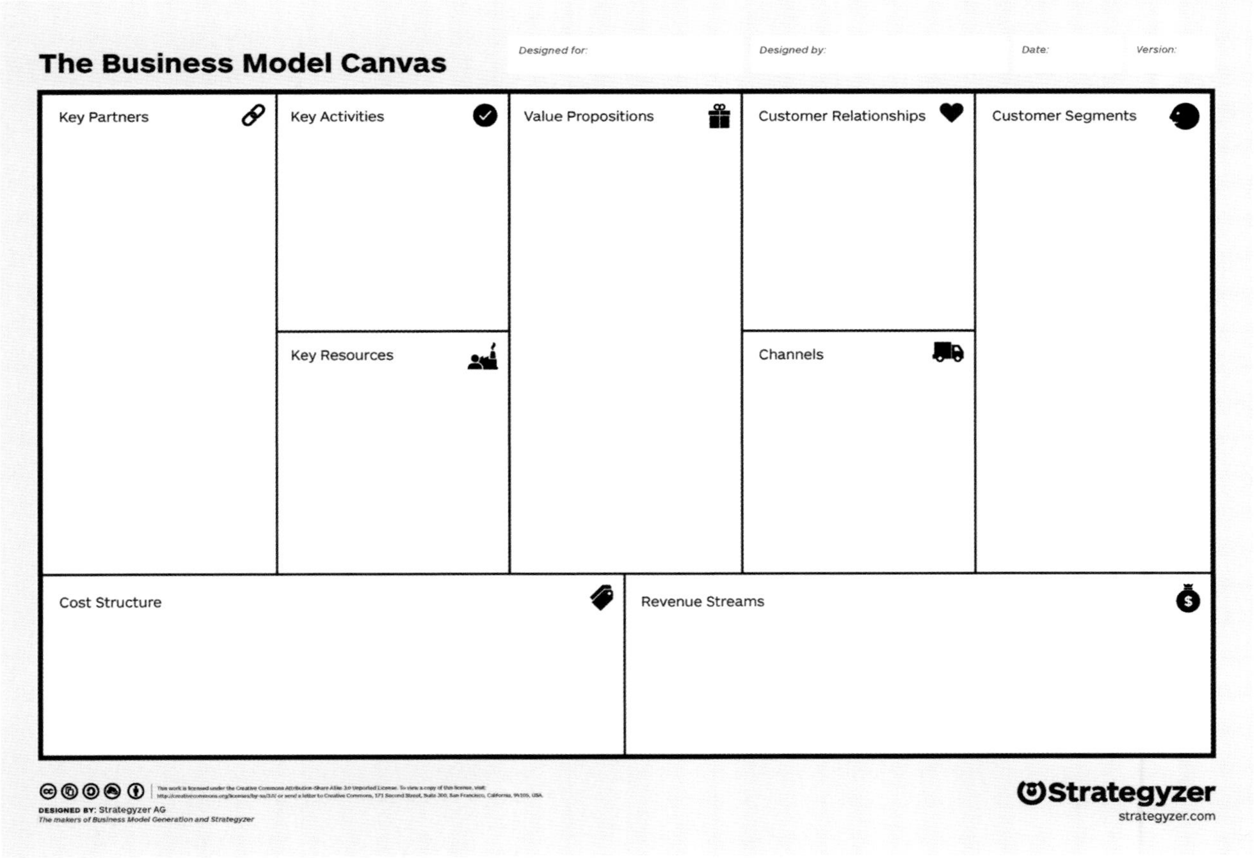
The Business Model Canvas
Designed for:
Designed by:
Date:
Version:
Key Partners
Key Activities
Key Resources
Value Propositions
Customer Relationships
Channels
Customer Segments
Cost Structure
Revenue Streams
DESIGNED BY: Strategyzer AG
The makers of Business Model Generation and Strategyzer
Strategyzer
strategyzer.com

Fig 11.10 The Business Model Canvas.

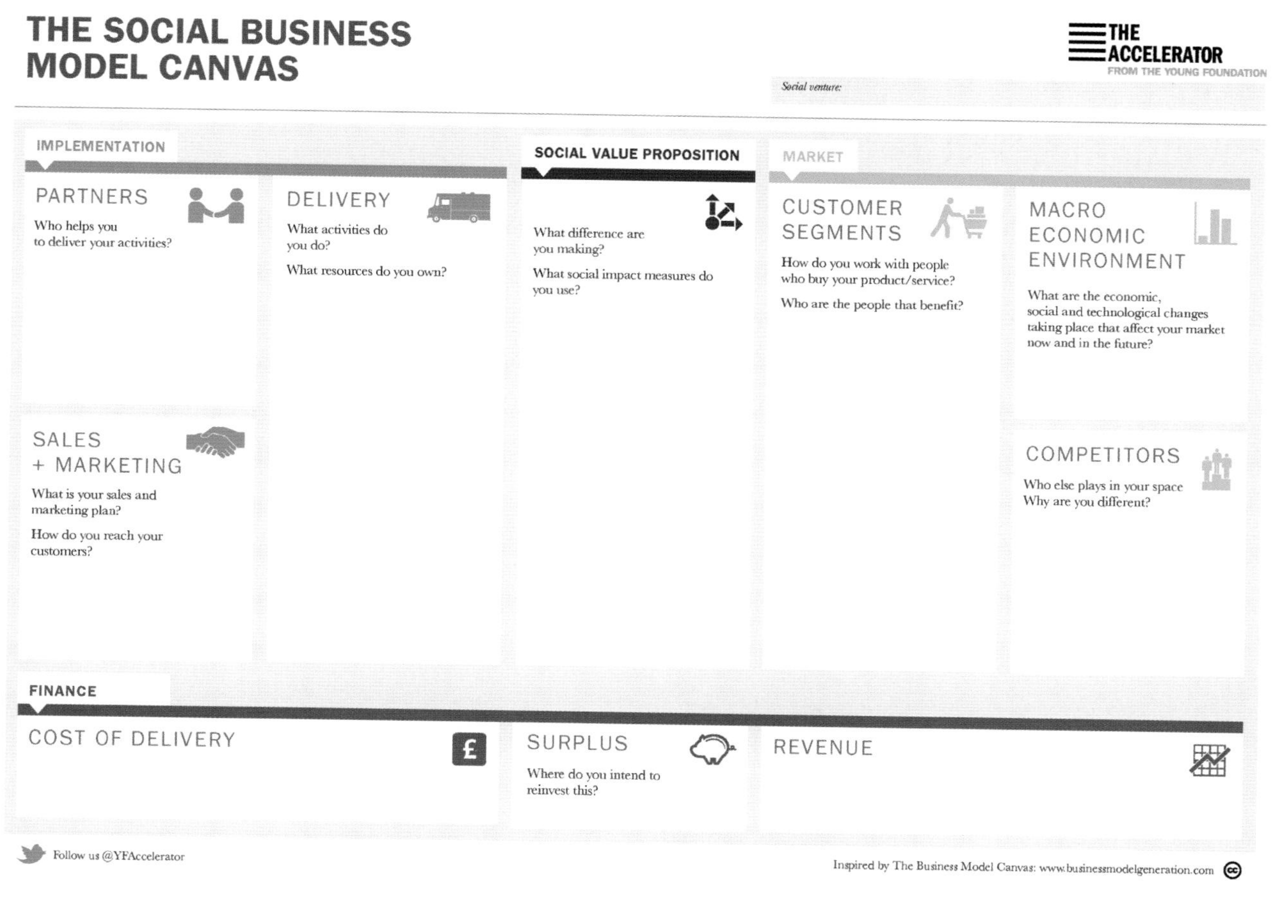
THE SOCIAL BUSINESS MODEL CANVAS
THE ACCELERATOR
FROM THE YOUNG FOUNDATION
Social venture:
IMPLEMENTATION
PARTNERS
Who helps you to deliver your activities?
DELIVERY
What activities do you do?
What resources do you own?
SALES + MARKETING
What is your sales and marketing plan?
How do you reach your customers?
SOCIAL VALUE PROPOSITION
What difference are you making?
What social impact measures do you use?
MARKET
CUSTOMER SEGMENTS
How do you work with people who buy your product/service?
Who are the people that benefit?
MACRO ECONOMIC ENVIRONMENT
What are the economic, social and technological changes taking place that affect your market now and in the future?
COMPETITORS
Who else plays in your space
Why are you different?
FINANCE
COST OF DELIVERY
SURPLUS
Where do you intend to reinvest this?
REVENUE
Follow us @YFAccelerator
Inspired by The Business Model Canvas: www.businessmodelgeneration.com

Fig 11.11 The Social Business Model Canvas, by The Accelerator from The Young Foundation.

Feedback strategies

The evaluation of services can be understood as a continuous form of cocreation. Users can tell service providers about problems and opportunities, informing management and staff of ways that they can improve and adapt accordingly. One main challenge is finding the appropriate feedback mechanisms to measure service experiences as they unfold.

The London Olympics case study offers an excellent example of feedback mechanisms that made use of mixed data to monitor service delivery and identify pain points on a daily basis. The service design team monitored data via questionnaires, registered complaints, and social media as well as through live observations, collecting not only hard quantitative data but also qualitative and anecdotal data. The mixed

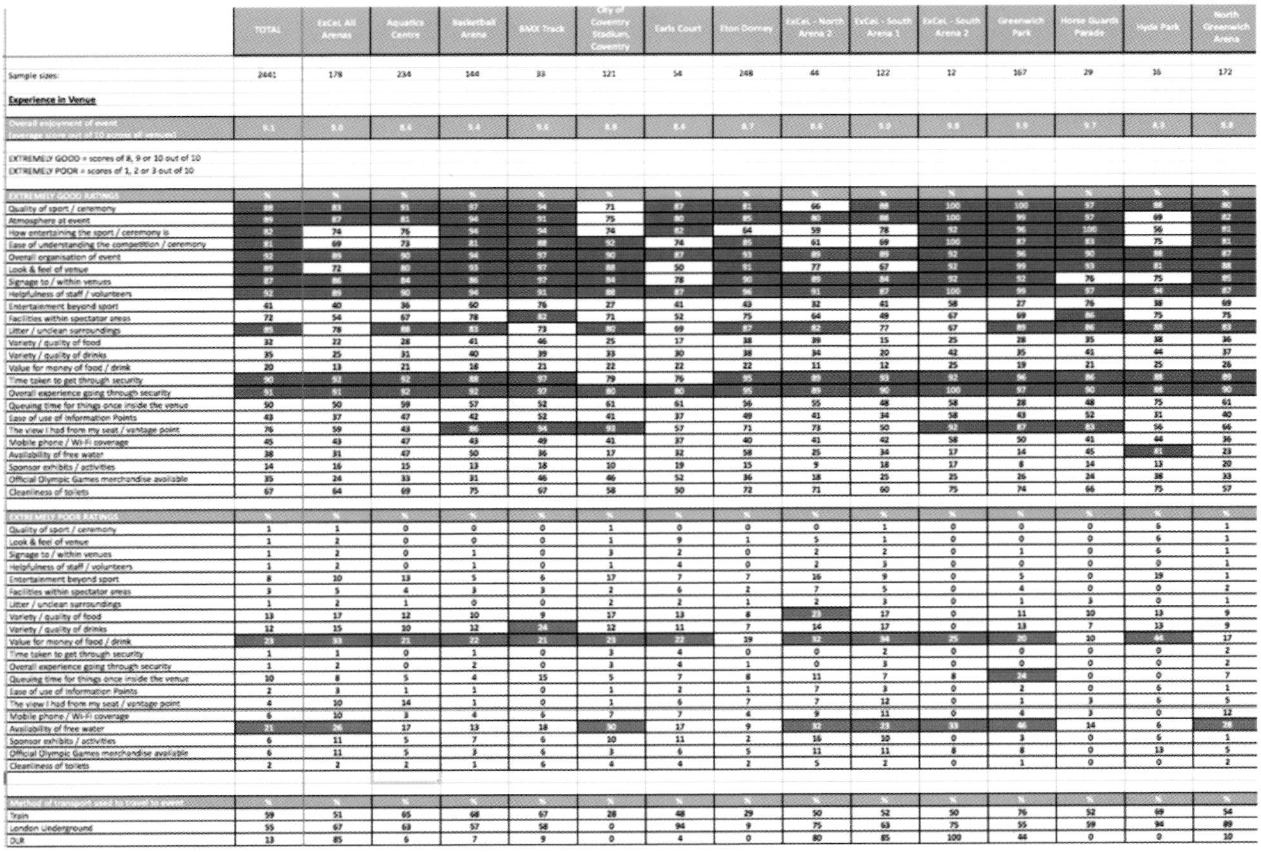

Fig 11.12 Example of a survey in the London Olympic Games, showing venue hotspots.

data capturing the public experience was compiled into daily reports containing insights that were translated into priorities and actions at the venues, working as an engine to drive continual improvement.

Questionnaires were solicited from the public at different venues, with questions addressing infrastructure (Wi-Fi coverage, availability of water fountains), communication (efficacy of signage), and experiential aspects (time in queue, look and feel of venue). The results were then compiled into spreadsheets aggregating data, highlighting the extremes, showing extremely good ratings and extremely low ratings at the different venues.

One key question asked of the public was: "If you could describe the emotions you felt while you were at the Olympic Park using three words or short phrases, what would they be?" A word cloud was the tool of choice to aggregate data about their reactions, providing glimpses into the public's experience.

Social media was another key channel for screening the spectators' experience in the London Olympic Games. In this case, social media was monitored as a barometer of the public's response; however, the team did not engage in replies, in part because of lack of capacity. In fact, social media is increasingly a vital communication channel between organizations and the people they serve. Several *social listening* tools are available to help organizations monitor their own customers' reactions, understand their target audiences, and benchmark their performance versus competitors. Nonetheless, many customer complaints via social media apparently still go unanswered, perhaps because engaging in conversations with the public is a bigger investment that might require new staff, such as a social media manager.

The final crucial question for feedback strategies is how quantitative and qualitative data from users can lead to decision making and eventually to the improvement of services. This depends, in great part, on who is reading these results and whether or not they want, or have the power, to implement the necessary changes.

In the case of the London Olympics, the daily report was a key tool of the "continual improvement engine" set up by the service design team, aggregating data collected from different sources. A one-page document full of rich data that was passed on to the International Olympic Committee (IOC) and the International Paralympic Committee (IPC) as well as managers at the different venues who interpreted the findings into direct actions at the venues.

Quant experiential
If you could describe the emotions you felt while you were at the Olympic Park using three words or short phrases, what would they be?
HAPPY
IMPRESSED
PROUD
EXCITED
OVERWHELMED
PATRIOTIC
FUN
TICKETS
ENJOYMENT
EMOTIONAL
RELAXED
DISAPPOINTED
AMAZED
PART
AWE
EXCITING
HAPPINESS
BRITISH
ATMOSPHERE
JOY
INSPIRED

Fig 11.13 Word cloud that provides a mix of qualitative and quantitative data of the public's experience in one day at the London Olympics.

Extended Spectator Research Summary

Olympics day 13 Thurs 9th Aug 2012

Summary – the lows

- Catering and queuing experiences need improvement at OLY, STA, WEA
- Mixed sentiments related to music (it's subjective)
- Empty seats – still an issue, but reducing
- Lack of GB gold generally leads to reduced venue scores

Contact Centre – Top complaint topics

Data source: Call Centre Period covered 11.01 08/08– 11.00 09/08

SEC (4) Staff behaviour (OPK, HGP, OLD, EXL)

CCW (4) Potential food poisoning (OPK)
Food shortage (MIL)
Payment (EXL)

EVS (4) Staff behaviour (GRP, AQC)

RIA (2) Noise pollution (EXL)
Seating malfunction (BBA)

18 total formal complaints received Thurs 9th

Social Media – Top negative topics

Data source: Twitter Period 18.01 8/08– 18.00 09/08

Catering and queuing at OPK, (also STA and WEA) *"Yet another Olympian water queue. Why oh why LOCOG & Seb is water so scarce in #olympic park? #citizencurators."*

Informed i can't buy chips on their own at the Fish & Chips stall because "McDonolds have bought the rights to selling chips on their own"

"It is a shame Lord Coe and #LOCOG never visited Twickenham on a match day to find out how stadium catering can work #ihatequeues #olympics."

Mixed sentiments related to music *"I don't know who the MC is at the **riverbank arena**, but im guessing he's a failed local radio DJ #oopadoodledoo." "YMCA in the Olympic stadium #omg."*

Empty seats update: The phrase was mentioned 250 times yesterday in Olympics conversation.
Compares to 45,000 times at its peak on the 29th

Key venues rating below average

Data source: Email. Period covered 8.00 08/08 – 13.15 09/08

Key drivers for below average scores

ACQ (8.2) The view I had from my seat – **23%**
Value for money of food and drink – **19%**
Variety / quality of drinks - **14%**

BMX (8.3) Value for money of food and drinks – **24%**
Availability of free water – **16%**

ETD (8.3) Value for money of food and drink – **22%**
Queuing time for things inside the venue – **14%**
Entertainment beyond sport – **13%**
Availability of free water – **13%**

Lowest rated spectator issues by FCC

Data source: Email. Period covered 8.00 08/08 – 13.15 09/08

% of spectators rating extremely poor

CCW Value for money of food / drink – **32%** (EAR), **31%** (ES1, NGA)
Availability of free water - **43%** (GRP), **32%** (ES2)
Queuing times inside – **51%** (GRP), **33%** (HGP)

EVS Availability of free water - **43%** (GRP), **32%** (ES2)

SPP Entertainment beyond sport - **20%** (ES2), View from my seat - **23%** (AQU)

What, if anything, about the Games has not been so good?
(Top 3 spectator mentions across all venues and FAs)

Tickets - too expensive / hard to obtain – **62%**
Empty seats at venue(s) – **45%**
Food too expensive – **29%**

Operational insights from SPX *Data source: SPX feedback Period 21.00 06/08– 21.00 07/08*

- More water fountains (GRP)
- More seating in spec zone & wayfinding to stadium (HGP)
- Continue to show key Olympic moments on the big screens (EXL)
- Not enough seating but people seem happy to sit on the floor (EAR)

Enjoyment and expectations

Day	-2	-2	0	1	2	3	4	5	6	7	8	9	10	11	12	13	14	15	16
Ave enjoyment	-	-	-	-	-	8.9	9.3	9.1	9.3	9.3	9.3	9.2	9.3	9.2	**9.3**				
Met or exceeded expectations	-	-	-	-	-	90	94	93	95	95	95	95	95	93	**95**				

Confidential LOCOG 2012

Extended Spectator Research Summary
The Venues

Olympics day 13 Thurs 9th Aug 2012

The highs

- Sport is top globally, Women's football, Dressage and particularly Hyde Park swimming, where they are in awe of how hardcore it is
- Spectators praise transport and the ease of getting to the games
- First impressions continue to be hugely positive, British Army and Volunteers are 'jolly', 'friendly' and 'welcoming'

Social Media – positive topics (High volume)

Data source: Twitter Period 18.01 08/08– 18.00 09/08

Sport is top conversation globally, Women's football, Dressage, particularly Hyde Park swimming, where they are in awe of how hardcore it is *"Can't believe ppl r swimming in that slimy duck pond! #london2012"*

Journeys and getting to the games *"Very impressed with the Javelin service from St Pancras to Stratford/Olympic Park."*

"Shouldn't have worried or got up so early. Green Park to Stratford is a half empty tube! Can't wait to see the magnificent aquatics centre!"

First impressions continue to be hugely positive *"The British army never fail to bring a smile to my face as I go through security at the Olympic Park. They are such a jolly bunch."*

*"We are **Eton Dorney** today- so well organised and all the volunteers are so friendly and welcoming."*

Venues rating above average Overall enjoyment (out of 10)

Data source: Email. Period covered 8.00 08/08 – 13.15 09/08

Greenwich Park (9.6, 9.6 yesterday)
- Quality of sport
- Look and feel of venue
- Helpfulness of staff / volunteers

Olympic Stadium (9.5 9.5 yesterday)
- Atmosphere at event
- Look and feel of venue
- Helpfulness of staff / volunteers

Basketball Arena (9.4 9.1 yesterday)
- Atmosphere at event
- Overall organisation of the event
- Overall experience going through security

Venues rating below average

Data source: Email. Period covered 8.00 08/08 – 13.15 09/08

Aquatics Centre (8.2, 8.8 yesterday)
- The view I had from my seat
- Value for money of food and drink
- Variety / quality of drinks

BMX track (8.3 - first day of sport)
- Value for money of food and drinks
- Availability of free water

Eton Dorney (8.3, 8.5 yesterday)
- Value for money of food and drink
- Queuing time for things inside the venue
- Entertainment beyond sport
- Availability of free water

Top rated Spectator Issues by FCC

Data source: Email. Period covered 8.00 07/08 – 13.15 08/08

SEC
Feeling safe and secure – **100%** (EN2), **96%** (STA)
Experience through security – **96%** (STA), **95%** (AWP)
Time through security – **96%** (STA), **96%** (AWP)

WF&S
Look & feel of venue – **99%** (GRP), **96%** (STA)
Signage to / within venue – **91%** (GRP), **93%** (EN2)
Look and feel on Park – **91%** (HOC), **90%** (STA)

TRA
Ease and efficiency of public transport around London **92%** (EN2), **91%** (HGP)
Getting home after attending your event - **100%** (HGP), **95%** (EN2)

Confidential LOCOG 2012

Figs 11.14 and 11.15
Extended Spectator Research Summary of Olympic Day 13, Thursday August 9, 2012—a daily report showing highs and lows, details about top complaints, positive topics appearing on Twitter, and venues ratings, among other details.

Evaluation frameworks: ROI, SROI, monetized blueprint, RATER, and the Theory of Change

Because of the complex nature of services, evaluation can be an elusive proposition. What and how do we measure services? And how do we define and measure *impact*?

ROI (return on investment) is the main assessment tool that organizations use, focusing primarily on financial impact. The basic formula used to calculate ROI is as follows:

$$\text{ROI} = \frac{\text{the return (net profit, or gross profit − expenses)}}{\text{resources that were committed (investment)}}$$

The ROI approach to evaluation centers on what can be monetized, thus defining value in financial terms. Quantifying impact, however, might go beyond monetization. Factors such as client relationships are hard to quantify in such a formula. The ROI model can be useful as a straightforward evaluation tool that resonates with a prevailing mindset in most organizations, industries, and sectors (private sector, public, or nonprofit) that often read value in largely economic terms.

So while ROI can be useful, designers might find themselves at odds with its general mindset of quantifying impact. Design is, after all, an exercise for anticipating new futures, and uncertainty is an intrinsic part of the creative process. It might take time to prove impact that is related to behavior change, for example.

SROI (social return on investment) is an impact assessment tool that expands the understanding of impact beyond financial aspects. It also includes the social and environmental impacts of a service. The guiding principle of SROI is that it accounts for all stakeholders' perspectives, including those who will actually be affected by the new service. It helps evaluate how a new initiative/service may transform or change lives in a broader sense. This is crucial, since the people determining goals and desired outcomes are not necessarily the same people who will have to live with the resulting experiences of these goals.

Service design author Lucy Kimbell (2014) proposes an approach toward measuring impact that considers framing service outcomes (and its desired impact) according to the specifics of each service context and domain.

DOMAIN	EXAMPLE OUTCOMES
Customer Service Operations	Reduced customer effort to resolve issues, increased customer loyalty, increased customer satisfaction, resolution of an issue in on phone call.
Healthcare	Quality adjusted life years, increased access to universal services by under-represented groups, reduced stigma for those experiencing mental health, excess weight in adults.
Crime	Reducing reoffending for those with a history of substance misuse, reduced fear of crime, a reduction in youth offending and anti-social behavior.
Community and Built Environment	Making somewhere a great place to live, an increased feeling of safety outside the home at night, an increase in recycling, increased feeling of pride in living somewhere, increased energy efficiency in the built environment.
Education	Increased educational attainment for children in families with complex needs, increased school attendance, reduced numbers of children excluded from school.
Social Care	Increased participation in activities for people experiencing mental health issues, fewer admissions to acute care, increased emotional wellbeing of looked after children.

Fig 11.16 Sample outcomes according to different service contexts.

Polaine, Løvlie, and Reason (2013) make an important case for measuring and evaluating service design by observing that managers and decision makers within private, public, and not-for-profit organizations need clear and tangible reasons to invest in service design. They need to be convinced that a return on investment is possible and that value is being created for their organizations and customers before investing in a service design project. Service designers need managers and decision makers to buy in to the process.

Polaine et al. propose a model that, like the ROI approach, focuses largely on financial aspects but puts them into the language of service design. *Monetized blueprints* are based on the service blueprint discussed in earlier chapters. The blueprint document ties together different key elements of a service, including two main service design concerns: (1) touchpoints and channels across time and (2) user experience and back-office operations.

Using the monetized blueprint, designers and managers can integrate business modeling as part of the design process, zooming in on specific moments in the user journey and verifying cost and revenue in relation to specific channels and touchpoints. In doing so, it is possible to study where in the journey costs can be reduced, where revenue can be generated, and where the creation of value is for users. It is also possible to identify questions of cost and value in relation to specific touchpoints and channels. The blueprint helps examine and deconstruct the economics of every single point of the service journey, while simultaneously providing a vantage point to zoom out and make sense of the service as a whole.

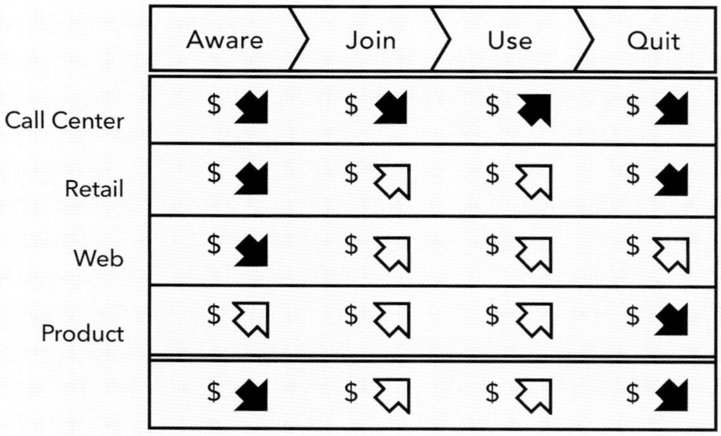
Aware
Join
Use
Quit
Call Center
Retail
Web
Product

Fig 11.17 The "business case" service blueprint tool, which uses the service blueprint to verify costs and revenues throughout the service journey across different channels and touchpoints.

RATER is a simplified version of SERVQUAL, a service evaluation framework created by service marketing scholars. RATER consists of a scale to measure services based on different dimensions of services. The principle behind this framework is that the quality of a service experience can be measured by considering the difference between users' expectations and their actual experience: when our expectations are higher than our actual experience, we perceive the service as low quality; when our expectations are lower than our actual experience, we perceive the service as high quality.

The five points of the RATER framework reflect five different dimensions where the gap can be measured.

The *Theory of Change* model was initially proposed by evaluation theorists and practitioners and became particularly popular with socially driven organizations such as nongovernmental organizations (NGOs), the United Nations, government agencies, and the philanthropic sector. Theory of Change is well suited for understanding complex systems; establishing goals, priorities, and benefits; and understanding the correlation between them, helping teams to test assumptions and detect risks.

The Theory of Change canvas can be used as a collaborative tool between the design team and various project stakeholders. The starting point is the definition of a main problem to be solved followed by the long-term vision to be accomplished. From there, other boxes include describing the main audience and the entry point for reaching them, defining where and how to start the action, and identifying the steps needed to achieve the goal. At each step, the theory suggests reflecting on the key assumptions behind each step and action in order to anticipate risks and opportunities.

Reliability	Organization performs the service in a reliable and accurate way.
Assurance	Staff is reassuring and courteous to customers, they know what they are talking about and they inspire trust and confidence.
Tangibles	Touchpoints, serviscapes, communication elements as well as staff is good.
Empathy	Staff relate to users in personable and relatable way.
Responsiveness	Staff and organization is willing to respond to users needs and promptly solve their problems.

Fig 11.18 RATER evaluation framework.

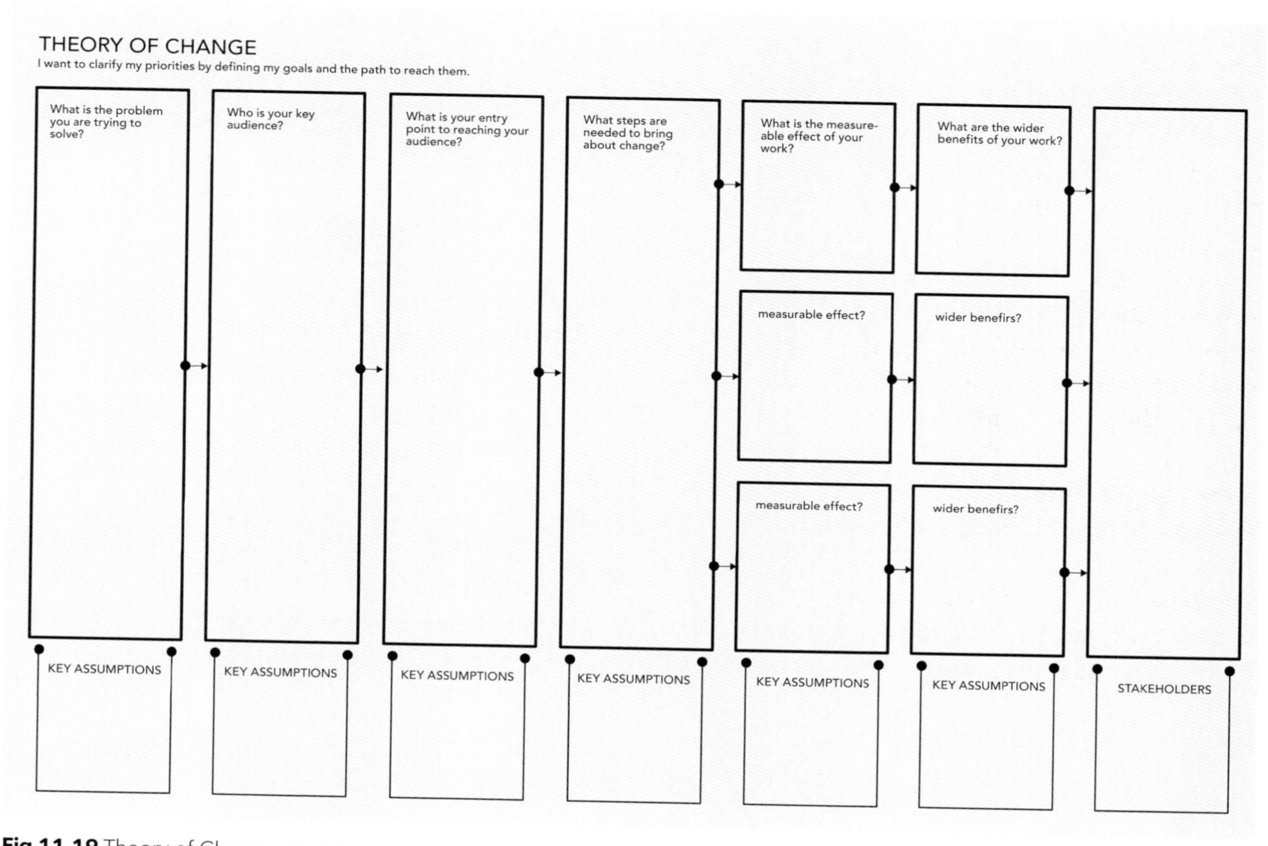
THEORY OF CHANGE
I want to clarify my priorities by defining my goals and the path to reach them.
What is the problem you are trying to solve?
Who is your key audience?
What is your entry point to reaching your audience?
What steps are needed to bring about change?
What is the measure-able effect of your work?
What are the wider benefits of your work?
measurable effect?
wider benefirs?
measurable effect?
wider benefirs?
KEY ASSUMPTIONS
KEY ASSUMPTIONS
KEY ASSUMPTIONS
KEY ASSUMPTIONS
KEY ASSUMPTIONS
KEY ASSUMPTIONS
STAKEHOLDERS

Fig 11.19 Theory of Change canvas.

11.6 Learning features

Activities

Business modeling

Working in teams, select a service recently designed by students. Define a specific social, economic, and geographic context and develop a business plan using the business canvas.

As a team, revisit existing service blueprints that you and your classmates have recently created. Gather insights from brainstorming, cocreation, and testing sessions to set the foundation for the business model of your service design proposal.

1. Discuss and decide on a specific socioeconomic (e.g., user group, target audience, service provider) and geographic context (e.g., rural, urban, small scale, or big scale).
2. Follow the steps of the Business Model Canvas or Social Business Model Canvas as a framework to communicate the values generated by your service design proposal.
3. Keep in mind that the Business Model Canvas is an agile method for strategy development and evaluation: you may use this tool to test your strategy and refine it later.

Comparative evaluation of services:

Select two or three evaluation tools (e.g., ROI, SROI, Monetized Blueprint, RATER) to conduct a comparative evaluation of an existing service.

1. The implementation of different methods to analyze the same service will help you get the best insight into the values generated and financial revenues, and will allow you to compare and test your assumptions from different angles.
2. Compare the results of each method, focusing especially on the financial aspects and contrast them to social impact.
3. Use these new insights, learnings, and tactics from your comparative analysis to revise and solidify your business model canvas.

Recommended reading

Kimbell, L. (2014). *The Service Innovation Handbook*. BIS Publishers.

Osterwalder, A., and Pigneur, Y. (2010). *Business Model Generation*. Wiley.

Polaine, A., Løvlie, L., and Reason, B. (2013). *Service Design. From Insight to Implementation*. Rosenfeld Media.

12 Service design core capabilities

This core capability may sound a bit overwhelming, especially for those coming from design rather than management. As Mauricio Manhães (2017) put it, a service designer does not have to know how to do everything. It's not about being a super-human. It's about developing a deep sense of understanding and knowing those who know and being able to connect the dots.

To summarize, service design scholar Lucy Kimbell (2014; read her interview at the end this chapter) points out the critical ability of service designers to zoom in and out. When designing a service touchpoint or contributing to the creation of a new business model or government policy, designers can play an important role of mediation and translation between senior management and frontline staff and between staff and their clients. According to Cameron Tonkinwise (read his interview in Chapter 5), by dictating the way staff is supposed to operate within a service situation, service designers are also designing the future of work and transforming labor conditions. Service designers are not only determining the service experience for service users, but also the working conditions of service workers and whether or not they might become redundant or lose essential labor rights. It's part of the service designer's responsibility to be able to *discern and balance organizational efficiency from the effects these might have for people* who sustain and enable a service through their work either at the front or back office. Navigating between these organizational scales, lines, and tasks requires designers to develop the capabilities described here, infused with a strong sense of responsibility and ethical integrity.

The case study presented in Chapter 7 about a public transportation company in Mantua, Italy, shows how the service design process can leave a profound impact on the organization's management structure and culture. Every step of the service design process can, in fact, open unexpected doors to change. *Cocreation sessions* (as described earlier in this chapter and in Chapter 9) are, for instance, opportunities *for organizational learning*. Through them, we see how different parts of the organization are forced to negotiate and start resolving internal challenges from within. Negotiating internal change is hard work, and such participatory design processes can provide the space to start this process in a collaborative way.

12.7 Interview with Lucy Kimbell

Lucy Kimbell is director of the Innovations Insights Hub at University of the Arts London (UAL). Previously, she was an Arts and Humanities Research Council research fellow in Policy Lab in the UK Government's Cabinet Office (2014–15). Lucy is also Associate Fellow at Said Business School, University of Oxford. She's the author of the book *The Service Innovation Handbook: Action-Oriented Creative Thinking Toolkit for Service Organizations* (BIS Publishers, 2014).

What do you think are the possible/most common learning paths toward service design practice?

I don't think there's just one kind of service design. I don't think there should be. You can't just have "design for services." You can have things like design for health-care services, design for emergency care, design for caring for older people, design for the public sector, education services design, customer services design in entertainment or hospitality, and so on. I think the future will be based on these kinds of specialisms and new ones will also emerge along with new kinds of business model, technologies and ways of organizing. So in many ways the learning paths will need to continue to develop in response to where these fields of practice end up going, with multiple intersections with other kinds of expertise and other learning paths in areas like technology, business, and social research as well as the humanities and the arts.

What do you think are the key capabilities and skills for service designers?

One of the major challenges for service design is prototyping. How do you prototype a service? And not just prototype the experience, but prototype the financial models, the operational models, the technical support required for service users, for customer service agents or volunteers, the infrastructures and capacities required for the ongoing cocreation of value. How do you prototype those things? I don't think we have seen it yet. One of the reasons is that it's incredibly hard to do, and it's actually about being deeply embedded in organizations and their networks of resources and capabilities, which extend beyond the boundaries of the firm. Sure, it's important to do some customer insights, but you can get that pretty easily these days. Generating ideas in workshops, everybody does that. What is crucial is understanding not just the current or future experience of the user, but the implications of service innovation for an organization and its network. This kind of understanding is what is needed to make key decisions about which direction to go in. I think this is a capability that doesn't yet exist, but design has much to contribute to it.

What is an essential skill for service designers if they want to influence organizational change?

For me, telling stories is critical for understanding organizations and shaping change. Stories can be made manifest in different ways, through different media, formats, and registers so people can engage, understand, think through, participate, and cocreate. That is so long as it's also accompanied by making maps. This is more than identifying and mapping stakeholders. Designers need to map the ecosystem of resources and capabilities that are brought together in an offering to cocreate value. But how do you really do that? If you want to change the ecosystem, which includes social practices, which are influenced by and shaped by wider cultural developments, how do you manifest that? This can't just be empathy and Post-it notes on the wall. Systems thinking, participatory design, and ethnographic research approaches all have angles on this. The main thing to remember is that there is no simple "inside" or "outside" the system. It's always relational. You need an understanding of the actors, the cultures, and infrastructures within which they come to exist and to act and the relationships that exist between them, which are dynamic and in flux. Designers need to understand that there are multiple sets of accountabilities and relations shaping how actors engage and what happens in a system. There needs to be an understanding of power relations, identities, subjectivities. Stories and maps provide pathways through and insights into all this.

How important is making (versus thinking) in the service design process?

What service design is doing is making relations. It's the making of new kinds of relations between different participants in some kind of society, system, organization, or economic and cultural context. Making physical or digital artifacts is absolutely critical because encountering such artifacts helps people to understand, change, or provoke insights into relations through inserting into a system or practice some kind of object with potential uses and experiences, thus revealing potential changes to social or organizational practices around it.

What do you understand to be the balance between analytical capability and creative synthesis (e.g., the need to create emotional experiences and translating them into logistics)?

There's a tension when designing services between the need to capture and define learning and decisions in documents or media that can be used and referred to later, and the need to keep on learning and changing things. There are other tensions between understanding the current situation, analyzing the implications of a proposal, and the generative work of coming up with proposals. Different people and functions in organizations (or networks of partners) collaborating to create a new service bring different expertise and mindsets to these tensions. A service design is not a thing that gets handed over to somebody else to implement. Those in charge of implementation, for example, operations teams and people tasked with detailing an overall design, need to be involved in doing the researching and designing. Participatory approaches would argue for users and other stakeholders to be involved too. So crafting a collective, iterative, multipartner journey that combines analysis and creativity, learning and doing, and brings in people with different perspectives, is a key task for service designers.

What are some ways to think about how to approach evaluation and validating impact in service design projects?

Evaluation is more of a problem for managers than for designers. It's only a problem for designers because somebody has to decide on things like budgets and investments, and making these decisions is a kind of power that designers typically don't have but want to have. The question of evaluating impact is tied to the premises of taking action. What are you trying to do and why? Who does this issue matter to? What outcomes do you want to achieve? What is the context or world associated with the issue? How do you imagine things might change (your "theory of change")? What resources do you have available? How will you know when you've been successful? Who is or should be involved in asking and answering these questions?

Management, and the social sciences more broadly, understands much of this and has many approaches, methods, and techniques to answer these questions, often much better ones than service designers have access to. So, let's hand the evaluation problem back to managers and say, "How can we, together, understand if the service leads to the desired outcomes?" But let's go with them on the journey of constructing evaluation frames, devices, and artifacts in relation to publics to whom a service matters, recognizing different time frames and accountabilities for understanding and assessing outcomes.

Let's give up on designers trying to understand their impact. Let's do it relationally with the people who typically have the resources, habits, power, and desire to evaluate things, and find new ways of evaluating impact with them—which might include problematizing a framing and the terms on which the value being cocreated is understood.

In terms of service design careers, and considering that many young designers are interested in promoting some kind of change, be it social or environmental, can we talk about self-led projects, or even a purpose-driven service design entrepreneurship? Is this a trend?

From what I see in design schools and design consultancies, this is a trend. But I think the exciting move is not to be a service designer but to be a person involved in redesigning services in domains that matter. Pick a topic that matters to you and work out why it matters to you. For example, health care or well-being. Then go work for a well-being charity or a health-care service provider. Don't take a job as a designer. Do designing through a job. Take a job in customer service and get to understand the frontline delivery experience and the operations side. Become a manager of a service. Then use your design skills and your understanding of the creative design process to promote change from inside the team where you have knowledge of the domain and a role that becomes how you do it, and where the consequences of the change will make a difference to you. Or, having learned about a domain, and worked out something that needs changing, set up a social enterprise. Join a political party or activist group and organize. If you want change to happen, go where there are things that need changing, learn from the people who are affected by and expert in an issue, and start making connections between these people and the resources and infrastructures required to make change happen.

Thinking about issues of where and how to work, how can service design influence projects and people toward better purpose, better scopes, and better projects?

Designers are really good at spotting things very early on, coming up with ideas very quickly and materializing future things so they can be considered and assessed. They make things. And not just beautiful things, but messy things that reveal and identify problems as well as proposing solutions. This can be done in lots of ways, through a mock-up, presentation, workshop, scenario, video, exhibition, or a graphic analysis. These outputs can help make the process of understanding and grappling with an issue or project tangible to the people who want to do something about it. If there's a project already in existence and you come along and say, "Here's some other perspectives on the problem. Here's some other ways in. That's not the real problem. This is the problem," you can shift the thinking about what the nature of the problem is. These are well-understood, core design capabilities. This kind of change making should be driven by an entrepreneurial, experimental spirit. Go and do it tomorrow. Don't just sit here finding things on the Internet or read incredibly interesting stuff. Don't just have great conversations here in the studio, get out, go learn from people and also take some stuff to them to trigger a rich, "thick" conversation. Deepen your and their understanding of the issue that you say you're interested in. Don't be interested inside the studio. Make the field a studio.

12.8
Learning features

Activities

Reflection roundtable:

- What has been the most meaningful experience you have been through on which you developed empathy?
- Design an interview guide for yourself and your team when engaging with different people and contexts.
- Revisit recent service cocreation sessions you have promoted or participated in. Sketch the team formation used during the session. Compare and contrast the facilitation done in different sessions.
- Pick a recent service design project you have worked on. Can you map the ways on which the project proposed or enacted some aspect of organizational change. In particular:
  - How important was it for you to observe and listen to different people in relation to your creative process?
  - What kinds of methods and tools did you use to obtain the buy-in from the different project stakeholders?
  - How did measurement and evaluation play a role in implementation?
  - What were the effects of your project for staff members and their labor conditions?

Jégou, F., and Manzini, E. (2008). *Collaborative Services: Social Innovation and Design for Sustainability*, Edizioni Polidesign.

Manzini, E. (2014). "Making Things Happen: Social Innovation and Design," in *Design Issues*, MIT Press, 57–66.

Meroni, A. (2007). *Creative Communities. People Inventing Sustainable Ways of Living*. Polidesign.

Mulgan, G. (2014, January). *Design in Public and Social Innovation: What Works and What Could Work Better*. NESTA.

Sangiorgi, D. (2011). "Transformative Services and Transformation Design." *International Journal of Design*, 5(2), 29–40.

Service Design Network (2016). *Service Design Impact Report*. Public Sector. Service Design Network.

Staszwoski, E., and Manzini, E. (Eds.) (2013). *Public & Collaborative: Exploring the Intersection of Design, Social Innovation and Public Policy*. DESIS Network.

UK Design Council, et al. (2013). *Design for Public Good*. SEE Platform. Sharing Experience Europe. Policy Innovation Design.

Chapter 5

Belletire, S., St. Pierre, L., and White, P. (2014). *The OKALA Practitioner Guide*. ISDA.

Bitner, M. J. (1992, April). "Servicescapes: The Impact of Physical Surroundings on Customers and Employees." *Journal of Marketing*, 56(2), 57–71.

The Designer's Oath. Available at http://designersoath.com/.

Hochschild, A. R. (2003). *The Managed Heart: Commercialization of Human Feeling*, 2nd ed. University of California Press.

ICOGRADA, or ico-D, International Council of Design. Available at www.ico-d.org/.

Jaffe, S. (2013, February 4). "Grin and Abhor It: The Truth Behind 'Service with a Smile.'" *In These Times*. Retrieved from http://inthesetimes.com/working/entry/14535/grin_and_abhor_it_the_truth_behind_service_with_a_smile.

Johnston, A., and Sandberg, J. (2008). "Controlling Service Work." *Journal of Consumer Culture*, 8(3).

Junginger, S. (2015, January). "Organizational Design Legacies and Service Design." *The Design Journal*, 18(2), 209–226.

Meadows, D. (2008). *Thinking in Systems: A Primer*. Chelsea Green Publishing Company.

Penin, L., and Tonkinwise, C. (2009, October). "The Politics and Theatre of Service Design," in *Proceedings of the IASDS (International Association of Societies of Design Research) Conference*. Seoul, Korea.

Polaine, A., Løvlie, L., and Reason, B. (2013). *Service Design. From Insight to Implementation*. Rosenfeld Media.

Shedroff, N. (2009). *Design Is the Problem*. Rosenfeld Media.

Tonkinwise, C. (2008). "Sustainability," in the M. Erlhoff and T. Marshall, Eds. Design Dictionary. Birkhäuser, 380–6.

Tonkinwise, C. (2016, October 22). "What Service Designing Entails. The Political Philosophy of Sculpting the Quality of People Interacting." Medium. https://medium.com/@camerontw/what-service-designing-entails-f718ac0ebcd6.

United States Department of Labor. (2009). "20 Leading Occupations of Employed Women. 2009 Annual Averages." Retrieved from http://www.dol.gov/wb/factsheets/20lead2009.htm.

Vezzoli, C. (2010). *System Design for Sustainability*. Maggioli Editore.

Vezzoli, C. A., and Manzini, E. (2008). *Design for Environmental Sustainability*. Springer.

Chapter 6

Binder, T., De Michelis, G., Ehn, P., Jacucci, G., Linde, P., and Wagner, I. (2011). *Design Things*. MIT Press.

Bitner, M. J. (1992), "Servicescapes: The Impact of Physical Surroundings on Customers and Employees." *Journal of Marketing*, 56(2), 57–71.

Björgvinsson, E., Ehn, P., and Hillgren, P-A. (2010). "Participatory Design and Democratizing Innovation." Paper presented at Participatory Design Conference, Sydney, Australia.

Blomkvist, J., and Homlid, S. (2010). "Service Prototyping According to Service Design Practitioners." ServDes Conference, Linköping, Sweden.

Brown, T. (2009). *Change by Design: How Design Thinking Transforms Organizations and Inspires Innovation*. HarperCollins.

Cross, N. (2001). "Designerly Ways of Knowing: Design Discipline

Versus Design Science." *Design Issues*, 17(3), 49–55.

Diana, C., Pacenti, E., and Tassi, R. (2009). "Visualtiles—Communication Tools for (Service) Design." First Nordic Conference on Service Design and Service Innovation. Oslo, Norway.

Enninga, T., et al. (2013) *Service Design, Insights from Nine Case Studies*. HU University of Applied Sciences, Utrecht Research Centre Technology & Innovation.

Meroni, A., and Sangiorgi, D. (2011). *Design for Services*. Gower.

Miettinen, S., and Valtonen, A. (Eds.) (2013). *Service Design with Theory. Discussions on Change, Value and Methods*. Lapland University Press.

Norman, D. A. (1988, 2002, 2013) *The Design of Everyday Things*. Basic Books.

Sanders, E. B. -N., and Stappers, P. J. (2012). *Convivial Toolbox. Generative Research for the Front End of Design*. BIS Publishers.

Stickdorn, M., and Schneider, J. (2010). *This Is Service Design Thinking. Basics – Tools – Cases*. BIS Publishers

Valentine, L. (Ed.) (2013). *Prototype. Design and Craft in the 21st Century*. Bloomsbury.

Chapter 7

AIGA (The Professional Association for design). *Professional Development (Resource Guide)*. Available at http://www.aiga.org/professional-development/.

Brown, T. (2009). *Change by Design: How Design Thinking Transforms Organizations and Inspires Innovation*. HarperCollins.

Design Council UK. *How to Commission a Designer*: Step 4—Brief Your Designer. Available at http://www.designcouncil.org.uk/news-opinion/how-commission-designer-step-4-brief-your-designer.

Engine Group. Available at http://enginegroup.co.uk/services/.

Manhães, M. C., Varvakis, G., and Vanzin, T. (2010). "Designing Services as a Knowledge Creation Process Integrating the Double Diamond Process and the SECI Spiral." *Touchpoint: The Journal of Service Design*, 2(2), 28–31.

Nessler, D. (2016, May 19). "How to Apply a Design Thinking, HCD, UX or Any Creative Process from Scratch." *Medium*. Retrieved from https://medium.com/digital-experience-design/how-to-apply-a-design-thinking-hcd-ux-or-any-creative-process-from-scratch-b8786efbf812#.g4x2mi7m0

The Project Brief Toolkit. Available at http://project-brief.casual.pm/.

Sangiorgi, D., and Prendiville, A. (Eds.) (2017). *Designing for Service: Key Issues and New Directions*. Bloomsbury.

Sangiorgi, D., Prendiville, A., Jung, J., and Yu, E. (2015). Design for Service Innovation & Development (DeSID) Final Report. Retrieved from http://imagination.lancs.ac.uk/sites/default/files/outcome_downloads/desid_report_2015_web.pdf.

Chapter 8

Adaptive Path (2013). *Adaptive Path's Guide to Experience Mapping*. Adaptive Path. Retrieved from http://mappingexperiences.com/.

AIGA. *An Ethnography Primer*. Available at http://www.aiga.org/Search.aspx?taxid=228.

Crouch, C., and Pearce, J. (2012). *Doing Research in Design*. Bloomsbury Academic.

Dubberly, H., Evenson, S., and Robinson, R. (2008, March–April). "The Analysis-Synthesis Bridge Model." *ACM Interactions*, Volume XV.2. On Modeling Forum. http://www.dubberly.com/wp-content/uploads/2016/02/ddo_interactions_bridgemodel.pdf.

Experience Fellow. Available at http://www.experiencefellow.com/.

Gimmy, G. (2006). *Shadowing*. Sennse.

IDEO (2015). *The Field Guide to Human-Centered Design*, 1st ed. Retrieved from http://www.designkit.org/resources/1.

Laurel, B. (2003). Design Research. *Methods and Perspectives*. MIT Press.

Martin, B., and Hannington, B. (2012). *Universal Methods of Design*. Rockport Publishers.

Remis, N., and the Adaptive Path Team at Capital One (2016). *A Guide to Service Blueprinting*. Adaptive Path.

Segelstrom, F. (2013). "Understanding Visualisation Practices: A Distributed Cognition Perspective," in S. Miettinen and A. Valtonen, Eds. *Service Design with Theory. Discussions on Change, Value*

and Methods. Lapland University Press, 197–208.
Service Design Tools. Available at http://www.servicedesigntools.org/.
Sitra. Ethnography Field Guide, V.1. Available at http://www.helsinkidesignlab.org/pages/ethnography-fieldguide.

Chapter 9

Dubberly, H., Evenson, S., and Robinson, R. (2008, March–April). "The Analysis-Synthesis Bridge Model." *ACM Interactions* Volume XV.2. On Modeling Forum. IDEO (2015). The Field Guide to Human-Centered Design, 1st ed. Retrieved from http://www.designkit.org/resources/1.
MakeTools. Available at http://MakeTools.com.
Manhães, M. C. (2016). "A Heuristic to Increase the Innovativeness Potential of Groups," In S. Miettinen, Ed., *An Introduction to Industrial Service Design*. Routledge, 105–9). Retrieved from https://www.routledge.com/An-Introduction-to-Industrial-Service-Design/Miettinen/p/book/9781315566863.
Martin, B., and Hannington, B. (2012). *Universal Methods of Design*. Rockport Publishers.
Montgomery, E. P. and Woebken, C. (2016, June 22). *Extrapolation Factory. Operator's Manual: Publication Version 1.0, includes 11 futures modeling tools*. CreateSpace Independent Publishing Platform.
Sanders, E. B. -N., and Stappers, P. J. (2012) *Convivial Toolbox*. Generative Research for the Front End of Design. BIS Publishers.
Service Design Tools. Available at http://www.servicedesigntools.org/.
Yin, R. K. (2013). *Case Study Research: Design and Methods*. Applied Social Research Methods. Sage.

Chapter 10

Koskinen, I., Zimmerman, J., Binder, T., Redstrom, J., and Wensveen, S. (2012). *Design Research Through Practice: From the Lab, Field, and Showroom*. Morgan Kaufmann/Elsevier.
Kuure, E., and Miettinen, S. (2013). "Learning through Action: Introducing the Innovative Simulation and Learning Environment Service Innovation Corner (SINCO)."
Martin, B., and Hannington, B. (2012). *Universal Methods of Design*. Rockport Publishers.
Sanders, E. B. -N., and Stappers, P. J. (2012). *Convivial Toolbox. Generative Research for the Front End of Design*. BIS Publishers.
SINCO Service Innovation Corner. Available at http://sinco.fi/.
Valentine, L. (Ed.) (2013). *Prototype. Design and Craft in the 21st Century*. Bloomsbury.
Warfel, T. Z. (2009). *Prototyping: A Practitioner's Guide*. Rosenfeld Media.

Chapter 11

The Accelerator from the Young Foundation. *The Social Business Model Canvas*.
Foglieni, F., and Holmlid, S. (2015). "Determining Value Dimensions for an All-Encompassing Service Evaluation." *The 2015 Naples Forum on Service*. Naples, Italy.
IDEO (2015). *The Field Guide to Human-Centered Design*, 1st ed. Retrieved from http://www.designkit.org/resources/1.
Kimbell, L. (2014). *The Service Innovation Handbook*. BIS Publishers.
NESTA/The Rockefeller Foundation. (2014). *DIY Development Impact & You. Practical Tools To Trigger & Support Social Innovation*. Also available at http://diytoolkit.org/.
Osterwalder, A., and Pigneur, Y. (2010). *Business Model Generation*. Wiley.
Polaine, A., Løvlie, L., and Reason, B. (2013). *Service Design. From Insight to Implementation*. Rosenfeld Media.
Strategyzer. *Business Model Canvas*. Available at http://www.businessmodelgeneration.com/canvas.
Zeithaml, V. A., Parasuraman, A., and Berry, L. L. (1988). "SERVQUAL: A Multiple-Item Scale for Measuring Consumer Perceptions of Service Quality." *Journal of Retailing* 64, 12–49.
Zeithaml, V. A., Parasuraman, A., and Berry, L. L. (1990). *Delivering Quality Service: Balancing Customer Perceptions and Expectations*. Free Press.

Chapter 12

Bens, I. (2012). *Facilitating with Ease! Core Skills for Facilitators, Team Leaders and Members, Managers, Consultants, and Trainers*. Jossey-Bass.
Cipolla, C., & Bartholo, R. (2014). Empathy or inclusion: A dialogical approach to socially responsible design. *International Journal of Design*, 8(2), 87-100.

Bibliography

Cross, N. (2007). *Designerly Ways of Knowing*. Birkhauser.

Diana, C., Pacenti, E., and Tassi, R. (2009) "Visualtiles—Communication Tools for (Service) Design." First Nordic Conference on Service Design and Service Innovation. Oslo, Norway.

IDEO (2015A). *The Little Book of Design Research Ethics*. IDEO.

IDEO (2015B). *The Field Guide to Human-Centered Design*, 1st ed. Retrieved from http://www.designkit.org/resources/1.

Kimbell, L. (2014). *The Service Innovation Handbook: Action-Oriented Creative Thinking Toolkit for Service Organizations*. BIS Publishers.

Maeda, J. (2016, March 14). "Design in Tech Report 2016." Kleiner Perkins Caufield & Byers. Retrieved from http://www.slideshare.net/kleinerperkins/design-in-tech-report-2016/8-Timeline_of_DesignInTech_MA_Activity.

Manhães, M. (2017, January 15). "The Service Design Show: Getting the Message Across." LinkedIn. Retrieved from https://www.linkedin.com/pulse/service-design-show-getting-message-across-mauricio-manhaes-ph-d-.

Polaine, A., Løvlie, L., and Reason, B. (2013). *Service Design. From Insight to Implementation*. Rosenfeld Media.

Segelstrom, F. (2013). "Understanding Visualisation Practices: A Distributed Cognition Perspective," in S. Miettinen and A. Valtonen, Eds. *Service Design with Theory. Discussions on Change, Value and Methods*. Lapland University Press, 197–208.

Simon, H. A. (1969). *The Sciences of the Artificial*. MIT Press.

Young, I. (2015). *Practical Empathy for Collaboration and Creativity in Your Work*. Rosenfeld Media.

Credits/Sources

Chapter 1

Chapter opener: Photo by Ulrich Baumgarten via Getty Images
Fig 1.1: Nisian Hughes / Getty Images
Fig 1.2: Photo by Justin Sullivan/ Getty Images
Fig 1.3: Afton Almaraz / Getty Images
Fig 1.4: Roy Mehta / Getty Images
Fig 1.5: Blend Images - JGI/Tom Grill / Getty Images
Fig 1.6: Thomas Barwick / Getty Images
Fig 1.7: Chris Hondros / Staff / Getty Images
Fig 1.8: David Pollack / Getty Images
Fig 1.9: Photo by Linda Davidson / The Washington Post via Getty Images
Fig 1.10: Granger Wootz / Getty Images
Fig 1.11: Dean Mitchell / Getty Images
Fig 1.12: Oktay Ortakcioglu / Getty Images
Fig 1.14: Christian Smirnow
Fig 1.15: Vargo and Lusch, 2016
Figs 1.20 to 1.22: Zipcar
Fig 1.23: Photographer: Andrew Harrer/Bloomberg via Getty Images
Fig 1.25: SAUL LOEB/AFP/Getty Images
Fig 1.26: Ole Spata / EyeEm / Getty Images

Chapter 2

Chapter opener: Airbnb
Fig 2.1: The World Factbook, Central Intelligence Agency. Retrieved March 28, 2014
Fig 2.3: Forrester Research, "The State of Service Design," 2013 (p. 8); base: 102 agencies (top five responses accepted)
Fig 2.4: British Library. © 2017. The British Library Board / Scala, Florence
Fig 2.5: Courtesy of Citi Community Development
Figs 2.6 to 2.9: Photos used with permission from CGAP [Consultative Group to Assist the Poor]
Fig 2.10: Photo by Melanie Stetson Freeman/The Christian Science Monitor via Getty Images
Figs 2.11 to 2.16: Mayo Clinic
Figs 2.17 to 2.20: Airbnb

Chapter 3

Chapter opener: Photo by Zhang Peng/LightRocket via Getty Images
Fig 3.1: Pew Research, 2013, 2014A, 2014B; Original illustration: Amy Findeiss
Fig 3.2: Pew Research, 2013, 2014A, 2014B; Original illustration: Amy Findeiss
Fig 3.3: TONY KARUMBA/AFP/ Getty Images
Fig 3.4: Original illustration: Amy Findeiss
Fig 3.5: Original illustration: Amy Findeiss
Fig 3.6: Lyft
Figs 3.14 to 3.16: Jawbone
Figs 3.17 and 3.19: Nest
Fig 3.20: Photo by Peter Macdiarmid/Getty Images
Fig 3.21: Original illustration: Amy Findeiss

Chapter 4

Chapter opener: Author
Fig 4.1: Author
Figs 4.2 and 4.3: Jeremiah Robinson, City of Boston
Figs 4.4 to 4.6: HPD PPL
Figs 4.7 and 4.8: Images provided by MindLab
Fig 4.11: Design for Europe and NESTA/La 27e Region
Fig 4.12: Photo by Chris Hondros/ Getty Images
Figs 4.13 and 4.14: Nottingham Circle

Chapter 5

Chapter opener: Photo by VCG/ VCG via Getty Images
Fig 5.1: Photo by NurPhoto/NurPhoto via Getty Images
Fig 5.2: Photo by Myung J. Chun/ Los Angeles Times via Getty Images
Fig 5.3: Photo by David M. Benett/ Getty Images for Virgin Atlantic
Figs 5.4 and 5.5: Siri Betts-Sonstegard
Fig 5.6: Susan Spraragen
Fig 5.7: Parsons School of Design, Transdisciplinary Design Program, 2015; Picture credit: Cameron Hanson
Fig 5.9: Steve Belletire, Louise St. Pierre, Philip White

Chapter 6

Chapter opener: Service Design Network.
Photo by Sophie Hou
Fig 6.1: Cibic Workshop; Photographer: Matteo Cibic
Fig 6.2: Courtesy IDEO
Fig 6.3: Adapted from Stickdorn and Schneider, 2010
Figs 6.4 and 6.5: Courtesy of Designit
Fig 6.6: Courtesy of Studio Thick
Fig 6.7: Service Design Jam Berlin

Chapter 7

Fig 7.17: Design Council UK
Fig 7.18: Adapted from Nessler, 2016
Fig 7.19: IDEO
Figs 7.20 and 7.21: Original Illustrations: Visualization of Lean and Agile Processes overview based on the following sources:

http://www.screenmedia.co.uk/blog/2014/08/what-is-agile-development-a-brief-introduction/and http://www.clevertech.biz/services/using-lean-agile-methodology-to-create-success.html

Fig 7.23: Adapted from Engine Group, http://enginegroup.co.uk/services/

Chapter 8

Fig 8.12: AIGA, An Ethnography Primer

Fig 8.13: Christian Smirnow

Figs 8.14 to 8.16: Christian Smirnow

Fig 8.17: Christian Smirnow, Stephanie Lukito

Fig 8.18: Sitra Ethnography Field Guide

Fig 8.19: Cassie Ang, Judy Lee, Misha Volf, Parsons School of Design

Fig 8.20: Courtesy of ExperienceFellow by More than Metrics, Austria

Fig 8.21: Service Design Studio at the New York City Mayor's Office for Economic Opportunity

Fig 8.24: Thesis project by Dongin Shin. MFA Transdisciplinary Design, Parsons School of Design, 2015

Fig 8.26: Parsons Transdisciplinary Design program, project on designing new services for immigrants in a public library. Credits: Noah Litvin, Melika Alipour Leili

Chapter 9

Figs 9.13 to 9.18: Designing for Financial Empowerment, by Parsons DESIS Lab in partnership with the city of New York (NYC Center for Economic Opportunity, NYC Consumer Affairs/Office for Financial Empowerment), the Food Bank, and funded by Citi Community and Mayor's Fund to Advance New York City

Fig 9.19: Illustration by Amy Findeiss

Fig 9.20: Illustration by Amy Findeiss

Figs 9.25 to 9.28: Parsons Transdisciplinary Design MFA, Alix Gerber, Valentina Branada

Fig 9.29: Illustration by Amy Findeiss

Fig 9.35: Parsons School of Design, Transdisciplinary Design Program, 2015

Chapter 10

Chapter opener: Hellon

Fig 10.1 to 10.17: Hellon

Fig 10.18: Sanders, E. B. -N., and Stappers, P. J., 2012; illustration by Amy Findeiss

Fig 10.19: Haijing Zhang

Figs 10.22 to 10.24: Simo Rontti

Fig 10.25: Tom Hagelberg

Chapter 11

Chapter opener and fig. 11.1: Photo by Jamie Squire/Getty Images

Fig 11.7: Courtesy Alex Nisbett

Fig 11.8: Courtesy Alex Nisbett

Fig 11.9: Parsons DESIS Lab

Fig 11.10: Osterwalder and Pigneur; tool distributed by Strategyzer, https://strategyzer.com/

Fig 11.11: http://youngfoundation.org/social-innovation-investment/introducing-the-social-business-model-canvas-2/

Fig 11.12: Courtesy Alex Nisbett

Fig 11.13: Courtesy Alex Nisbett

Figs 11.14 and 11.15: Courtesy Alex Nisbett

Fig 11.16: Kimbell, 2014

Fig 11.17: Polaine et al., 2013; illustration Amy Findeiss

Fig 11.18: illustration Amy Findeiss

Fig 11.19: Nesta/The Rockefeller Foundation, DIY Development Impact & You, Practical Tools to Trigger & Support Social Innovation, www.diytoolkit.org; illustration Amy Findeiss

Chapter 12

Chapter opener: Cameron Hanson

Fig 12.4: Segelström, 2013

Fig 12.5: Diana, Pacenti, and Tassi, 2009; and Segelström, 2013

Index

Index

Index